BILINGUALISM
THROUGH
SCHOOLING

Arnulfo G. Ramirez _____

BILINGUALISM THROUGH SCHOOLING _____

*Cross Cultural Education
for Minority
and Majority Students*

STATE UNIVERSITY OF NEW YORK PRESS   ALBANY

Published by
State University of New York Press, Albany

© 1985 State University of New York

Printed in the United States of America

For information, address State University of New York
Press, State University Plaza, Albany, N.Y., 12246

Library of Congress Cataloging in Publication Data

Ramirez, Arnulfo G., 1943–
    Dimensions of language and bilingual schooling.

    Bibliography: p.
    1. Education, Bilingual—United States. 2. English
language – Study and teaching (Elementary) – Foreign
speakers. 3. English language – Study and teaching –
Bilingual method. 4. Children of minorities – Education –
United States. I. Title.
LC3731.R28 1984   371.97   83-24246
ISBN 0-87395-891-8
ISBN 0-87395-892-6 (pbk.)

10 9 8 7 6 5 4 3

CONTENTS _____

PREFACE _____

This book explores various dimensions of language and bilingual schooling which have a direct bearing on the education of ethnolinguistic minority children and majority, English-speaking pupils. Bilingualism as an individual and societal phenomenon can be examined from linguistic, psychological, and sociocultural perspectives. Bilingual education often involves a link between language and ethnicity and is manifested by diversified curricular goals and patterns in many parts of the world.

The particular concerns associated with bilingual education programs serving the needs of language-minority children are not the same as those involved with the schooling of mainstream, English-speaking pupils in the United States. These differences are generally contrasted in terms of compensatory versus enrichment bilingual programs and subtractive versus additive types of bilingualism. For limited English-proficient pupils, questions related to language testing are extremely important since *entry* and *exit* to "compensatory" bilingual programs is based on language proficiency criteria. Equally important are issues related to the acquisition of English language skills. For language-majority children, questions are usually directed at the acquisition of functional proficiency in the second language, the development of first language skills, academic achievement, and the effects of different types of "immersion" bilingual approaches.

Language teaching strategies, classroom discourse processes, and language/cultural attitudes are important dimensions of language operating within a bilingual school context. Language policies, often reflecting societal goals, priorities, and intergroup relations, however, have a more direct influence on the mission and ultimate success of bilingual schooling for both minority and majority schoolchildren.

The topics discussed in this book include material from different sources — federally funded research projects, doctoral dissertations, journal articles, texts, and unpublished reports. The many studies reviewed vary with respect to research standards (e.g. design, methodological approaches, and controls) and educational significance, but each contributes to our understanding of the many dimensions of language and bilingual schooling.

ACKNOWLEDGMENTS

This book evolved with the help of many persons. My first debt of gratitude is to those students from the University of California at Los Angeles, Stanford University, and the State University of New York at Albany, who attended my graduate courses dealing with issues in language learning and bilingualism and who taught me about the dimensions of language and bilingual schooling. My special thanks go to those students from Albany attending my course "Perspectives in Bilingual Education" during 1980–1983, who provided me with their insights, experiences, and questions regarding many of the topics included in this book. Robert L. Politzer offered valuable comments regarding the structure and contents of the text, and Russell Campbell extended the opportunity to study the effects of Spanish immersion education in California. For meticulous reading of the manuscript and suggestions for stylistic changes, I am grateful to Paola Bonissone and Nomi Hahn. For typing and clerical assistance, I am most appreciative of Peggy Weissleder's work. Finally, to my family — my wife Maria Esther and my children Cristina and Dominica — I extend thanks for their understanding and kindness.

LINGUISTIC DIVERSITY AND BILINGUAL EDUCATION ___

INTRODUCTION

Linguistic diversity is a basic characteristic of most nations. The degree and type of multilingualism around the world can be characterized from different perspectives (e.g. the linguistic and sociological status of the languages used, the interrelationship between state boundaries and linguistic communities, and the presence or absence of individual and societal bilingualism). Language diversity can also be found in the United States. Persons with non-English language backgrounds live in every state, ranging from fewer than one hundred thousand to more than one million in seven states. Population estimates indicate the number of non-English language background persons will increase from 28 million in 1976 to 39.5 million in the year 2000. The number of school-age children (ages 5–14) of limited English language proficiency is expected to increase from 2.4 million in 1976 to 3.4 million in 2000.

A number of factors (e.g. demographic, social, cultural, political, and linguistic) influence the degree of language maintenance or shift among ethnolinguistic groups. The rate of linguistic assimilation (shift to English) ranges from 80 percent among United States citizens of German and Scandinavian descent to 30 percent among Spanish language background persons. The language shift pattern (home language to English) usually occurs over a period of three generations.

Bilingual schooling (the use of two languages as mediums of instruction) is utilized around the world to varying degrees. Many countries recognize two or more languages as "official" and use them for governmental and educational purposes. Bilingual education can serve a number of educational and social functions, offering advantages to ethnolinguistic minorities as well as to culturally dominant groups. Bilingual education can also contribute to the development of a "global" perspective.

MULTILINGUALISM

Multilingualism appears to be a characteristic of most human societies. According to Mackey (1967), more areas of the world are marked by linguistic diversity than by monolingualism. Mackey and Ornstein-Galicia (1977:121–22) note there are approximately five thousand living languages in the world distributed among roughly 250 sovereign nation-states. The number of languages within national systems of education can range from hundreds in the Soviet Union, the United States, or Asian countries to a few as in Spain or Sweden. Lewis (1978) points out that a high incidence of multilingualism can be found in large urban centers in the United States and the Soviet Union as well as in rural areas of African countries, where six or seven native languages can be heard along with several European languages. The incidence of multilingualism in urban and rural areas is related to the country's historical development (e.g. annexation, migration, and colonization). In Brussels, for example, standard Dutch and French are present along with various dialectal variants. Some speakers are bilingual, while others are monolingual in French or Dutch. Flemish and Walloon immigrants use their language varieties and often master different varieties of French and Dutch (Beardsmore 1982).

The languages in a particular situation could differ in terms of linguistic and sociological status. One of the languages, for example, could consist of a "cluster of dialects like those of the Pamirs" in the USSR (Lewis 1978:xii), without standardization or an alphabet. Russian and Georgian are fully developed, standardized, literary languages, but Russian enjoys a "higher" status. It is the *lingua franca* (national language) promoted by the central government in Moscow.

LANGUAGE-NATION TYPOLOGIES

Various classification schemes have been proposed to characterize multilingualism within and across state boundaries. Rustow (1968) formulated the notion of "linguistic constellations" to show how state boundaries and linguistic communities are interrelated. Three aspects — number/size of linguistic communities, degree of similarity/difference between the languages, and degree of standardization among the languages — are combined to yield six major patterns.

1. Distinct language predominates (Turkish, Mongolian)
2. Single language predominates throughout several neighboring countries (Spanish in Latin America; Arabic in the Middle East and North Africa)
3. Closely related languages, one serves as official language (Malayo-Indonesian in Indonesia; Swahili in Tanzania; Tagalog in the Philippines)
4. A number of unrelated languages, one with a substantial literary tradition (Arabic in the Sudan; Spanish in Mexico or Ecuador)
5. A number of unrelated languages without literary traditions (tropical Africa with English and French as colonial languages)
6. A number of unrelated languages, each with its own literary tradition (India, Cyprus)

Kloss's typology (1968) includes four sets of variables to describe linguistic pluralism among nation-states.

1. The type of national language — endoglossic (indigenous) as in the case of Amharic in Ethiopia, or exoglossic (imported) as with Spanish in Bolivia
2. The linguistic status of a specific language (e.g. degree of standardization)
3. The juridical status of the speech community (e.g. dominant ethnic group[s])
4. The relative numerical strength of the ethnic group in power relative to the general population and the type of representativeness it offers — "genuine" or "section based" (subjection of other ethnic groups — Amharic in Ethiopia; "consensus based" — Tagalog in the Philippines)

SOCIETAL BILINGUALISM

Another way of examining language diversity is by relating individual bilingualism to societal bilingualism. Social bilingualism, described as diglossia by sociolinguists (Ferguson 1959; Fishman 1967, 1982), represents an enduring societal arrangement in which there is stable compartmentalization in the allocation of the two languages. This social compartmentalization may be along such lines as formal-informal contexts (as in Paraguay—Spanish in school/government spheres, Guarani in the home environment) or the written-spoken modalities of language (as in Switzerland—High German in written texts, Swiss German in oral communication). Societies may differ both in the presence or absence of diglossia and individual bilingualism. Fishman (1982) describes four types of relationships:

1. Bilingualism and diglossia (Paraguay—Guarani and Spanish are used in different societal domains, most individuals are bilingual)
2. Diglossia without bilingualism (Switzerland—government or political diglosia, German in Zurich, French in Geneva)
3. Bilingualism without diglossia (United States—bilingualism among immigrants groups or language minorities)
4. Neither bilingualism nor diglossia (Korea, Portugal, or Norway—countries have relatively little immigration and almost no indigenous minorities)

These four types of linguistic situations characterize individual bilingualism in the context of societal bilingualism.

LANGUAGE DIVERSITY IN THE UNITED STATES

Non-English speakers live in every state of the Union. Figures based on the 1976 Survey of Income and Education, conducted by the Bureau of the Census, indicated that approximately 28 million persons, including about 5 million school-age children (6–18 years old), spoke mother tongues other than English or lived in households in which non-English languages were spoken. According to these data, one person in eight in the United States had a non-English language background. Spanish language background persons accounted for more than 33.3 percent (10.6 million) of all minority language speakers and 60 percent of school-age children. Italian and German language background persons numbered nearly 3 million individuals each. Nearly 2 million persons were of French language background, and another 2 million persons were of Asian American origin (Chinese, Filipino, Japanese, Korean, or Vietnamese). The relative population density by state is presented in Figure 1. Seven states (California, Florida, Illinois, New Jersey, New York, Pennsylvania, and Texas) had more than one million language-minority persons, and another seven states had between five hundred thousand and a million. Eighteen other states had between one hundred thousand and five hundred thousand non-English background persons. In states like Hawaii, with its large Asian American population, and New Mexico, with its many persons of Spanish language and Native American backgrounds, over 25 percent of inhabitants use languages other than English.

Projections for the number of non-English language background-English persons in the United States to the year 2,000, using 1976 as a base year, have been completed by Oxford et al. (1981). The study was requested by the United States Congress in order to identify the approximate number of children of limited English proficiency needing bilingual education and related services. The major findings are summarized as follows:

1. The number of non-English language background (NELB) persons is projected to grow from 28 million in 1976 to 39.5 million by the year 2000 unless there are unexpected shifts in migration, fertility, and mortality patterns
2. The number of Spanish language background persons is expected to increase from 10.6 million persons (38 percent) in 1976 to 18.6 million (46 percent) by 2000
3. The strong geographic concentration of NELBs in the three states of California, New York, and Texas is expected to increase from 45 percent of NELBs in 1976 to 48 percent in 2000
4. The total number of limited English proficiency (LEP) children, ages 5–14 is projected to increase from 2.4 million in 1976 to 3.4 million in 2000
5. Spanish language background LEP pupils accounted for 71 percent of all LEP children in 1976, and is projected to increase to 77 percent by 2000
6. The highest LEP rates (LEP/NELB ratio) among non-English language groups are expected to be found among Spanish (.75), Vietnamese (.75), Navajo (.66) and Yiddish (.60)

Figure 1. Number of Persons with Non-English Mother Tongues by State
LOCATION OF LANGUAGE-MINORITY PERSONS

States with 1,000,000 or more
States with 500,000 to 999,000
States with 100,000 to 499,000
States with fewer than 10,000

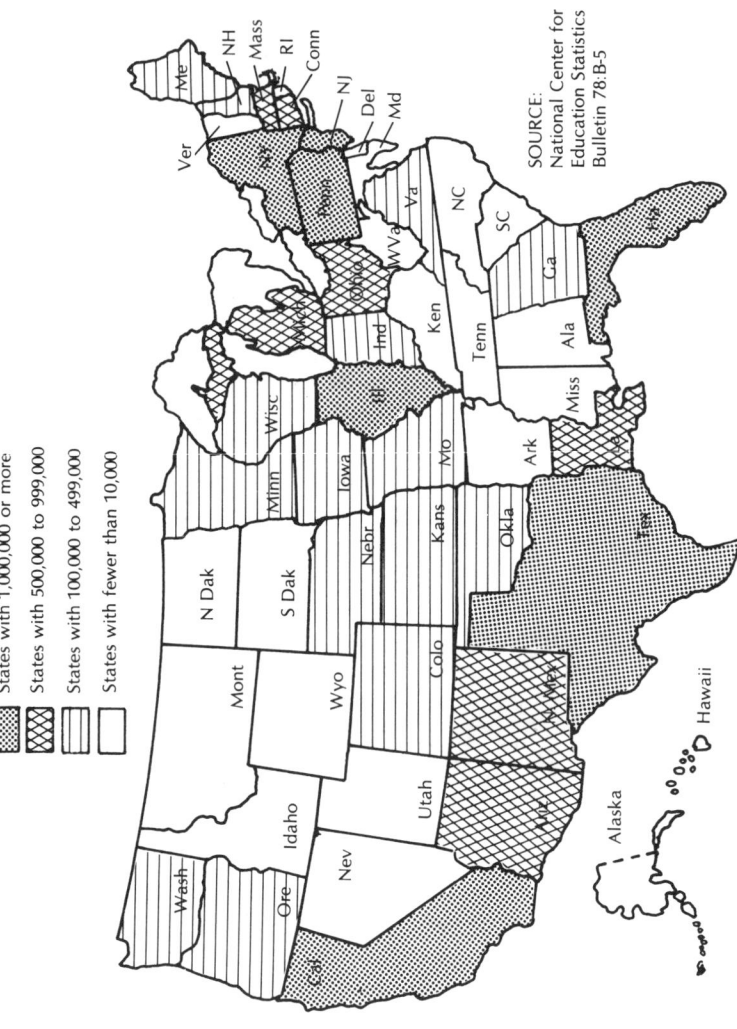

SOURCE:
National Center for
Education Statistics
Bulletin 78:B-5

LANGUAGE MAINTENANCE AND LANGUAGE SHIFT

Some ethnolinguistic communities can be regarded as stable bilingual situations (the two languages can be used for different functions) while others may experience a language shift (one language gradually displacing the other). The prospect for language maintenance of marked languages in the United States, according to Fishman (1966), can be examined from the demographic strength of various speech communities. A comparison of the census data for 1940 and 1960 indicates that six languages — Italian, Spanish, German, Polish, French, and Yiddish — have the best prospects for maintenance. Only Spanish registered a gain among the "big six" over the twenty-year period. Other languages such as Ukrainian, Serbo-Croatian, Dutch/Flemish, and Greek also gained speakers.

A number of factors affect language maintenance or language shift among ethnolinguistic groups. Some of the variables are related to the status of the group (economic standing, political power, social mobility, and occupations) and of its language (attitudes about and uses of the language, international or local language, standard written language or nonstandard variety); other factors are demographic (size of group, birthrate, immigration patterns — recent arrival and/or continuing immigration — geographic proximity to the homeland, geographic concentration, and isolation from other minority or majority groups) or institutional/ governmental (e.g. use of native language, and/or second language in the mass media, education, and government services; laws pertaining to languages and educational policies; and cultural support by a foreign state) in nature. Conklin and Lourie (1983:172) conclude there are

> . . . many factors affecting language retention and language loss. They range from cultural and emotional associations with the language to family and community structure, number and proximity of speakers, and outsiders' attitudes toward the speakers. Demographics, social and political context, cultural values and language factors all contribute to create an environment that encourages or inhibits language shift. A single factor may have one effect in one community and the opposite in another. Racism and nativism, for example, isolate minorities and immigrants. Targeted populations may respond by retaining a separate and supported ethnic and language community by seeking rapid assimilation into mainstream society. This latter option is open only to people who resemble the majority population in physical characteristics.

A specific example of the relative degree of language maintenance or language shift among persons of Spanish language background can be seen in a study conducted by Laosa (1975). He compared the degree of bilingualism and the contextual use of language among three Hispanic groups in the United States — Mexican Americans from central Texas, Cuban Americans living in Miami, and Puerto Ricans residing in New York. He found the Puerto Rican group exhibited the greatest degree of maintenance of Spanish while the Mexican American group showed the highest degree of language shift from Spanish to code switching (alternation between English and Spanish) to English. The Puerto Ricans apparently had less contact with English-speaking institutions (i.e. highest degree of unemployment and lowest occupational status) and maintained close contact with the island. The Mexican American group evidenced the greatest length of stay in the United States. The children from the Mexican American group and Cuban American sample tended to use less Spanish when compared to adults in the familial context. Interestingly, Cuban children born in the United States used more Spanish than Cuban-born pupils in interactions with peers in school or recreational contexts.

LINGUISTIC ASSIMILATION

Veltman (1980) projects varying rates of linguistic assimilation for different ethnolinguistic groups in the United States. Using the 1976 National Survey of Income and Education which includes language data, he notes the following rate of anglicization (shift to English):

1. 80 percent shift to English monolingualism among United States citizens of German and Scandinavian origins
2. 60 percent shift to English among persons from Native American, Filipino, Italian, and French-speaking groups
3. 40 percent switch to English among persons from Portuguese, Chinese, and Greek American backgrounds
4. 30 percent switch to English among Hispanic American groups

The rate of language shift to English is affected by the proportion of young adults and older persons in each language group. The number of French, German, and Italian speakers is expected to decline within a generation since a large proportion of persons are over forty years old. Speakers of Spanish, Native American languages, and Chinese are expected to increase during the next generation since these language groups have a significant number of young persons between the ages of twenty and thirty in the parenting years. Within the Hispanic group, the anglicization rate varies depending on the geographic region (highest rates occurring in the Rocky Mountain states, lowest rates in Texas).

Fishman (1964) notes most immigrant communities in the United States follow a language shift pattern that can be characterized in relation to four stages.

Stage 1: Immigrants learn English through their mother tongue. English is utilized in only those domains (e.g. work) where the mother tongue cannot be used. (This may be the case in the first generation.)

Stage 2: Immigrants learn more English and can use this language or their own in various domains (e.g. neighborhood or recreation). There is still a dependency on the mother tongue.

Stage 3: Speakers become bilingual, being able to use both languages with almost equal ease. Language separation does not occur by domain. (This is usually the case of the second generation).

Stage 4: English displaces the mother tongue, except in the most intimate domains (e.g. family affairs or religious services). (This may occur in the third generation.)

Veltman (1980) suggests that three conditions must be met if non-English languages are to survive in this country without the support of continued immigration:

1. Parents who shift to English must use their first language frequently
2. Their children must learn the non-English language as a second language
3. These children must maintain their own bilingualism so that they can pass it on to their children

According to Veltman, the educational system must undergo changes to promote minority language maintenance if bilingualism is to be nurtured as a national asset.

INTERNATIONAL DIMENSIONS OF BILINGUAL EDUCATION

Bilingual education (the use of two languages as mediums of instruction) has been utilized around the world to resolve a number of issues related to linguistic diversity. The presence of bilingual education around the world varies partly because of issues related to cultural homogeneity as well as historical and political considerations. Fishman (1976:75) found in his study of the relative presence of bilingual education programs among 117 countries that the states tended to cluster around five dimensions:

1. Category I countries included thirteen states (e.g. Australia, Burma, Liberia, West Indies) which tended "to be at the outskirts of spheres of interest rathern than at their center or at their intersection".

2. Category II countries included twenty three states (e.g. Bolivia, Guatemala, Kenya, Sudan) in which attempts were being made to recognize the language of minority groups.

3. Category III countries consisted of twenty four states (e.g. Brazil, England, Peru, United States) in which there is either vacillation "between decreasing it (as their foreign colonies shrink by assimilation or expulsion) and increasing it (as neglected indigenous minorities gain recognition)."

4. Category IV countries are marked by heterogeneity and include thirty three states (e.g. Albania, Canada, Cyprus, Yugoslavia) which have recognized the use of minority languages in education.

5. Category V countries are marked by diglossia and stable intragroup bilingualism; twenty-four states (e.g. Algeria, Hong Kong, Philippines, Sri Lanka) compose this group.

The number of countries recognizing two or more languages as "official" is growing. Official languages are used for governmental affairs as well as in schools and the business sector. In some countries, the central (national) government may use one official language (e.g. Spanish in Spain) in dealing with its various ethnolinguistic regions (Catalan, Basque, Galicia). Each region may use the local language for intragovernmental affairs. A list of countries where two or more languages are given official status has been compiled recently by the National Clearinghouse for Bilingual Education (Table 1). The list may grow as newly independent states recognize local languages, sometimes supplanting former colonial languages.

The recognition of two or more languages as "official" is usually reflected through the use of various types of bilingual programs.

Table 1   Countries with Official Bilingualism

Afghanistan
Pushtu & Dari (a Persian dialect)
Algeria
Arabic; French is quasi-official
Belgium
French, Flemish (Dutch) & German
Brunei
Malay: English is quasi-official
Burundi
Kirundi & French
Cameroon
English & French
Canada
English & French
Channel Islands (U.K.)
English & French
Cyprus
Greek & Turkish
Czechoslovakia
Czech & Slovak
Finland
Finnish & Swedish
Hong Kong
Chinese & English
India
Hindi (official national language)
English (quasi-official language;
used as an official language in
some of the Indian territories)
Assamese, Bengali, Kannada,
Kashmiri, Malayalam, Marathi,
Oriva, Punjabi, Sanskrit, Sindhi,
Tamil, Telegu, Urdu
Ireland
English and Gaelic
Israel
Hebrew & Arabic
Italy
Italian; German has regional
official status in the Alto-Adige
region
Kenya
English & Swahili
Luxembourg
French, German & Letzeburgesch

Madagascar
Malagasy & French
Malta
Maltese & English
New Hebrides
French & English
Nauru
Nauruan & English
Peru
Spanish & Quechua
Philippine Islands
Pilipino, English & Spanish
Rwanda
Kinyarwanda & French
Seychelles
English & French
Singapore
Malay, English, Chinese & Tamil
Republic of South Africa
English & Afrikaans
U.S.S.R.
Russian (official national language)
Official regional languages include:
Armenian, Byelorussian, Ukrainian,
Georgian, Lithuanian, Latvian,
Estonian, Moldavian, Uzbek,
Tadjik, Kazakh, Azerbaijani
Spain
Spanish (national, official language)
Official regional languages:
Catalan, Basque and Gallego
Sri Lanka
Sinhalese; Tamil recognized for
some purposes
Swaziland
English & SiSwazi
Switzerland
French, German, Italian &
Rumansch

SOURCE: NCBE FORUM, vol. 1, no. 6 (August 1978), pp. 1–2.

BILINGUAL EDUCATION GOALS

In his survey of the ancient world through the Renaissance, Lewis (1977) examined the various conditions which created individual and societal bilingualism. These included *reciprocal bilingualism,* motivated by trade and commerce, in which both groups had to learn each other's language; *territorial bilingualism*, resulting from conquest, the superordinate group imposing its language; and *unilateral transitional bilingualism*, created by migration and with a tendency toward assimilation into the new language/cultural group. He also noted the different types of bilingual education during the various efforts of linguistic unification directed by such groups as the Babylonians, Greeks, and Romans. Some of these efforts can probably be seen in the list of implicit goals of contemporary bilingual education programs outlined by Ferguson, Houghton, and Wells (1977):

1. To assimilate individuals or groups into the mainstream of society (e.g. young speakers of the provincial vernaculars Alsacian and Breton in France)
2. To unify a multilingual society (e.g. Russian language policy to educate Soviet children in their mother tongues—Ukranian, Georgian, Armenian, etc.)
3. To enable people to communicate with the outside world (e.g. Dutch children learn English and German)
4. To gain as economic advantage for individuals or groups (e.g. Japan trains large numbers of personnel in English, necessary for jobs in business, government, and technology)
5. To preserve ethnic or religious ties (e.g. Irish children are exposed to the Irish language in the schools to help promote its restoration)
6. To reconcile different political or socially separate communities (e.g. English-speaking pupils in Canada learning French)
7. To spread and maintain the use of a colonial language (e.g. the use fo French in the Ivory Coast)
8. To embellish or strengthen the education of elites (e.g. United Nations International School in New York City for the children of UN officials)
9. To give equal status to languages of unequal prominence in the society (e.g. the use of Finnish in Swedish schools)
10. To deepen understanding of language and culture (e.g. the study of Greek or Latin among Europeans)

Clearly, some of these bilingual education goals serve the needs of ethnolinguistic minority children, while others are intended to promote bilingualism among culturally dominant groups.

BILINGUAL EDUCATION AND GLOBAL PERSPECTIVES

One of the important goals of bilingual education, according to Rand (1981), is to contribute, in terms of both human and material resources, to our current efforts to provide students with a functional language competence as well as with an in-depth understanding of the history and culture influencing the values, beliefs, and attitudes of a different cultural group. The President's Commission on Foreign Language and International Studies, established under Carter, presented the report *Strength Through Wisdom: A Critique of U.S. Capability* by J. A. Perkins and others (1979), which noted that our lack of "foreign" language and international studies was detrimental to the economic and security interests of the United States. At the same time, our involvement in world affairs and interdependence—economic, political, and ecological—with other nations makes it imperative for us to perceive and understand local/global relationships. The concern for an interdependent world has manifested itself as "global" education. Global education includes such areas as citizenship with a global focus, transnational organizations, global issues—property, pollution, and energy—and cultural variability. The Minnesota State Department of Education, for example, has identified the following goals for a global citizenship program (1981):

1. Understanding diversity: The awareness that diversity offers opportunity for growth but also poses potential conflicts.
2. Understanding the world as a series of emerging interdependent systems: The awareness that no one nation alone can successfully deal with contemporary and future world problems.
3. Developing effective working relationships with others: The awareness of similarities and differences between interpersonal and international relations.
4. Understanding the nature and process of change: The awareness that change is a permanent part of history.
5. Understanding prevailing world conditions: The awareness that the world is made up of differing cultural value systems.
6. Understanding emerging global trends: The awareness that

there are varying alternatives and difficult decisions for the future.

The global education movement, however, has not addressed the issue of how student citizens are to be prepared to cope in a multilingual world. In 1978 the American Council on the Teaching of Foreign Languages called for the establishment of a national policy to preserve, develop, and strengthen second language education in this country. The National Advisory Council for Bilingual Education in its fifth annual report (1980–1981), *The Prospects for Bilingual Education in the Nation*, recommended the establishment of a multiple language educational policy for the nation to address the needs of both monolingual English-speaking students and minority-language pupils. One of the recent developments has been the establishment of the Joint National Committee for Languages (JNCL), a coalition of organizations concerned with language teaching (e.g. National Association for Bilingual Education, the Modern Language Association, Teachers of English to Other Speakers, and the American Council on the Teaching of Foreign Languages). These language organizations have just begun to identify the need to establish and develop language programs which can produce competent bilinguals able to cope with a highly interdependent, multi-lingual world.

SUMMARY

In summary, we have seen that linguistic diversity, a characteristic of most human societies, is related to a country's historical development. Multilingualism can be found in both rural and urban areas throughout the world; the languages in each situation may vary in terms of linguistic and sociological status. Different classification systems have been proposed to characterize language diversity. These include various frameworks for depicting multilingualism.

    I.   "Linguistic constellations" formulated by Rustow to show the interrelationship between state boundaries and linguistic communities, expressed in terms of six major patterns.

    II.   Kloss's typology of linguistic pluralism, based on four sets of variables:

        A. endoglossic or indigenous national language; exoglossic or imported national language

        B. linguistic status of a specific language

      C. juridical status of the speech community

      D. relative numerical strength of ethnic group

III. Societal bilingualism, described as diglossia and representing an enduring societal arrangement in which there is stable compartmentalization of the two languages. Individual bilingualism and diglossia can exist in four different types of relationships.

      A. bilingualism and diglossia

      B. diglossia without bilingualism

      C. bilingualism without diglossia

      D. neither bilingualism nor diglossia

Language diversity is also a characteristic of the United States. Non-English speakers live in every state, including some 28 million persons, according to a 1976 survey, of which 5 million are school-age (6–18 years old) children. More than seven states have more than a million language-minority persons and another seven have betwen five hundred thousand and a million. Projections for the year 2000 suggest increases in the number of non-English language background persons as well as in the number of limited English-speaking children (ages 5–14), with high geographic concentrations in California, New York, and Texas.

Some ethnolinguistic communities are characterized as stable bilingual situations, others may experience a language shift. Numerous factors affect language retention or language loss among ethnolinguistic groups. These include, for example:

1. the status of the group (economic/political power, social status);
2. the status of its language (attitudes and use of the language, linguistic status);
3. demographic considerations (group size, birthrate, immigration patterns); and,
4. institutional/governmental support (use of language in school, mass media, and government).

Linguistic assimilation of different ethnolinguistic groups in the United States appear to be affected by the proportion of young adults and older persons in each language group. The language shift patterns for these groups have been characterized into four stages:

1. Learning English via mother tongue
2. Learning more English; used in various domains
3. Bilingualism
4. English displaced mother tongue

In order for non-English languages to survive in the United States, three conditions must be met:

1. Parents must use first language
2. Children must learn non-English language as a second language
3. Children must maintain bilingualism

The educational system must also promote bilingualism if it is to flourish in the United States.

Bilingual education around the world varies because of factors associated with cultural homogeneity, political issues, and historical processes.

Throughout history, various conditions created individual societal bilingualism. These include: reciprocal bilingualism motivated by trade; territorial bilingualism motivated by conquest; and, unilateral transitional bilingualism created by migration. In fact, some of the implicit goals of contemporary bilingual education programs seem to be very similar to the efforts of linguistic unification directed by such groups as the Babylonians, Greeks, and Romans.

Bilingual education can influence values, beliefs, and attitudes of students. It can also provide language-majority children with the opportunity to become functionally proficient in a second language. Lack of foreign language competence and knowledge about other cultures can be detrimental to the economic and security interests of the United States. Because of our involvement in world affairs and economic, political, and ecological interdependence with other nations, highly competent bilinguals may be essential for the well being of the country. This concern can be approached through "global" education. Although various departments of education have attempted to identify goals for a global citizenship program, few, as yet, addressed the issue of how students are to cope with a multilingual world.

Various language organizations in the country have asked for the establishment of a coordinated national language policy. Bilingual education programs can serve the linguistic needs of both language-minority children and English-speaking pupils, and, at the same time, respond to the demands for an education with a global perspective. The various kinds of bilingual education programs and their instructional features will be examined in the next chapter.

SUGGESTED READINGS

Articles

Braun, C. M., ed. "Language of Instruction in a Multicultural Setting: Symposium." *International Review of Education* 24: no. 3 (1978): 237–421.

Caliguri, J. P. et al. "An Annotated Bibliography Guide to the Literature on Bilingualism and Multicultural Education" (1980). (Eric Document Reproduction Service No. ED 205365)

Verdoodt, A. "Education in a Multilingual and Multicultural Context." *Education Documents and Information*, no. 204 (1977): 9–44.

Books

Conner, M. W., ed. *A Global Approach to Foreign Language Education.* Skokie, Ill.: National Textbook Company, 1981.

Fishman, J. A. *The Sociology of Language.* Rowley, Mass.: Newbury House Publishers, 1972.

Grosjean, F. *Life with Two Languages: An Introduction to Bilingualism.* Cambridge, Mass: Harvard University Press, 1982.

Hartford, B. and A. Valdman, eds. *Issues in International Bilingual Education.* New York: Plenum Publishing Corporation, 1982.

Lewis, E. G. *Bilingualism and Bilingual Education.* Albuquerque: University of New Mexico Press, 1980.

Spolsky, B. and R. L. Cooper, eds. *Case Studies in Bilingual Education.* Rowley, Mass.: Newbury House Publishers, 1978.

Weinreich, U. *Languages in Contact* The Hague: Mouton and Company, 1970.

TYPES OF BILINGUAL EDUCATION PROGRAMS __

INTRODUCTION

This chapter examines the various types of bilingual programs. Bilingual programs, for example, can be characterized from the point of view of a nation's language policy, educational linguistic goals, and the curricular use of the two languages, as well as the sociolinguistic status of each language. Specific instructional arrangements have been developed to specify language use during the presentation of subject matter as well as the utilization of various teaching personnel. Bilingual programs can be used for compensatory or enrichment purposes. The California State Department of Education has proposed specific program models designed to address the needs of language-minority children attending elementary and secondary schools. The New York State Education Department offers a number of second language/bilingual program options as approaches for promoting intercultural skills and a functional proficiency in second language particularly among English-speaking children.

BILINGUAL EDUCATION AND NATIONAL LANGUAGE GOALS

Bilingual programs can be characterized from a sociolinguistic perspective and as "implementation agents for a nation's language policy" (Garcia 1982:128). According to Garcia, there are at least four distinct types of bilingual instructional programs, designed with various national goals in mind. These include programs of

1. vernacularization, designed to restore an indigenous language and establish it as the national standard (e.g. Tagalog in the Philippines);
2. internationalization, intended to create proficient bilinguals who can function in the international community (e.g. English for Greek students);
3. assimilation, designed to incorporate immigrant groups or linguistic minorities (English for Greek immigrants in Australia); and
4. pluralization, created to allow different language and cultural groups to coexist within a nation (bilingual programs for Navajos in the American Southwest).

BILINGUAL EDUCATION MODELS

In addition to national goals, bilingual programs can be categorized by their linguistic goals. Fishman and Lovas (1970) have classified them as such:

1. Transitional bilingualism — L_1 (mother tongue) is used as an interim medium of instruction until fluency in L_2 (second language) is acquired so that pupils can be incorporated into the "regular" classroom in an L_2 curriculum;
2. Monoliterate bilingualism — L_1 is developed and used in oral communications and to teach content areas;
3. Partial bilingualism — L_1 and L_2 are used for both literacy instruction and the teaching of subject matter; more content areas (e.g. math, science) are taught in L_2, and L_1 is ordinarily used for ethnic-related areas (e.g. social studies, literature); and

4. Full bilingualism — students develop all skills in both languages in all domain.

These programs are characterized in Figures 2-A through 2-D.

Mackey's (1971) models of bilingual education focus on the curricular use of the two languages and the status of each language. His typology accounts for ninety different types of bilingual schools on the basis of

1. the use of one (single medium) or two (dual medium) languages for instruction;
2. transfer or maintenance linguistic goals;
3. trends toward cultural assimilation (gradual or abrupt transfer) or resistance toward assimilation (accultural maintenance); and
4. modes of language interaction (use of L_1 and L_2 in the home, school, region, and nation).

Saravia-Shore (1979:338–339) notes that various models from Mackey's classification system can be found in United States bilingual education efforts. These include the following models:

1. Dual Medium Equal Maintenance — both languages are used as mediums of instruction and given equal treatment (method: alternate mornings and afternoons or days or weeks, etc.)
2. Dual medium differential maintenance — each language has a different function in a different domain
3. Dual medium accultural transfer — initial use of both languages as a preparation for eventual, exclusive use of the mainstream language of wider communication
4. Single medium irredental maintenance — the marked language is maintained only as a subject, not as a medium of instruction
5. Single medium irredental transfer — only the marked language (i.e. Spanish in an immersion bilingual program) is used as a medium of instruction
6. Single medium accultural transfer — English as the sole medium of instruction
7. Dual medium irredental transfer — ESL (English as a second language) as a subject only; the marked language used as a medium of instruction

Valencia's (1976) model of nineteen types of programs represents a partial adaptation of Mackey's typology and is directed at Spanish-speaking pupils differing significantly in their proficiency in English and Spanish and in their familiarity with the standard forms of both languages. His program models include diverse patterns of transition from L1 to L2 (gradual, abrupt, partial, complete) with enrichment components, such as SSP (Spanish for Spanish speakers) and SSL (Spanish as a second language).

Saravia-Shore (1979) suggests that bilingual education models need to be placed in the context of cultural factors (e.g. pluralism or assimilation tendencies — degree of options among majority and minority cultural values and behavioral patterns) and social structural dimensions (e.g. integration — access to higher education, occupations, political power; separatism — separate institutions; segregation — discrimination and token access to higher education, positions of prestige, and political power). Moreover, "bilingual education program models need to be based in specific learning theories which are compatible in order to guide the development of components which mutually support or supplement one another to become a coherent, cohesive whole" (Saravia-Shore 1979:42). To illustrate how the various components of a bilingual education program interact and articulate particular goals, Saravia-Shore (1979:343) contrasts two program models, shown in Table 2.

BILINGUAL INSTRUCTIONAL MODELS

Within the bilingual program, several instructional models have been developed to address language use during the presentation of subject matter. These models include the following:

1. Preview-review approach — the introduction to the lesson is given in one language by an instructor who is the model for that language. The body of the lesson is taught in the other language by another instructor who is both the teacher and the model for the language medium being used. The review is provided either by dividing the students into dominant language groups — each with a model instructor — or by maintaining a language-mixed group and using both languages interchangeably.

2. Concurrent model — the two languages are used interchangeably, with an attempt to avoid direct translation. One instructor may teach the lesson using both languages, or two teachers can present the lesson, each modeling a different language.

3. Alternate language approach — lessons are presented one day (or

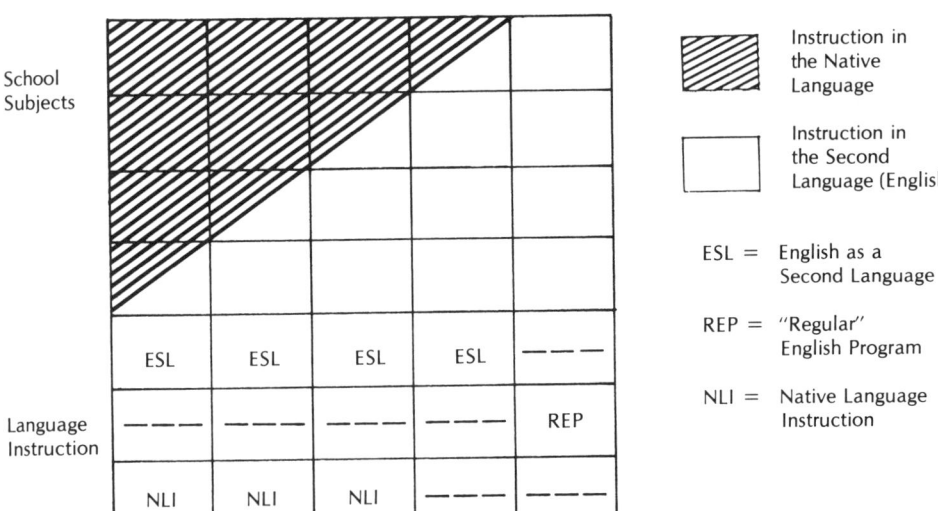

Figure 2-A. Transitional Bilingualism

Figure 2-B. Monoliterate Bilingualism

Figure 2-C. Partial Bilingualism

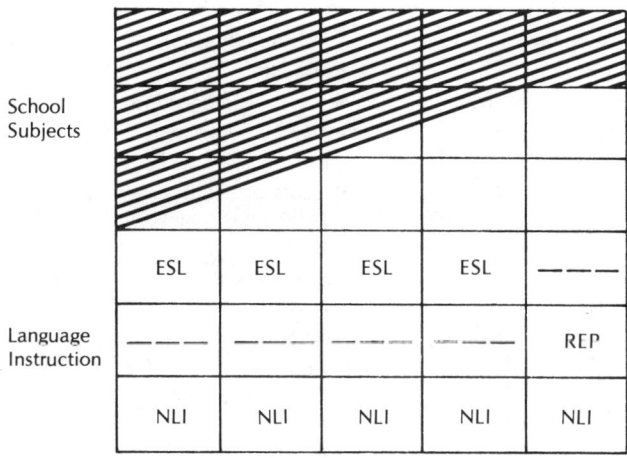

School
Subjects

| ESL | ESL | ESL | ESL | — — — |

Language
Instruction

| — — — | — — — | — — — | — — — | REP |

| NLI | NLI | NLI | NLI | NLI |

Grade Level

Figure 2-D. Full Bilingualism

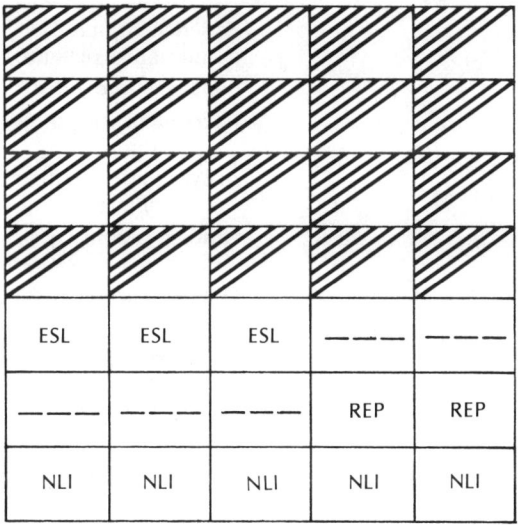

| ESL | ESL | ESL | — — — | — — — |

| — — — | — — — | — — — | REP | REP |

| NLI | NLI | NLI | NLI | NLI |

Grade Level

Table 2. Two Bilingual/Multicultural Program Models with Congruent and Distinctive Features

	Goals	
Languages:	Developmental	Transitional
Culture:	Pluralism	Assimilation
Social Structure:	Structural integration	Structural integration
Model:	*Child Development*	*Behaviorist* (audiolingual)
	Process oriented following Piaget, Chomsky	Product oriented following Skinner
	Teacher speaks L_1 and L_2	Teacher models L_2
	Aide speaks L_1	Aide speaks L_1
	Dominance integration L_2 acquired from peers in natural settings	Dominance segration
	Two-Way program	One-way program
	Ethnic culture is integral	Token cultural activities
	Parent advisory role	Token parent involvement
	Pluralistic context	Mainstream cultural context
	Experiential, multi-cultural curriculum	Objective-based curriculum
	Languages separated	Languages separated
	Curriculum content learned in L_1 first	Curriculum content taught in L_2
	Integration of reading and content	ESL is a subject
	Reading first in L_1	Reading learned first in L_2
	Gradual introduction to L_2	Rapid introduction to L_2
	Language experience approach	L_1 is a subject
	Bilingual program articulated with monolingual	Pull-out programs

during one occasion) in one language and then repeated in the other language on another day (or another time).

In an experiment conducted in the Philippines, Tucker (1970) reports that an "alternate days approach" was followed in bilingual schools using English and Filipino. The material covered on day two was not a repetition of the content presented the first day, but was simply a continuation of the previous day's lesson in the other language which, apparently, was not posing major problems to students or teachers. The alternate language approach can be based on an alternate week model (e.g. English used as a medium of instruction for one week and Chinese utilized the following week), or the half-day model (e.g. French used as the medium of instruction during the morning and English used for the same functions during the afternoon). Instruction in language arts and reading in both languages, whether as a first or second language, is usually conducted on a daily basis, following the goals of the bilingual education program.

From the teacher's perspective, various instructional arrangements are possible:

1. Bilingual resource teacher — assists monolingual (L_2) teachers with native language instruction and specific content areas that are taught bilingually
2. Bilingual aide — assists monolingual (L_2) teacher with native language instruction, though the aide (parent) may lack educational preparation and pedagogical training
3. Team teaching approach — two model bilingual teachers, each consistently using one language with a group of pupils (González and Lezama 1976); or two basically monolingual teachers (one in L_1 and the other in L_2), each providing instruction in language and content areas.

COMPENSATORY VERSUS ENRICHMENT BILINGUAL PROGRAMS

Bilingual instruction in the United States has existed since the Spanish colonization of the Southwest during the sixteenth century. Garcia (1982) characterizes the history of bilingual education in this country according to four major periods:

1550–1815: bilingual instruction for religious reasons (Franciscan missionaries used tribal dialects to christianize Native Americans)
1816–1887: bilingual instruction for maintenance of native language (German-English bilingual schools in Cincinnati)
1880–1960: decline of bilingual instruction
1960–present: establishment of bilingual programs for equalization/ compensation in public schooling (non-native, English-speaking children of diverse language backgrounds attend bilingual programs)

The rationale for federally funded bilingual education programs in the United States (Bilingual Education Act of 1968 — Title VII — and Comprehensive Bilingual Education Act of 1973) rests on the "linguistic mismatch" hypothesis. This assumption is based on the belief that switching between the home language (L_1) and the school language (L_2) results in academic retardation and eventual school failure among language-minority pupils. To compensate for home-school language differences, bilingual programs, usually of the transitional type, are established using the marked language as a co-medium of instruction briefly until the unmarked language (English) is sufficiently learned for use as the sole medium of instruction. Fishman (1982) notes transitional, compensatory bilingual programs constitute most of United States bilingual effort, while this model represents only one-third of the worldwide bilingual effort in such places as the USSR, Francophone West Africa, Anglophone East Africa, and Latin American countries populated by major Indian groups (Mexico, Peru, Guatemala, etc.). Fishman (1982:23–24) points out that transitional, compensatory bilingual education efforts in the United States may not be "conspicuously successful in importing English skills to marked student populations," but they do "provide children with teachers of their own ethnic extraction who can serve as role models" and offer the possibility of "identificational mainstreaming" with the unmarked cultural group.

Enrichment bilingual education, which constitutes about one-third of the worldwide bilingual enterprise, is generally associated with private and church school efforts (Fishman 1982). These "elite" bilingual schools exist in many European countries, Canada (French immersion programs), and the United States (partial and total immersion programs in French, Spanish, German, Italian, and Russian). Bilingual education through immersion (initial L_2 instruction) for children from the majority population can be described "as an 'additive' form of bilingualism, implying that children, with no fear of ethnic/linguistic erosion, can add to one or more foreign languages to their accumulating skills and profit immenscly—in psychological, social, and even economic domains—from the experience" (Lambert 1980:3). The success of enrichment bilingual education programs can be attributed to the "advantaged" status of the students along with their parents who share in the control of various aspects of the programs (staff selections, budgetary decisions, etc.). These programs appear to be "an effective means of developing a functionally bilingual citizenry," and to "the extent that mainstream children are sensitized to and educated in another language and culture, the better the chances are of developing a fairer, more equitable society" (Lambert 1980:2-3).

BILINGUAL EDUCATION AND ENGLISH AS A SECOND LANGUAGE (ESL) PROGRAM DESIGNS

The following program guidelines are offered by the California State Department of Education (1974:34-38) for planning bilingual programs to serve the needs of both English-speaking pupils and limited English-speaking students. Six different program designs are outlined for elementary schools and four types of programs are suggested for secondary schools.

I. ELEMENTARY PROGRAMS*

Elementary Program Design A

Schools able to initiate a fully bilingual program with an all bilingual teaching staff (teachers and aides) may wish to explore the following program design:

1. Begin only at the kindergarten level (or preschool level, depending on the school organization) and operate in all classrooms at that level. If possible, one-half of the students in each classroom should represent the English-speaking culture.
2. The following year, incorporate all classrooms at the first grade

---

*Reproduced from *Bilingual-Bicultural Education and English-as-a-Second Language Education*. Sacramento: California State Department of Education, 1974, 34-38.

level into the program. Thereafter, add one grade level per year.

3. Organize the physical environment in all classrooms for provision of learning centers and individualized instruction.
4. Make provision in the daily schedule to meet the needs of learners in the following areas:
   a. Concept acquisition
   b. Retention and development of home languages
   c. Literacy in home language
   d. Second-language acquisition
   e. Literacy in second language
   f. Self-concept development
5. Group learners according to ability (not according to home language) for concurrent bilingual instruction in the concept or content areas.
6. Group learners according to home language for monolingual reading instruction in that language at the appropriate reading ability level. This approach requires two separate and distinct reading periods.
7. Group learners according to home language for bilingual instruction in the second language which eventually includes reading instruction in that language.
8. Group bilingual learners according to reading ability in each of the two languages. These students participate in both reading periods.

Elementary Program Design B

Schools able to provide only a strand of the bilingual program described in Elementary Program Design A may consider the following procedure:

1. Begin only at the kindergarten level (or preschool level, depending on the school organization) and operate in at least one of the classrooms at that level (with a bilingual teacher and aide). If possible, one-half of the students in such classroom, or classrooms, should represent the dominant English-speaking culture.
2. The following year, provide for continuation of the bilingual strand in at least one of the classrooms at the first grade level. Thereafter, continue the stranding process, adding one grade level per year.

3. This program design also incorporates the features described in items 3 through 8 under Elementary Program Design A.

Elementary Program Design C

Schools able to provide only a bilingual-monolingual team-teaching approach may consider the following program design, which requires bilingual aides in each classroom:

1. Begin only at the kindergarten level (or preschool level, depending on the school organization) and operate in all classrooms at that level. If possible, one-half of the students in each classroom should represent the dominant English-speaking culture.
2. Organize the bilingual-monolingual teaching team in such a manner that each of the classrooms involved receives daily instruction from the monolingual English-speaking teacher during one-half of the day and instruction from the bilingual teacher during the other half. Either the teachers or the students may exchange classrooms for instruction. The bilingual aides may or may not exchange classrooms, depending on the need for their skills.
3. The following year, incorporate all classrooms at the first grade level into the program. Thereafter, add one grade level per year.
4. This program design also incorporates the features described in items 3 through 8 under Elementary Program Design A.

Elementary Program Design D

Schools able to provide only a strand of the bilingual-monolingual team teaching approach may consider the following design, which also requires bilingual aides in each classroom:

1. Begin only at the kindergarten level (or preschool level, depending on the school organization) and operate in at least two of the classrooms at that level. If possible, one-half of the students in each classroom should represent the dominant English-speaking culture.
2. The following year, provide for continuation of the bilingual strand in at least two of the classrooms at the first grade level.

Thereafter, continue the stranding process, adding one grade-level per year.
3. This design also incorporates the features described in items 3 through 8 under Elementary Program Design A.

Elementary Program Design E

Schools able to initiate only English-as-a-second language (ESL) programs may wish to consider the following procedures:

1. Offer the program at any grade level on the basis of student needs.
2. Offer the physical environment to facilitate the learning of a second language by providing a teaching station for that purpose.
3. Assign pupils to a group according to language proficiency. If possible, group pupils in the lower grades and pupils in the upper grades separately.
4. Organize instruction on a self-contained type basis (from two to three hours daily) during which time pupils are given instruction in the language skills as well as in content areas. The balance of the school day is spent in the regular program. Examples of this approach include:
    a. Extended daily instruction for beginning students in separate ESL stations, with the aide following students back to the classroom for reinforcement in ESL instruction and tutoring in other areas of instruction
    b. Combinations of separate station instruction and (within) classroom instruction, depending on cluster grouping in regular classroom assignments
    c. Team approach within classroom between ESL specialist and regular classroom teacher
5. Establish a traveling teacher design. The teacher travels from the teaching station for a limited period of time where the teacher provides ESL instruction to pupils identified for that purpose. Coordination of the regular classroom activities and ESL instruction is essential to a meaningful educational experience for pupils.
6. Pull-out programs may be established in which students are pulled out of the regular classroom to a separate teaching station to receive ESL instruction. Recognize that this procedure,

as with the traveling teacher, offers only a limited amount of time with students.

    a. Provide instruction in a separate ESL station, with daily reinforcement in the regular classroom by the ESL specialist or aide.

    b. Provide instruction in a separate station for individuals with special ESL needs.

7. Provide resource help to the regular classroom teache by the specialist, with teacher doing his own instruction.

Elementary Program Design F

Schools may combine the features of elementary program designs "A" through "E" to organize additional modified bilingual-ESL programs.

II. SECONDARY PROGRAMS

Secondary Program Design A

Schools able to initiate a fully bilingual program with completely bilingual teaching staff may wish to explore these possibilities:

1. Establish the bilingual program as a separate department with a designated department chairperson.
2. Provide bilingual instruction in each of the subject areas.
3. Assign monolingual teachers to teach the ESL classes where students receive intensive English instruction.
4. Assign bilingual staff to teach the content areas for concept development.
5. Assign bilingual staff to teach elective courses on language literacy.
6. Assign paraprofessionals to tutor small groups of students for reinforcement purposes or to help on individual needs, as recommended by staff.
7. Schedule English instruction classes of different proficiency levels at the same time block to provide for the greater flexibility of movement from one ability group to the other as rapidly as possible.

8. Provide opportunities for the bilingual program students to interact in all areas of the total school environment, such as music, fine arts, physical education, industrial arts, and the humanities.

Secondary Program Design B

Schools able to initiate only an ESL program may wish to consider the following procedures:

1. Establish the ESL program as a separate department with designated department chairperson.
2. Organize instruction on a developmental basis.
3. Group and assign students according to language proficiency:
   a. ESL beginning level for students with limited or no proficiency in English
   b. ESL intermediate level for students with increased competencies of proficiency in English
   c. ESL advanced level for students with adequate mastery of English but with a need to develop an appreciation for literature and to refine their composition skills
   d. ESL transition level for students preparing to undertake a regular instructional program
4. Provide a core program which offers intensive instruction in the first year of ESL. This is essential for success.
5. Decrease ESL instruction gradually each year or semester until the students are phased into a complete regular program.
6. Carefully schedule students into other subject areas in which limited speakers of English can function with confidence and achieve success.
7. Assign students to the program only as long as they need it and move them along as rapidly as possible on the basis of teaching staff recommendations.

Secondary Program Design C

Schools may combine the features of secondary program designs "A" or "B" to organize modified bilingual-ESL programs.

SECOND LANGUAGE IMMERSION INSTRUCTIONAL MODELS

In contrast to the types of bilingual education programs already mentioned, second language/bilingual program designs appropriate for majority-language children in elementary schools have been suggested by the New York State Education Department (1982:9–12) as appropriate models for implementing the state's plan for "education for a global perspective." The global dimension in education will require schools to promote intercultural skills (cognitive and affective) and a functional proficiency in a second language. To achieve both these goals will mean the reintroduction of "foreign" language programs beginning at the elementary school level. The models range from total or partial immersion to the "switch" approach, involving trading classes between the bilingual education teacher and the English-speaking, common branch subject teacher, responsible for instruction in the various content areas.

I. EARLY LANGUAGE IMMERSION (ELI)*

1. Description
    (ELI) programs are designed for English-speaking children who live in an English-speaking environment. Of the foreign language instructional models in elementary schools, ELI sets the highest goal: functional proficiency in a foreign language by grade 6. By the time ELI students complete grade 6, they are able to function as sixth graders in a country where the foreign language is spoken (Rhodes, 1981:9). They also perform as well on tests of English as their peers taught only through English (Rhodes, 1981:9). As reported by an ELI school principal, "Immersion students have suffered no loss in any academic area and have even achieved beyond expectation in some of them" (Jacobs, 1978:41).
    ELI begins in kindergarten or grade 1. During the first three years (grades K-2 or 1-3), all of the common elementary-school subjects are taught in the foreign language. Thereafter, English is phased in and increased gradually as the medium of instruction. By grade 6, the foreign language/English ratio of instruction is generally 50%/50%. However, there may be variations to this ratio in grade 6.
    Although ELI teachers use only the foreign language during the first three years of instruction, students initially respond in English.

*Reproduced from *Education for a Global Perspective, a Plan for New York State*. Albany: State Education Department, Sept. 1982, pp. 9–12.

They begin to respond in the foreign language gradually and by the end of the first year they communicate with the teacher (but not yet among themselves) primarily in the foreign language. During the second year, students begin communicating with each other in the foreign language as well. By the end of the third year, most of them can switch from one language to the other.

ELI programs require teachers who are fluent in the foreign language and trained to teach all elementary-school subjects in that language. In addition, they must have a thorough understanding of the psychology of elementary-school students whose native language and environment is American English.

2. Modified/Partial ELI

A school day in a modified or partial early language immersion program is the same as in a total immersion program, except that one or more of the subjects are taught in English from the beginning. In such programs, the one subject that is almost always taught in English is language arts. In total immersion programs, English is phased in as the medium of instruction after the first three years.

Schools may decide to introduce a modified or partial rather than a total ELI program for any number of reasons.

Partial ELI - A Compromise. While research reports that ELI is effective for developing fluency without a negative influence on either English language acquisition or other common branch subjects, it represents such a substantial departure from conventional approaches that partial ELI is often adopted as a compromise. However, partial ELI loses some of the advantages of total immersion.

Availability of qualified personnel. Until teacher-training institutions develop appropriate pre-service training programs, the supply of adequately trained ELI teachers will be limited. Because of the shortage of qualified teachers, schools may initiated a partial ELI program in which 50% of the subjects are taught in the foreign language by an ELI teacher and 50% of the subjects are taught in English by a regular common-branch teacher.

Contractual agreements. In some school districts, including New York City, teachers' contracts provide for one or more daily periods of preparation time. Floating teachers (or cluster teachers) instruct students during the regular teacher's preparation time. Unless floating teachers are competent to give instruction in the foreign language, the subject area assigned to them would be taught in English in a modified ELI model.

II. SELF-CONTAINED CLASSROOM

1. Description

The self-contained classroom models require no additional personnel to provide foreign language instruction in elementary schools. In a self-contained classroom all of the common elementary-school subjects are taught in English. In addition, the same classroom teacher (rather than an additional foreign language specialist) teaches the foreign language. Foreign language instruction may begin in grade 1 or later with frequencies varying from three to five times a week. Instruction in listening and speaking tends to be emphasized. Students' development of foreign language skills is commensurate with exposure time and type of instructional emphasis. The teacher is trained to teach common elementary school subjects in English, has proficiency in the foreign language, and has a knowledge of the people whose language is taught.

2. Floating Teacher or Cluster Model

The floating teacher model is a variation of the self-contained classroom model. It is used where schools have teachers who instruct classes during the regular classroom teachers' contractually negotiated preparation periods. Instead of hiring all common-branch subject teachers, schools hire, as floating or "cluster," teachers a sufficient number to conduct foreign language instruction during those periods.

3. Switch Model

The "switch" model is another variation of the self-contained classroom model. It uses existing personnel other than the regular common-branch classroom teacher to teach a foreign language to English-speaking students.

The "switch" model can be applied in schools with bilingual programs for non-English-dominant students. In it, the bilingual education teacher and the English-speaking, common branch subject teacher trade classes during one instructional period, so that the bilingual teacher teaches the foreign language to the English-speaking students and the common branch teacher teaches English to the non-English-dominant students.

A diagram comparing the time distribution of school subjects in a typical day in elementary schools (primary and intermediate levels) with or without a foreign language program is presented in Figure 3. The inclusion of the foreign language component does not seem to have a major effect on the other school subjects in the curriculum. The allocation of instructional time for specific subjects seems based on other priorities rather than on foreign language considerations.

SUMMARY

Bilingual education programs can be characterized from a sociolinguistic perspective and can be viewed as the "implementation of a nation's language policy." This policy includes programs designed for: (1) vernacularization, (2) internationalization, (3) assimilation, and (4) pluralization. Various bilingual eduation models have also been designed based on linguistic goals: (1) transitional bilingualism, (2) monoliterate bilingualism, (3) partial bilingualism, and (4) full bilingualism.

Mackey's typology is based on ninety different types of bilingual schools and focuses on the curricular use of the two languages and the status of each language in respect to (1) single medium or dual medium language instruction, (2) transfer or maintenance, (3) cultural assimilation or accultural maintenance, and (4) use of L_1 and L_2 in home, school, region, and nation. Saravia-Shore notes that bilingual programs need to be placed in the context of (1) cultural factors, (2) social structural dimensions, and (3) learning theories.

The issue of language use when presenting subject matter has been addressed through the use of various models: (1) preview-review approach, (2) concurrent model, and (3) alternate language approach. In addition, various arrangements have been proposed to make use of teaching personnel with different language capabilities and skills: (1) bilingual resource teacher — assists monolingual teacher with instruction in the content areas and the native language, (2) bilingual aide — assists monolingual teacher with instruction, and (3) team teachers — two bilingual teachers each using one language with a group of students.

Four main periods in the history of bilingual education in the United States were mentioned. The main reason behind the present-day legislation known as the Bilingual Education Act of 1968 rests on the linguistic "mismatch" hypotheses. To compensate for home-school language differences, different bilingual education programs have been established to address language needs. Most programs in the United States are of the transitional, compensatory type, while around the world enrichment ("elite") bilingual programs predominate. The New York State Educa-

Figure 3.
Representational Diagram of Typical Class Days for Elementary
School with or without Foreign Language Programs

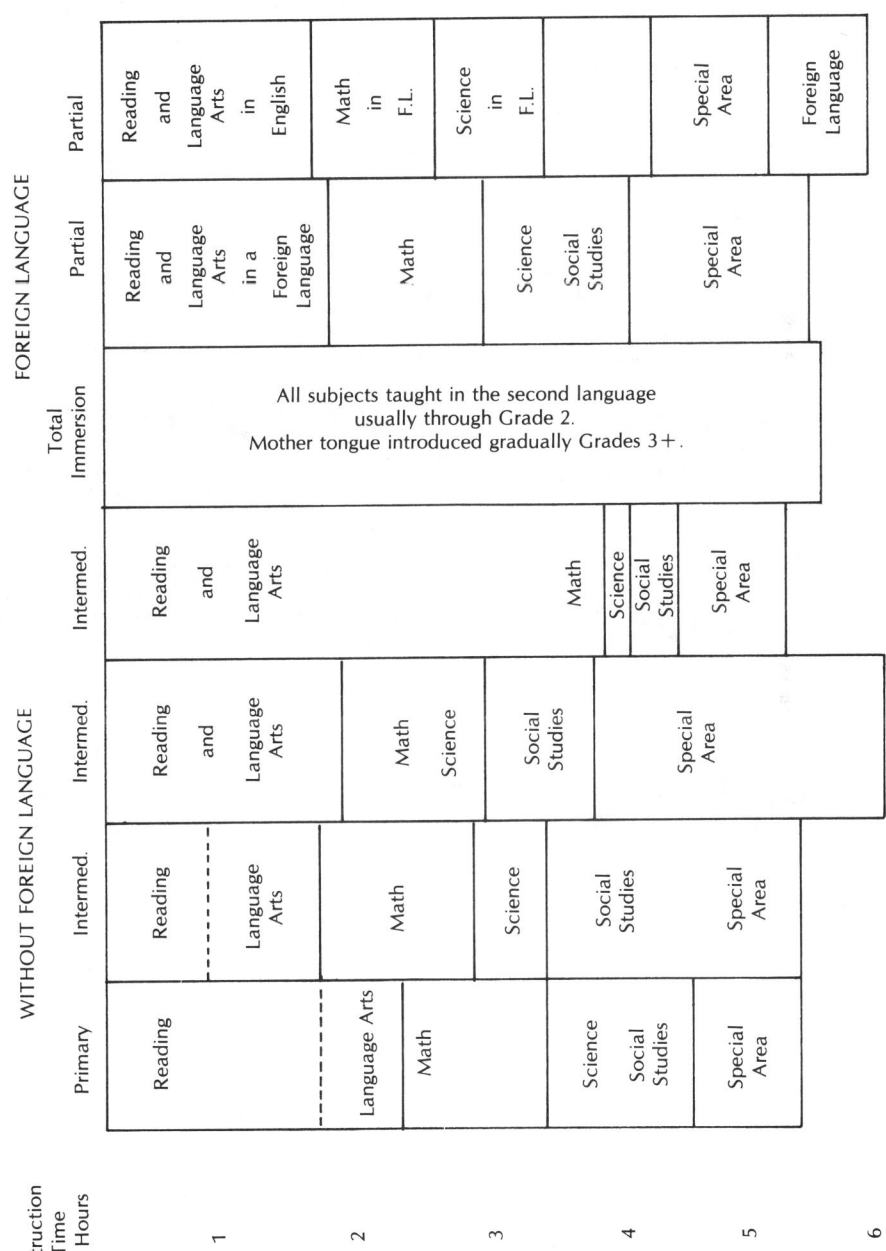

tion Department has proposed a number of models designed to implement the state's plan for global education. The proposed models range from total immersion to the "switch" approach.

In the following chapter, the important topic of assessing bilingual proficiency will be discussed. Various factors associated with the assessment of bilingual proficiency abilities will be examined, along with the educational implications of language testing.

SUGGESTED READINGS

Anderson, T. and M. Boyer, eds. *Bilingual Schooling in the United States.* Austin, Texas: National Educational Laboratory Publishers, Inc., 1978.

Chu-Chang, M., ed. *Asian- and Pacific-American Perspectives in Bilingual Education.* New York: Teachers College Press, Columbia University, 1983.

Donoghue, M. R. and J. F. Kunkle. *Second Languages in Primary Education.* Rowley, Mass.: Newbury House Publishers, 1979.

Fishman, J. A. and G. D. Keller, eds. *Bilingual Education for Hispanic Students in the United States.* New York: Teachers College Press, Columbia University, 1982.

Trueba, H. T. and C. Barnett-Mizrahi, eds. *Bilingual/Multicultural Education and the Professional.* Rowley, Mass.: Newbury House Publishers, 1979.

ASSESSMENT OF BILINGUAL PROFICIENCY _____

INTRODUCTION

The measurement of bilingual proficiency is influenced by conceptions regarding language itself, developments in language testing theory, and educational issues (e.g. identification of "limited" English-speaking pupils and assignment of students to different educational programs based on language proficiency levels). Individual bilingualism is usually expressed in terms of the person's knowledge of the two languages. This proficiency can include relative knowledge of different aspects of language (grammar, vocabulary, pronunciation), language skills (listening, speaking, reading, and writing), and sociolinguistic dimensions of language (style, language varieties, functions). The depiction of bilingual proficiency from a behavioral-structural model of language tends to be associated with discrete-point testing, involving specific linguistic items scored on the basis of grammatical accuracy. The assessment of bilingual competence from a communicative perspective focuses on an "integrated," global ability, involving the functional use of language in a given sociolinguistic situation. Communicative competence testing is an active field in language research, but most assessment instruments used in bilingual programs serving ethnolinguistic minority children focus on grammatical skills. The choice of a particular language test can influence educational decisions regarding the entry/exit criteria used in bilingual programs for language-minority schoolchildren in the United States.

CONCEPTIONS OF BILINGUAL PROFICIENCY

Bilingualism is usually measured by an individual's knowledge of his two languages. Cohen (1975) draws from Bordie (1970), Macnamara (1967), and Cooper (1968, 1970) in depicting the degree of bilingualism by five linguistic levels — semantics, syntax, morphemes, phonemes/graphemes, and lexicon — four language skills — two (reading and listening) which are receptive and two (speaking and writing) which are productive — various language varieties — refering either to a dialect (e.g. Southwest Spanish or "standard" Mexican Spanish), register type (e.g. classroom Spanish), or level of formality (e.g. academic/literary Spanish or colloquial Spanish).

From the perspective of language-testing theory, Cohen's model (see Figure 4) follows the behavioral-structural mode of language learning. His attention to "language variety" takes into account variability in language use due to the situation or speaker's dialect. In addition, he focuses on the area of orthography by including graphemes (the written representation of phonemes) with the written skills involved in writing and reading.

LANGUAGE DOMINANCE

Zirkel's (1974) conceptual framework for determining and depicting language dominance includes the four language skills, five linguistic components, and three sociolinguistic contexts (home, community, and school). He describes his diagram, shown in Figure 5, by saying:

> The four basic language skills and the cultural substratum are represented as a series of continua which are interrelated to the socio-linguistic domains and linguistic levels within a three-dimensional matrix (*sic*). Each continuum can be constituted of quantifiable units in Spanish and English depending on the dominance measure that is utilized. Each dimension could be further analyzed and segmented (e.g., listening skill into comprehension and phonetic discrimination; speaking skill into pronunciation, intonation, etc.) (Zirkel 1974:12).

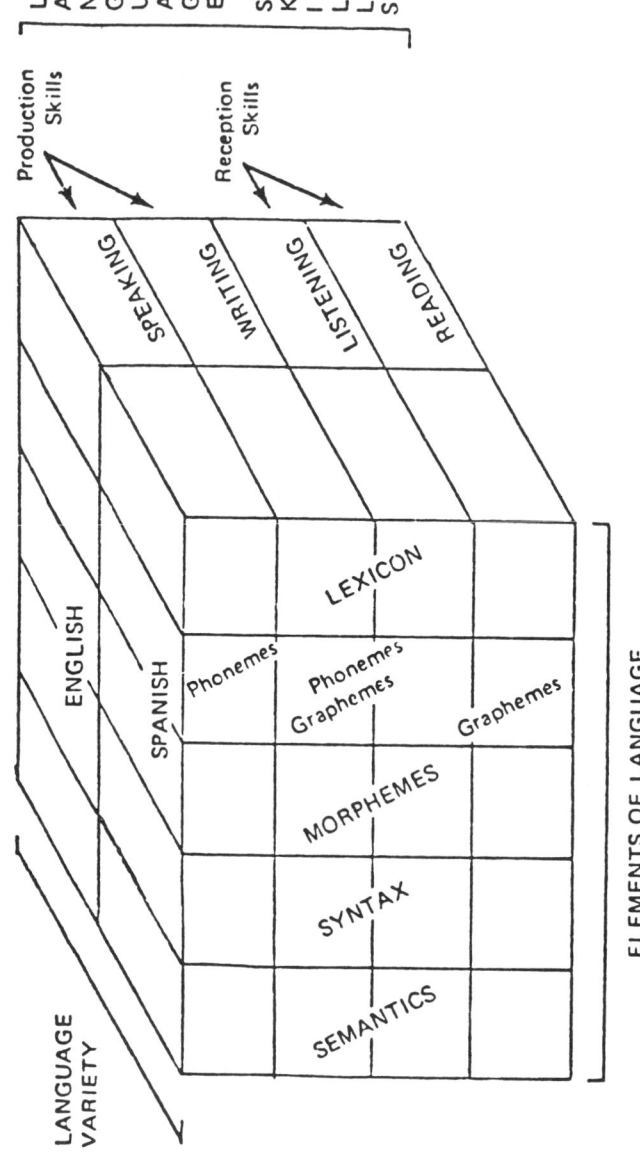

Figure 4. Cohen's Model of Language Testing (1975, p. 9).

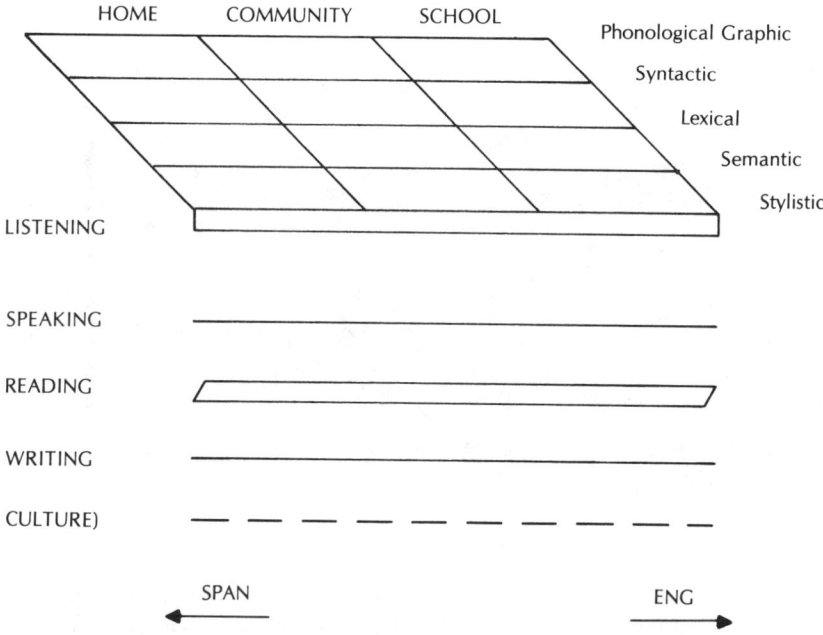

Figure 5. Representation of Bilingual Dominance Matrix. Reprinted, by permission, from P. A. Zirkel, "A Method for Determining and Depicting Language Dominance" *TESOL Quarterly,* 8:1 (March 1974): 12.

While Zirkel's model explains bilingual dominance in relation to a series of continua composed of "quantifiable units," his concern for the speaker's ability to understand and use language appropriately (his stylistic category) in various situations reflects a context-sensitive view of language. Bilingual dominance could then be seen in a multidimensional perspective. Ramírez (1979) illustrates how bilingual proficiency could vary in the area of vocabulary in different contexts (home, neighborhood, church, and school and in specific school subject areas (math and art). Figure 6 represents parallel vocabulary tests of eight items in English and Spanish for each of the six contexts. A "balance" (dominance) now can be derived for each area by contrasting the correct number of items obtained in each language.

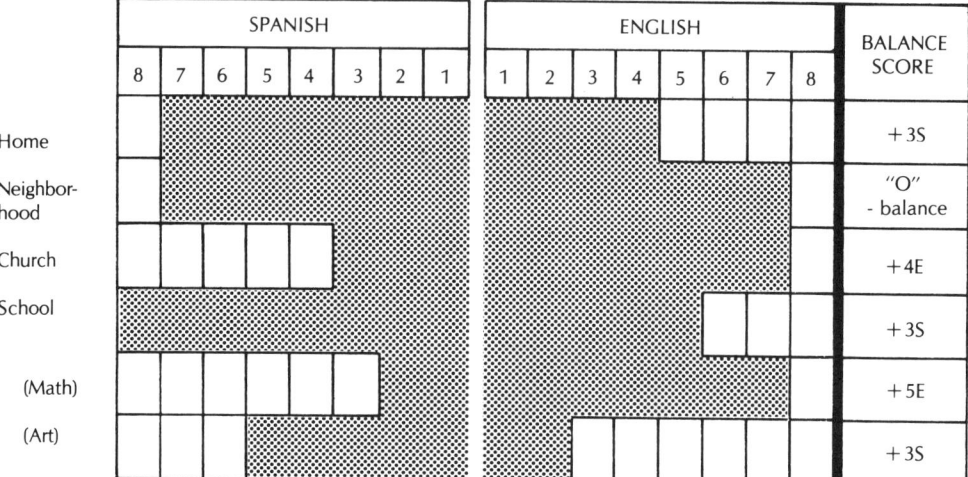

Figure 6. Vocabulary-by-Domain Test. Reprinted, by permission, from A. G. Ramírez, "Language Dominance and Pedagogical Considerations" In E. J. Briere, ed. *Language Development in a Bilingual Setting* (Los Angeles: National Dissemination and Assessment Center, California State University, 1979a): 161.

LANGUAGE DOMINANCE AND BILINGUAL PROFICIENCY

Hernández-Chávez, Burt, and Dulay (1978) characterize language dominance in relation to three major dimensoins: (1) the linguistic components—phonology, syntax, semantics, and lexicon; (2) modality—the oral channel (spoken production and listening comprehension) and the written channel (reading and writing); and (3) sociolinguistic performance—usage (style and function) and language use (variety and domain). They suggest that a three-dimensionsl matrix could be constructed with sixty-four possible intersections of "independently measurable" language proficiencies; however, an attempt to measure each component in the model would be a monumental task (see Figure 7.). Even if some of the components could be combined with others or eliminated because of

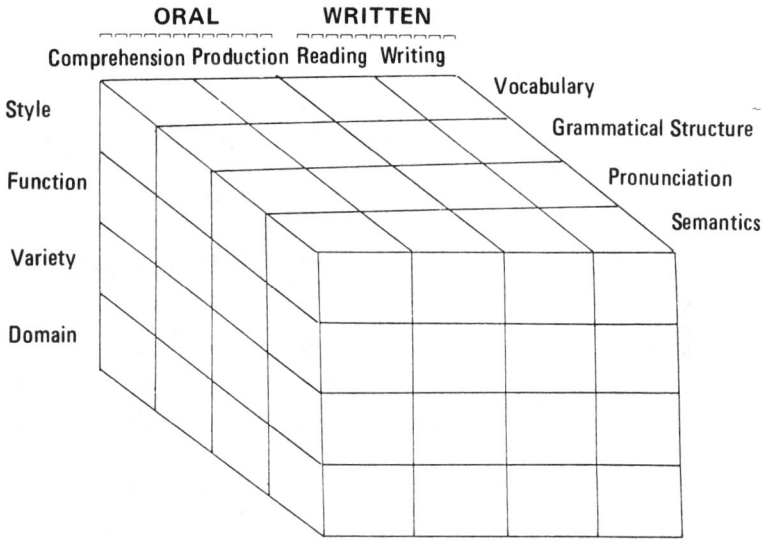

Figure 7. Linguistic Parameters Relevant to Proficiency Testing. Reprinted by permission, from E. Hernández-Chávez, M. . Burt, and H. C. Dalay, "Language Dominance and Proficiency Testing: Some General Considerations" *NABE Journal* 3:1 (Fall 1978): 43.

nonsignificance, testing equivalent proficiencies in both languages is problematic since the use and function of two languages in society is unequal. Spanish may be used only in the oral modality (conversations in the context of the home and neighborhood, or in radio programming) in a given locality, while English is utilized in both the oral and written modalities and employed in the domains of school, work, government, and church. In addition, the particular variety of Spanish may include borrowing from English as well as "nonstandard" and/or archaic Spanish features. It may also be the case that some speakers may alternate (code switch) from one language to the other while performing communicative acts (e.g. asking for permission, apologizing, explaining, etc.). Apparently, then, measuring language dominance without examining the nature of societal bilingualism could greatly distort any conclusions about an individual's bilingual proficiency.

Recent development in language testing has been devoted to characterizing the different linguistic aspects tapped by various tests (see Jones and Spolsky 1975; Valette 1977; Davies 1978; Oller and Perkins 1980; and Oller 1979). Language testing associated with the behavioral-structural model of language learning divides language skills according to linguistic levels (phonology, morphology, syntax, vocabulary) and into performance skills which are either receptive (reading, listening) or active (writing, speaking). These skills are usually tested according to a discrete-point approach which allows for high (specific item based) reliability.

Linguistic competence usually refers to the ability to produce (and recognize) structures which are grammatically correct. Davies (1978: 149) describes this ability as an "analytical discrete" skill reflected in the speaker's mastery of the formal grammar of the language. Palmer (1979:170) views this competence as a "compartmentalized control" of language.

AREAS OF LANGUAGE ASSESSMENT

Vocabulary

Studies of bilingual proficiency focusing on "discrete" elements of language have examined various linguistic dimensions. In the area of vocabulary, Cohen (1976) asked Spanish/English bilingual pupils to name objects found in settings associated with the domains of home, education, religion, and neighborhood. These domains were based on the findings of Greenfield and Fishman (1971) who investigated language use patterns among members of a Puerto Rican community in Jersey City. Cohen selected the settings of kitchen, school, church, and street and asked each child to name as many objects as possible for each location within a period of forty five seconds. The task was given in both English and Spanish, thus yielding the relative size of the child's active vocabulary in each language according to the four contexts.

Along the same lines, Ramírez and Politzer (1975a) developed a vocabulary-by-domain test consisting of four sections (home, neighborhood, church, and school), each with eight items, and requiring the pupil to match one of three sentences with a picture. a "balance" score for each domain could be derived by contrasting the correct number of items obtained for English and Spanish. Figure 6 illustrates graphically the notion of vocabulary-by-domain for these four areas as well as for subject matter vocabulary associated with math and art.

Hinofotis (1977) explored the notion of lexical dominance in Greek and English using a picture vocabulary test and word association tasks. The picture vocabulary test consisted of two sets of sixty pictures, each depicting simple objects to be named by the pupil in each language. A language dominance score was determined for each subject by calculating the difference in seconds between the mean times for the two sets of pictures in Greek and English. The word association task involved two procedures — first, naming in each language as many words as possible associated with nine stimuli objects (e.g. a doll, phonograph record, spoon, towel, pencil, apple, stuffed animal); second, requiring each subject to name words in each language associated with seven word classes (toys, furniture, animals, fruits, clothes, sweets, and kitchen). Each task yielded a mean number of words by language and by category, thus indicating the subject's relative control of each language.

Grammatical Structure

The assessment of relative bilingual proficiency by grammatical categories has been characterized from different perspectives. Carrow (1971) compared preschoolers' comprehension of English and Spanish structures, including such aspects as nouns, pronouns, plurals, negatives, tense markers, and noun phrases with adjective modifiers. Peña (1967) measured among first graders the productive use of six basic sentence patterns and five basic transformations (e.g. negation, questions, passives) for both English and Spanish based on *The Grammatical Structures of English and Spanish* by Stockwell, Bowen, and Martin (1965). Ramírez and Politzer (1975b) assessed bilingual proficiency by asking pupils in grades 1, 3, 5 and 7 to perform linguistic operations requiring the (1) change from singular to plural, (2) change from plural to singular, (3) change from present to past, (4) change from affirmative to negative, (5) indication of location, (6) conversion of indirect to direct question, (7) conversion of indirect to direct command, (8) conversion of direct to indirect question, (9) conversion of direct to indirect command, and (10) change from positive to comparative in adjectives and adverbs. Two items were included in each category and each item was accompanied by two related pictures, one described in a sentence by the test administrator and one completed by the student.

Relative bilingual proficiency can be depicted in relation to a pupil's control of specific grammatical categories in both languages. Figure 8 illustrates the performance of a student exhibiting a greater mastery of Spanish grammar (total score = 15) when compared to a parallel English test (total score = 9). Another method for indicating relative proficiency involves the use of performance levels. Performance on the two parallel tests, each with twenty items, could be expressed in terms of five levels, each level including four correct/acceptable responses. Figure 9 represents the performance of four pupils. Student A (S_5 E_5) has a higher degree of "balance" than student D (S_3 E_3), and student B (S_4 E_2) is more dominant in Spanish while student C (S_2 E_4) is the opposite.

Category	Item	English		Spanish	
I	1, 2	+	−	+	+
II	3, 4	+	−	✓	+
III	5, 6	✓	✓	+	+
IV	7, 8	+	+	−	+
V	9, 10	+	✓	+	+
VI	11, 12	−	−	−	−
VII	13, 14	−	−	✓	−
VIII	15, 16	−	−	+	+
IX	17, 18	−	−	−	✓
X	19, 20	−	−	+	✓
TOTAL		5 + 3 = 8 correct		11 + 4 = 15 correct	

+ = correct response
✓ = acceptable response
− = incorrect response

Figure 8. Relative Bilingual Proficiency in Grammatical Categories

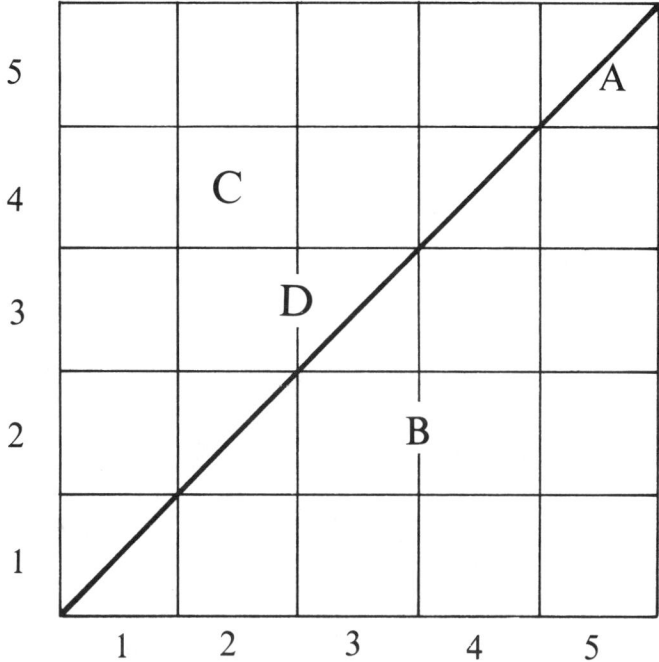

Figure 9. Relative Bilingual Proficiency in Terms of Performance Levels

TESTS OF LANGUAGE SKILLS

Some individuals could be classified as passive bilinguals (oral proficiency in one language, receptive language skills — listening comprehension — in the other), others as productive bilinguals (oral abilities in both languages — mastery of formal and informal varieties in one language, informal/colloquial variety in the other language), and some as biliterate bilinguals (oral and written competence in both languages — mastery of formal and informal varieties in both languages, literary variety in one language). Figure 10 presents possible types of bilinguals according to language skills. Student A can be described as a productive bilingual since he/she comprehends and speaks both languages. Student D is both

Language	A		B		Student C		D		E	
Skill	L_1	L_2	L_1	L_2	L_1	L_2	L_1	L_2	L_1	L_2
Listening	+	+	+	+	+	+	+	+	+	+
Speaking	+	+	+	+	+	+	+	+	+	−
Reading	−	−	+	−	−	+	+	+	+	−
Writing	−	−	+	−	−	+	+	+	+	−

Figure 10. Bilingual Proficiency According to Four Language Skills

bilingual and biliterate, whereas student B is literate only in L_1, and student C is able to read and write in L_2. Student E has a passive knowledge (oral comprehension) of L_2.

Studies of English and Spanish bilingualism in terms of language skills have been conducted with test development efforts in various states. Brown and Zirkel (1977) report on some of the results using New York City's *Language Assessment Battery*, and Agrawal (1979) describes the construction of Chicago Board of Education's *Short Tests of Linguistic Skills*. Language skills in French and English have been assessed in Canadian "immersion" bilingual projects (Swain and Lapkin 1982). Cohen (1976) investigated the development of English and Spanish language skills among pupils in a bilingual program in California. These same pupils were tested by Chun and Politzer (1975) and Merino (1982) with measures to determine comprehension and production of various grammatical features. Merino included items from seven categories (number, gender, past tense, word order, Spanish subjunctive/English equivalents, relatives, and conditions). Chun and Politzer examined fourteen categories (e.g. singular/plural, present/past, mass/-count noun, subject pronouns, active/passive sentences with agent/object reversals). The fourteen categories for both the comprehension and production tasks were translated into French and were used to assess language development among pupils attending a French/English bilingual school in grades K, 1, 3, and 5 in San Francisco.

LINGUISTIC COMPETENCE TESTS

Many of the assessment instruments available and currently used within the context of bilingual education programs have been described by Silverman et al. (1976) and Pletcher et al. (1978). The majority of the instruments focus on linguistic competence and concentrate on the oral channel of communication, testing pupils' speaking ability. Most of the instruments can be classified in one of three categories:

1. Those that determine language dominance at the level of vocabulary (e.g. Crane Oral Dominance Test, James Lanugage Dominance Test, Dos Amigos Verbal Language Scales)
2. Those that establish language dominance through the mastery of grammatical features/syntactic structures or sentence complexity (e.g. Bilingual Syntax Measure, Basic Inventory of Natural Language, MAT-SEA-CAL Instruments for Assessing Language Proficiency)

3. Those that determine establishment of dominance according to the four language skills — listening, speaking, reading, and writing (e.g. Language Assessment Battery, Marysville Test of Language Dominance).

A few tests, such as the Language Assessment Scales (LAS I and II), include various linguistic components:

1. Phonology (phonemic distinctions)
2. Lexicon (word identification through pictures)
3. Syntax (associating a picture with a sentence and recalling a story)
4. Pragmatic use of language (teacher rates the child's ability to complete tasks requiring language — playing with peers, shopping at the store). This fourth dimension is not included in the scoring calculations, but may be used as a comparison with the pupil's final proficiency level.

COMMUNICATIVE COMPETENCE PERSPECTIVES

Communicative competence is often characterized as an "integrated control" (Palmer 1979:170) of language, reflected in the speaker's ability to understand and use language appropriately for communicating in various situations. The theoretical basis for the communicative competence construct comes from the anthropological, sociolinguistic, and pragmatic view of language. The testing of communicative competence is associated with a global ability (integrating the different elements of language — grammar, vocabulary, etc.) to perform communicative acts — giving direction, requesting permission, apologizing, etc. In most instances, the specific situations are described by the examiner and rating scales are used to evaluate how effectively the examinee performed the communicative act.

ASPECTS OF COMMUNICATIVE COMPETENCE

Definitions of communicative competence are often relatively broad. One definition, for instance, includes the ability to adapt the totality of one's communicative resources, both linguistic and functional (i.e. extralinguistic and paralinguistic) to a given situation" (Legarreta

1979:523). Recent attempts undertaken by communication experts (Wiemann and Backlaud 1980) or applied linguists (Canale and Swain 1980) to define the concept of communicative competence have only demonstrated the multiplicity of possible components involved. Seemingly, at least three distinct traditions of inquiry are merging in the communicative competence field:

1. Psychologists and communication specialists view communicative competence primarily as the ability to understand, organize, and convey information (e.g. Flavell et al. 1968; Wang et al. 1973

2. In the tradition of philosophers of language like Austin (1962) or Searle (1969), communicative competence is viewed as the ability to perform speech acts efficiently

3. Sociolinguistic tradition, itself often influenced by the philosophy of language mentioned above, defines communicative competence with regard to situational appropriateness of language use (Hymes 1971; Shuy 1979)

Canale (1981), for example, depicts communicative competence according to four areas:

1. Grammatical competence (mastery of the language code — lexical items, rules of word formation, sentence formation, literal meaning, pronunciation, and spelling)

2. Sociolinguistic competence (mastery of appropriate language use in different contexts, with emphasis on appropriateness of meanings and forms)

3. Discourse competence (mastery of how to combine meanings and forms to achieve a unified text in different modes — telephone conversation, persuasive essay — through the use of cohesion devices relating utterance forms and coherence rules to organize meanings)

4. Strategic competence (mastery of verbal and nonverbal strategies to compensate for breakdowns in communication due to insufficient competence or performance limitations — use of dictionaries, paraphrasing — and to enhance communication effectiveness)

This model incorporates the oral and written modalities of languages within various communicative situations (e.g. writer to reader — friend or stranger; speaker to listener — student to teacher or student to friend).

The testing of communicative competence is a very active and prolific field. Although less than a decade ago communicative competence testing was still a relatively new field (Savignon 1972; Briere 1971), it is now a much discussed area of research (see Davies 1978; Marrow 1977, Briere 1979). The measurement of communicative competence faces many problems, some of them related to the already mentioned vagueness of the concept or trait to be measured. The measurement problems are compounded by the fact that the usual measurement of communicative competence is based on global rating scale approaches, while linguistic competence is generally measured in tests using a discrete item method. As a result, the suggestion has been made that in many situations a presumed difference between measured linguistic and communicative competence may reflect a difference in method of measurement rather than in the trait or constructs being measured (Corrigan and Upshur 1978; Stevenson 1979).

One of the challenges in constructing communicative competence tests is to resolve what has been referred to as the reliability/validity tension in language testing (Davies 1978). Highly reliable discrete point tests which present language out of context lack the communicative situation and, therefore, have little face validity. Tests which elicit a genuine communicative type of response have validity, but often depend for their reliability on inter-rater agreements based on rating scales.

MEASURES OF COMMUNICATIVE COMPETENCE

Several studies comparing the relationship between linguistic and communicative competence among bilinguals have been conducted. Overall (1978) determined the extent to which grammatical tests were accurate measures of communicative competence. Thirty Spanish-speaking students enrolled in a bilingual program were administered two grammatical tests of English and a sociolinguistic measure (SLM) developed by the researcher. The SLM consisted of role-playing situations using puppets to represent the participants (e.g. teacher, student, principal) in various communicative contexts. The students' verbal performance of the various speech acts (e.g. requesting, explaining, etc.) involved in the different situations were tape-recorded and then scored by a panel of three judges in terms of fluency, effort to communicate, completeness, and grammaticality. The correlational analysis among the three language tests indicated a strong linear relationship; however, a closer examination of the results, using scattergrams, revealed a curvilinear relationship between the measures. The higher correlation was due to the cluster of scores at the lower and upper ends of the curve. Separate correlations for these two groups tended to be much lower than the overall correlations. The finding suggests that discrete-point grammatical tests may not reveal a student's communicative ability, particularly at the beginning or advanced levels of language proficiency.

Ramírez (1984) examined the relationship between performance on a linguistic competence test (Bahia Oral Language Test with twenty items) and three aspects of communicative competence — active communicative competence, receptive communicative competence, and sociolinguistic competence. Active communicative competence (ACC) was measured in a test involving four tasks. In task one ("transmitting information"), students were asked to describe simple line drawings (e.g. apples falling from a tree) in such a way that the picture could be reproduced by an interlocutor who could not see the picture. Task two ("giving directions") involved giving directions that would enable another person to find his or her way to a party. Task three ("giving instructions") consisted of extending an invitation to a party on the basis of pictoral information (time indication, address, picture of projected activities). Task four ("giving descriptions") was reporting an accident depicted in a series of line drawings. Scoring the test was based on a content analysis of the task. The content of each task (i.e. the description of the picture or the events of the accident) was analyzed into smaller units of information with each unit forming a discrete item of the test. The replies of the testees were taped and then scored by examiners who checked each bit of information on the task analysis sheet as the information appeared in the examiner's reply. This procedure of analyzing student replies turned out to be nearly "objective." Variation in test scores obtained by three different examiners were minor, and agreement (checked for five different students) was in the 90 to 99 percent range.

Receptive communicative competence was defined as the ability to follow directions or instructions and consisted of three parts: (1) following directions on a map; (2) filling out a standardized form; and (3) following instructions by underlining and circling words in a written text. Each task was treated as a discrete item and the scoring of this test was entirely objective.

Sociolinguistic competence (SC) was defined as the ability to recognize the intent of speech acts. It was tested by a receptive, discrete item test. The stem of each item described the communicative intent of a teacher or pupil in a specific classroom situation. The stem was followed by four choices, two of which constituted possible ways of expressing the intended speech act. In one of the two correct choices the speech act was expressed overtly; in the other, it was stated in a covert manner. Overt and covert speech act recognitions were scored as separate test items;

thus, the test led to a double score: overt and covert speech act recognition. The overt speech acts were expected to be recognized more easily than covert ones. The difference between the SC covert and SC overt scores were to furnish an indication of sociolinguistic sensitivity.

The tests in both English and Spanish were administered to pupils in four different settings:

San Francisco Bay area schools

School 1 (senior high school, N = 65)
Students were in a Spanish/English bilingual program. Approximately one-third had been born in the United States, another third had lived in the United States between four and eight years, and a third were recent arrivals (one to two years) from Latin America (primarily Mexico)

School 2 (bilingual elementary school, N = 18)
Students were in the fourth and fifth grades.

School 3 (monolingual elementary school, N = 18)
Students were mainly in the fourth and fifth grades and were English dominant.

Los Angeles area

School 4 (bilingual elementary school, N = 28)
Students were in the fourth and fifth grades. (The active communicative competence measures were not administered to these pupils.)

Several pattens emerged from the results of the three bilingual schools:

1. Linguistic competence in English and Spanish were negatively related

2. Active communicative competence in English and Spanish were moderately related ($r = .51, p = .001$), for the high school group, but almost unrelated for the elementary group of school 2 ($r = .05$)

3. Receptive communicative competence across languages is almost unrelated in two schools ($r = .14$ for the high school, $r = .17$ for school 2) and moderately related ($r = .58, p = .05$) in school 4

4. Sociolinguistic competence, consisting of the recognition ot overt and covert speech acts, correlated highly within English and Spanish and across the two languages in the two elementary schools

5. Sociolinguistic competence and receptive communicative competence are related across languages in three of the schools
6. Active communicative competence and sociolinguistic competence are moderately related within each language for the high school and bilingual elementary school (school 2)

Based on the instruments used in this study, one can conclude that linguistic competence in English and Spanish is unrelated. Knowledge of the grammatical structures of one language seems to have no association with grammatical knowledge in the other. Communicative competence in English and Spanish seems to differ according to school (age) groups. For the high school group, there was a relatively high correlation ($r = .51$) between ACC English and ACC Spanish tests, but this relationship was not found among elementary school pupils. Sociolinguistic competence correlated across the two languages in the bilingual elementary schools, thus suggesting the presence of linguistic ability somewhat different from the active communicative measure.

Politzer, Shohamy, and McGroarty (1981) analyzed the oral English tapes collected as part of the active communicative competence (ACC) measure. The analysis consisted of rating the tapes on a global scale, a five-point scale similar in format to the FSI Oral Interview ratings which include considerations of pronunciation, vocabulary, grammar, fluency, and comprehension. The reason for using this procedure was to explore the relationship between global proficiency ratings with the amount and accuracy of information scored previously as discrete items. The global ratings were correlated with the original scores based on the amount and accuracy of information conveyed in the ACC measure as well as the scores on the linguistic competence (BOLT English grammar test) measure. The two methods of scoring communicative competence—discrete and global—influenced the results. The global rating was more closely related to linguistic competence ($r = .74$) for school 1 (high school) than for school 2 (elementary) with a negative correlation ($r = -.06$). The correlations of the scores on the amount/accuracy of information with the linguistic competence measure was considerably higher ($r = .67$) for school 1 than for school 2 ($r = .27$). The scores using global rating scales were similar to the performance rated by the amount/accuracy of information transmitted by high school students ($r = .54$) but not for elementary pupils ($r = -.05$).

Other communicative assessment procedures include the number of different linguistic forms used to perform specific speech acts, variation in linguistic patterns due to sociolinguistic setting, conversational abilities in small groups, and observational checklists to analyze children's communicative behavior. Walters (1979) utilized the notion of language variation (the number of different structures a child can produce or comprehend) as an alternative procedure to assess communicative abilities. Thirty-two elementary schoolchildren of Latino background were classified as balanced or nonbalanced bilinguals according to their performance on the Peabody Picture Vocabulary Test. Request strategies in English and Spanish were elicited with the use of puppets in simulated situations. Balanced bilinguals produced more variation in each language than the nonbalanced bilinguals, half of whom were Spanish dominant and the other half English dominant.

The ethnographic work of Rodríguez-Brown and Elías-Olivares (1981) focuses on the variation of discourse patterns among bilingual children as a result of different levels of language proficiency and/or differences in sociolinguistic settings (home, community, and school). The discourse is analyzed in terms of recurrent speech events across the different settings and according to the hierarchical analytical system developed by Sinclair and Coulthard (1975) which includes turn-taking sequences and speech acts categories.

Wiedemann (1982) utilized a small group discussion procedure adapted from Barnes and Todd (1977) to examine the communicative abilities of Portuguese-English pupils in a California high school. Pupils in groups of three were formed according to grade level (9–12), sex, and date of arrival in the United States (early versus recent immigrants). Each group met for six recording sessions (three in English and three in Portuguese), alternating from one language to the other for each period. The conversational topics included controversial conversational themes (e.g. crime, love, teenagers, drinking). The performance of each pupil was analyzed by three native-speaking judges, trained to rate each participant in terms of five dimensions: (1) effort to communicate, (2) amount of relevant communication, (3) comprehensibility, (4) fluency, and (5) appropriateness. Each dimension was rated on a five-point scale. Using this procedure, she found that early immigrants performed better than recent immigrants on all five aspects of communicative (conversational) competence in English. Recent immigrants had higher scores than the early immigrants on the fluency and comprehensibility scales in Portuguese.

Omark (1981) suggests the use of pragmatic and ethological techniques for the observational assessment of children's communicative abilities. He offers examples of various instruments that can be used by teachers, parents, and observers. The checklist for the teacher includes a list of statements (e.g. rarely asks questions, omits sounds in words, unable to tell a comprehensible story or sequence of events, usually quiet and passive) that could be used for initial identification of children with possible problem areas (in personality, culture, intelligence, language, hearing). The questionnaire for the parent can be used to assess the child's past verbal and behavioral characteristics. The questionnaire was developed to assess the pragmatic uses of language (e.g. pro-test/complain, understanding commands/requests, conversational abilities). The form to be used by an observer consists of a list of speech acts (e.g. threats, questions, promises, descriptions, words) with a place to record the data of occurrence/observation. These instruments provide the opportunity to view the child in different situations and different interpersonal relationships (with parents, teachers, and aides).

COMMUNICATIVE COMPETENCE TESTS

The majority of assessment instruments designed to measure communicative proficiency have been designed for adult second language learners (Day 1980). The approaches include such forms as (1) the Foreign Service Institute (FSI) Oral Interview, consisting of a conversation with a trained tester and designed with a five-level global rating scale (S-1 elementary proficiency to S-5 nativelike proficiency) with subscales for accent, grammar, vocabulary, fluency, and comprehension; (2) the Savignon (1972) communicative competence tests, which ask the student to discuss, obtain information, report, and describe; and (3) the Ilyin Oral Interview (1976), consisting of a series of pictures initially presented by the examiner and then described by the student until he/she reaches the frustration level. The instruments developed by the High/Scope Educational Research Foundation (Cazden et. al., 1977) for program evaluation purposes suggest alternate ways for assessing the communicative abilities of children through the manipulation of real objects (productive language assessment tasks — reporting and narrating) and problem-solving tasks (e.g. mother and child baking cookies together) that consist of authentic verbal interactional situations.

COMPARABILITY OF LANGUAGE TESTS

Rodríguez-Brown and Elías-Olivares (1981) attempted to establish the congruence between some of the widely used proficiency tests (James Dominance Test and the Bilingual Syntax Measure) and pupils' communicative behavior. They noted that tests which included communicative skills were better predictors of language proficiency levels than those instruments assessing basically grammatical skills. Discrete item language tests which focus on one aspect of language also tend to limit the range of communicative abilities which need to be considered in determining relative language proficiency. Factors such as the type of setting or activity can affect children's use of different language functions — interrogatives and requests for action, permission, and information gathering — and this kind of variability is not usually tapped by language tests.

Ulibarri, Spencer, and Rivas (1981) administered three language tests — Language Assessment Scales (LAS), Bilingual Syntax Measure (BSM), and the Basic Inventory of Natural Language (BINL) — to 1,100 first, third, and fifth grade Spanish and English pupils of California schools to determine the comparability of assessment instruments. Since the entry/exit criteria to bilingual programs for minority schoolchildren is based on performance on language tests, proficiency levels — non-English (NES), limited-English (LES), and fluent-English (FES) — become an important educational issue. The breakdown of levels by grades and proficiency test are presented in Table 3.

Apparently, at the first grade level the three tests do not identify the same percentage of NES/LES/FES pupils. The LAS and BINL appear

Table 3. Percentage Breakdown of NES, LES, and FES by Language Test and Grade Level

Grade/Level	LAS	BSM	BINL
First			
NES	44%	8%	16%
LES	26	79	26
FES	30	13	58
Third			
NES	14	8	14
LES	20	88	34
FES	66	4	52
Fifth			
NES	14	3	3
LES	80	87	31
FES	6	10	60

Source: D. M. Ulibarri, M. L. Spencer, and G. A. Rivas, "Language Proficiency and Academic Achievement: A Study of Language Proficiency Tests and Their Relations to School Ratings as Predictors Academic Achievement," *NABE Journal* 5: 3 (Spring 1981): 47-80.

to be closer at grades three (61 percent agreement) and five (65 percent agreement). With the LAS instrument, a decrease in the proportion of LEP students is reflected from grades one to five, while the BINL shows a similar number of FES pupils across the grades, and the BSM identifies a very high number of LES pupils at each grade level. Apparently, then, the use of a particular language test may not reflect a child's total range of communicative abilities, and, at the same time, the test may under- or overestimate the student's proficiency for entering/exiting a bilingual program.

SUMMARY

The degree of bilingualism can be depicted according to such areas as:

1. aspects of language — grammar, vocabulary, pronunciation;
2. receptive and productive control of language skills — listening, reading, speaking, writing; and
3. language use — varieties, stylistics, domains, functions.

Language testing associated with the behavioral-structural model of language learning generally divides language skills according to three areas:

1. Linguistic levels — phonology, morphology, syntax, and vocabulary
2. Receptive performance skills — listening and reading
3. Active performance skills — speaking and writing

A number of research studies have focused on "discrete" elements to examine bilingual proficiency. Vocabulary testing by domain and lexical dominance testing through the use of pictures were discussed here. Other tests compare the comprehension and production of various linguistic patterns in the two languages. Based on language proficiency according to the four skills, various classifications of bilinguals have been noted. Bilinguals can be classified as:

1. passive bilinguals — speaking abilities in only one language;
2. productive bilinguals — listening and speaking abilities in both languages; and
3. biliteral bilinguals — oral and written competence in both languages.

Considerable research has been done regarding the measurement of grammatical competence at the level of comprehension and production. Most of the assessment instruments currently used in bilingual education programs focus on linguistic competence. The instruments measure language proficiency according to vocabulary, grammar, or language skills. Few tests assess language proficiency as an "integrated" ability involving the functional use of language in a sociolinguistic context.

The testing of communicative competence focuses on the student's language use in communicative situations. Communicative competence can involve such aspects as grammatical, sociolinguistic, discourse, or strategic competencies. Measurement problems associated with communicative competence testing is partially due to the use of "global" rating scales, while linguistic competence is generally measured as a series of discrete items.

Various studies have been conducted to compare the relationship between linguistic and communicative competence among bilinguals. Some studies determined the extent to which grammatical tests are accurate measures of communicative competence, while others examined the relationship between performance on a linguistic competence test and different aspects of communicative competence. Most assessment instruments designed to measure communicative proficiency have been designed for adult second language learners. Language testing is a basic feature of bilingual programs serving language-minority children in the United States. The use of a particular test, for example, can affect the number of children identified as fluent-, limited-, or non-English-speaking.

SUGGESTED READINGS

Alatis, J. E., ed. *Current Issues in Bilingual Education*. Washington, D.C.: George-town University, 1980.

Beardsmore, H. B. *Bilingualism: Basic Principles*. Clevedon, England: Multi-lingual Matters, 1982.

Carroll, B. J. *Testing Communicative Performance*. New York: Pergamon Press, Ltd., 1980.

Kelly, L. G., ed. *Description and Measurement of Bilingualism*. Toronto, Can-ada: University of Toronto Press, 1969.

DEVELOPMENT OF
BILINGUAL PROFICIENCY ___

INTRODUCTION

The process of becoming bilingual is influenced by social and individual factors as well as by language learning contexts. Second language learning is part of an acculturation process involving, in part, a willingness to identify with a target ethnolinguistic group. The nature of interethnic relations can influence the acquisition of nativelike proficiency of the dominant group's language by members of a subordinate group. From an individual's perspective, differences in bilingual proficiency are often related to learning conditions – i.e. the two languages were both learned from infancy (simultaneous bilingualism) as opposed to one language being introduced first (sequential bilingualism).

Children learning two languages simultaneously follow a number of linguistic stages (e.g. language mixing, code separation). Studies of sequential bilingual acquisition among language-minority children have documented the role of first language interference and the use of specific cognitive and social strategies in second language learning. Code switching (alternating between the two languages in an utterance or conversation) appears to be an important aspect of child bilingualism, governed by grammatical and sociolinguistic norms. Bilingualism through schooling can be influenced by such factors as the status of the first and second language, geographic location (e.g. learning Spanish near or far away from the Mexican border), and the pupils' initial degree of bilingualism. Among majority schoolchildren, the type of language program (e.g. immersion versus traditional second language program) can greatly affect the degree of bilingualism attained.

LANGUAGE LEARNING IN INTERETHNIC CONTEXTS

The development of bilingual proficiency can be affected by factors beyond societal influences (e.g. ethnolinguistic vitality of the group, regional differences — Spanish in Texas versus Kansas) or the type of educational program (e.g. transitional or full bilingual program). The student, as a learner, has a particular set of personal characteristics he brings to the task. These traits can include differences such as age, home language behavior, sex, motivation, degree of acculturation, and learning style.

Second language learning can be described as an acculturation process (Shumann 1978) involving a willingness to identify and/or adopt the linguistic and nonlinguistic aspects of behavior that characterize the target ethnolinguistic group. Individual characteristics can interact with social and instructional factors resulting in differential outcomes. Giles and Byrne (1982) present an intergroup approach to second langugae learning. They offer a comparison of Gardner's (1979) and Clement's (1980) models. Figure 11 is a schematic representation of Gardner's model. The model includes four major categories:

1. Social milieu (cultural beliefs) regarding the learning of L_2 or becoming bilingual
2. Individual differences (the role of intelligence, language aptitude, motivation, and situational anxiety/tension — the four variables considered important in L_2 acquisition research)
3. Second language acquisition contexts (formal classroom instruction and amount/quality of informal language experiences — communication with L_2 speakers, exposure to television/radio in L_2
4. Outcomes (linguistic oral proficiency, vocabulary range; nonlinguistic, positive attitudes toward L_2 group, interest in continuing language study).

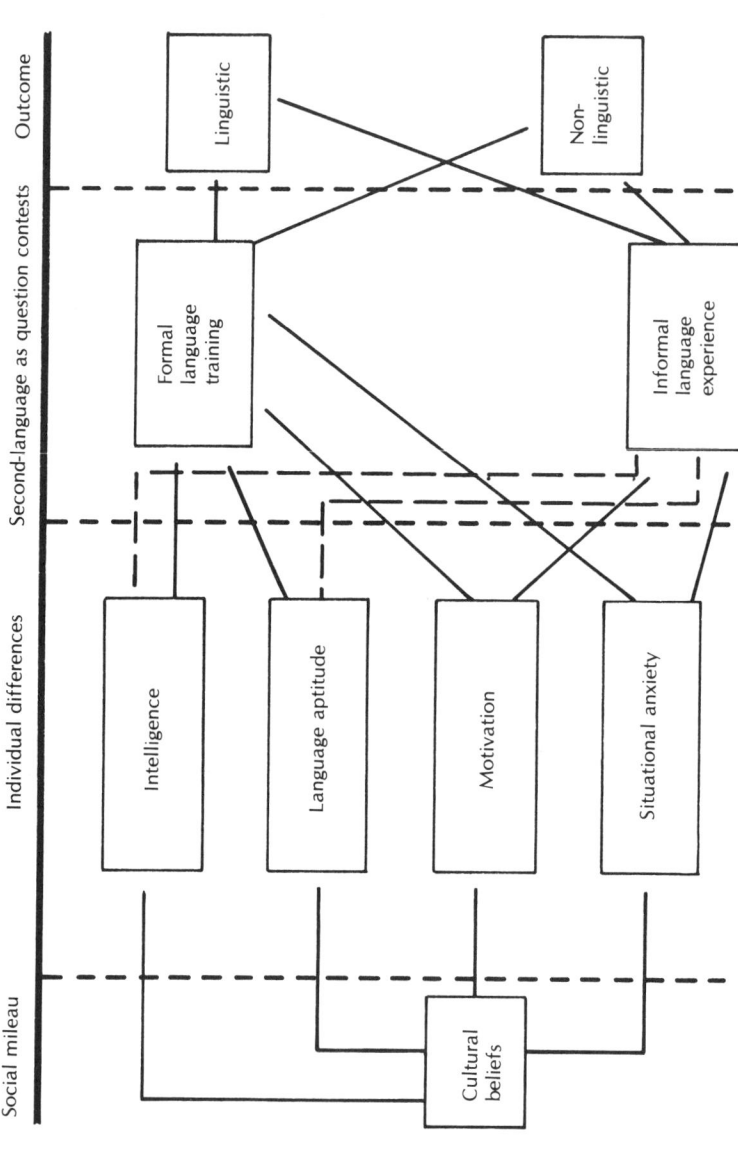

Figure 11. Schematic Representation of Gardner's (1979) Model. Reprinted, by permission, from H. Giles and J. L. Byrne, "An Intergroup Approach to Second Language Acquisition" *Journal of Multilingual and Multicultural Development*, 3:1 (1982): 27.

Clement's model, represented by Figure 12, highlights the social milieu context which provides the "primary motivational process" (willingness to integrate or fear of assimilation) leading to positive or negative avoidance) tendencies in interethnic language behaviors. Individuals participating in a common milieu experience share predispositions (self-confidence and secondary motivational processes — desire to become an accepted member of the L_2 culture or unwillingness to learn L_2 for fear of losing L_1 cultural affiliation) which, in turn, determine the degree of L_2 communicative competencies. Individual outcomes give rise to collective consequences for the group (assimilation or integration).

Giles and Byrne point out that the two models do not give adequate treatment to a number of concepts or processes associated with intergroup theory. These factors can influence the degree to which individuals identify with their ethnic group or the perceptions they have regarding the type of social relationships that exist within and between the ethnic groups. Giles and Byrne (1982: 34–35) offer the following two proposals to explain the acquisition or the lack of acquisition of nativelike proficiency in the dominant group's language among members of the subordinate group who have an instrumental value for learning L_2. Acquisition of nativelike proficiency occurs if:

1. ingroup identification is weak and/or L_1 is not a salient dimension of ethnic group membership;
2. quiescent interethnic comparisons exist (e.g. no awareness of cognitive alternatives to inferiority);
3. perceived ingroup vitality is low;
4. perceived ingroup boundaries are soft and open; and
5. strong identification exists with many other social categories, each of which provides adequate group identities and a satisfactory intragroup status.

Nativelike proficiency does not occur when:

1. ingroup identification is strong and language is a salient dimension of ethnic group membership;
2. insecure interethnic comparisons exist (e.g. awareness of cognitive alternatives to inferiority);
3. perceived ingroup vitality is high;
4. perceived ingroup boundaries are hard and closed;
5. weak identifications exist with few other social categories, each of which provides inadequate group identities and an unsatisfactory intragroup status.

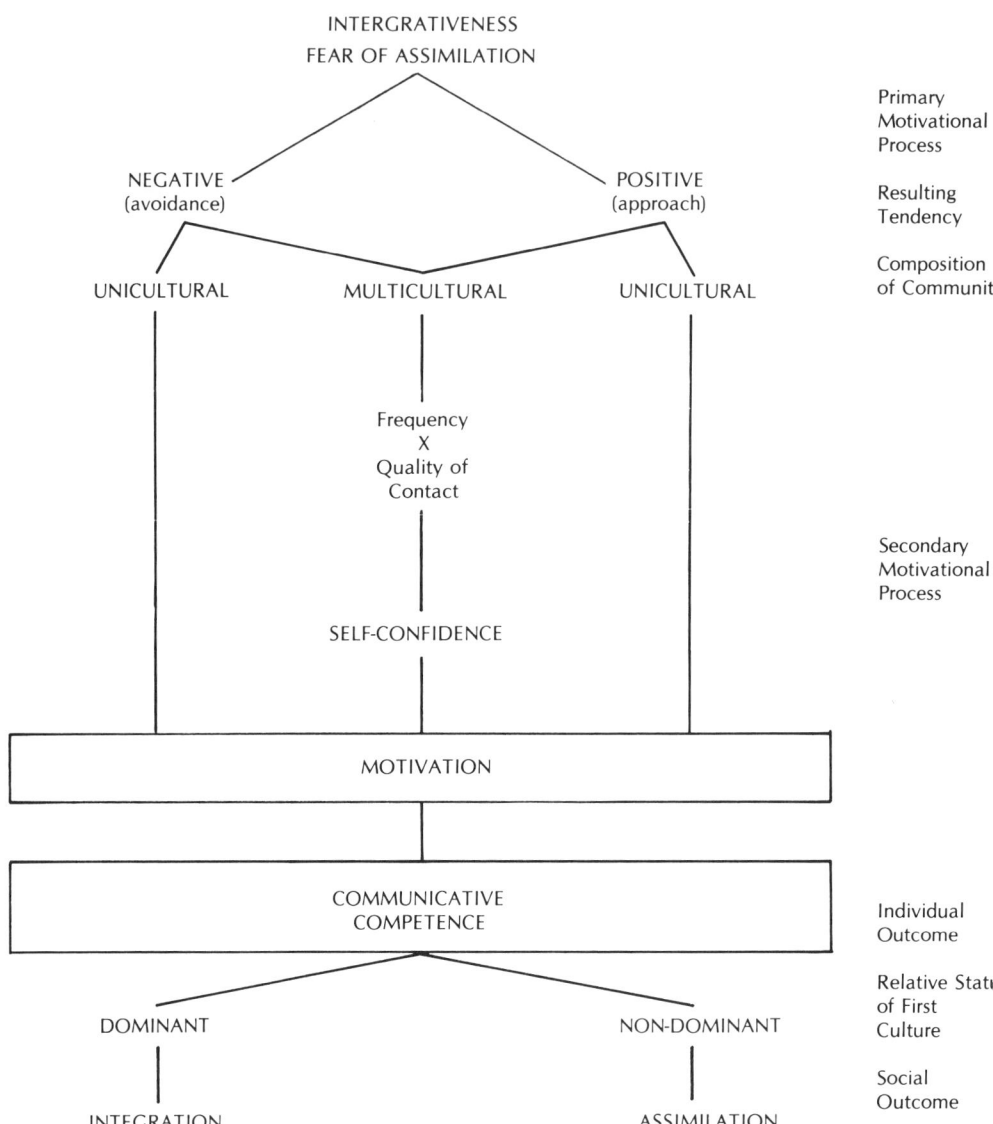

Figure 12. Schematic Representation of Clément's (1980a) Model. Reprinted, by permission, from H. Giles and J. L. Byrne," An Intergroup Approach to Second Language Acquisition" *Journal of Multilingual and Multicultural Development*, 3:1 (1982): 30.

INDIVIDUAL BILINGUALISM AND LEARNING CONTEXTS

The development of individual bilingualism can be examined within the context of sociolinguistic factors (e.g. cultural beliefs, interactional patterns between the two language groups, and functional uses of the two languages), individual differences (e.g. motivation, personality variables – anxiety, extrovertedness), and learning situations (e.g. formal language training, informal language exposure). Differences in bilingual acquisition are often related to learning conditions.

In simultaneous bilingualism, the child is exposed to both languages from infancy. The exposure to each language may be person specific (e.g. the father speaks German, the mother uses English) or bound by setting (Greek at home, English in the community).

In sequential bilingualism, the child obtains some degree of competence in the first language before exposure to the second one. This exposure can occur at an early age (e.g. when the child enters a nursery/elementary school) or at a later age (e.g. English-speaking pupils learning French in Canada at the intermediate school level.

SIMULTANEOUS BILINGUAL ACQUISITION

One of the major questions considered in simultaneous bilingual acquisition is whether the two languages are acquired as a single system initially and later differentiated or whether the two languages develop as separate linguistic systems. Various studies support the "interdependent" developmental hypothesis. Leopold's (1978:25) work, which remains the most extensive in this area, concluded that "infants exposed to two languages from the beginning do not learn bilingually at first, but weld the double presentation into one unified speech system." At first, his English-German bilingual daughter noted and produced "only the coarsest contrasts" and later was able to make finer distinctions in learning linguistic patterns (e.g. phonemic patterns, word structures, and syntactic relationships). The child was not really bilingual during the first two years. She often combined elements of the two languages into a "hybrid" form, particularly in the area of compound nouns and verbs. By the third year, the child became conscious of her bilingual situation and slowly began to separate the two languages.

Imedadze (1978) described her daughter's acquisition of Russian and Georgian, each language separated by person (parents spoke Georgian and the grandmother and nurse spoke Russian to the child). The acquisition process was quite similar to the stages reported by Leopold. In the initial stage the child mixed elements of both languages, then, after a period of twenty months, the child began to separate the two linguistic systems.

Findings based on studies of young French-English bilingual children have led Swain (1972, 1977) to the conclusion that simultaneous acquisition of two languages does not differ significantly from the acquisition of one language, insofar that in both cases the child begins with a single set of rules in response to the linguistic environment. The children approach their task of learning two languages as if they were learning only one. This approach can be seen in the "mixing" of vocabulary in the early stage (words are stored without differentiation to language) and in the formulation of linguistic devices (for signalling question forms, for example), which emerge in the same order for these bilingual children as for their monolingual counterparts. An analysis of code interaction by Nygren-Junken (1977) indicated that the children followed three stages of development during the linguistic differentiation period:

1. In the language cooperation period, the child uses items from both languages in a complementary fashion since most items are available in only one language
2. In the linguistic interference phase, the child acquires words from both languages to designate same item, action, or function but may occasionally produce "mixed" utterances
3. In the code separation stage, the child separates the two linguistic systems with minimal "mixing".

Volterra and Taeschner (1978) also identified a three-phase developmental pattern based on the data of two young sisters acquiring German and Italian. By focusing on the lexical system, they were able to examine which items had or did not have a corresponding word in the other language. During the first phase, each child possessed one lexical system composed of both Italian and German items, with a few two to three word utterances containing a mixture from both languages. In the second stage, the child became aware of equivalent words from the two languages and began to translate from one language to the other. Utterances still contained a "mixture" from both languages, suggesting that only one set of syntactic rules applied to both languages. In the third period, the child formulated phrases in each language, the choice depending on the interlocutor. By this stage, the child had separated each language at both the lexical and syntactic levels, though some syntactic interference was still detected in situations of conflict (e.g. during interactions with persons speaking different languages or when asked to perform language functions usually conducted in the other language).

Other researchers argue that from the beginning bilingual infants use two distinct sets of rules in language production. Even in mixed utterances, Padilla and Liebman (1975) noted that English morphemes were pronounced according to English phonological rules, and Spanish morphemes were realized without interference from the English sound system. The mixed utterances, which accounted for only 2 to 3 percent of the language samples obtained, reflected an appropriate use of word class (e.g. using a Spanish verb for a corresponding English verb) and word order (e.g. using a Spanish article before an English noun or placing the Spanish imperative verb form before the English direct object). Bergman (1976:94) has pointed out that "early mixing in child bilinguals is not so much evidence of a lack of linguistic competence but rather a lack of sociolinguistic norms of language use." Mixed utterances in children's speech could also be influenced by exposure to mixed language patterns commonly heard in the speech of adults, particularly in the American Southwest. See appendix A for a description of "The Language of the Spanish/English Bilingual."

Though there are a number of difficulties with early bilingualism studies (e.g. the influence of sociolinguistic factors — functional allocation of the two languages, interactional patterns), McLaughlin (1981:23) offers the following three generalizations explaining the processes of simultaneous bilingual acquisition:

1. Children experiencing balanced exposure to two languages develop both languages as do monolingual speakers of either language. Initially, children seem to work from a single set of rules and there is a stage of language mixing, especially lexical mixing, but gradually two sets of rules become differentiated.

2. When exposure to the languages is less balanced, there may be more persistent linguistic transfer and more frequent introduction of the vocabulary of one language into the grammatical system of the other.

3. There is a single language system that underlies both languages of the bilingual child. It is unparsimonious to postulate separate linguistic systems and more economical to regard the bilingual's two languages as separate linguistic subsystems, analogous to the linguistic codes of a monolingual speaker.

SEQUENTIAL BILINGUAL ACQUISITION

Becoming bilingual after the age of three or during preschool years is often accomplished by interacting with native speakers of the language in the immediate community (children, adults) or in the school setting (teachers, classmates). Since children of this age group already possess basic linguistic skills and communicative abilities in the first language, questions regarding the nature/degree of L_1 interference and L_2 acquisition processes have attracted scholarly attention.

Linguistic studies have focused on various aspects of English language development (e.g. vocabulary [Yoshida 1978], interrogative and negative constructions [Huang and Hatch 1978], grammatical morphemes [Hakuta 1974]. Studies have also described L_2 acquisition processes in different languages — French (Ervin-Tripp 1974), German (Wode 1978), Spanish (Dato (1970). The influence of L_1 on the acquisition English as a second language (ESL) among Spanish-speaking children has been analyzed within the context of specific grammatical constructions (Dulay and Burt 1974), and of story narration (Politzer and Ramirez 1973). Dulay and Burt (1974) classified the errors from the speech of 179 Spanish-speaking children (5–8 years old) learning ESL into three categories: developmental (errors similar to those made by children learning English as a first language), interference (errors similar in structure to a semantically equivalent phrase or sentence in Spanish), and unique (errors neither "developmental" nor "interference" in nature). The findings, based on 513 utterances containing errors drawn from seven grammatical patterns, indicate the following proportion of errors: developmental, 87 percent; interference, 4.7 percent; and unique, 8.2 percent. The L_2 acquisition process, thus, appears to be quite similar to that found among monolingual English-speaking children. Wode (1978) found that the developmental sequence for negative constructions among four English-speaking children, ages 3 to 7½, learning German as a second language, was very similar to the process followed by German monolingual children. The sequences for German-speaking children learning ESL, however, were different from those noted among English-speaking monolingual children. The differences were largely the result of first language influence (German word order — the negative after the verb) and/or overgeneralization (analogy based on the English rule of placing the negative after auxiliaries). Differences due to first language interference have been observed between Spanish- and Cantonese-speaking pupils on the correct use of English articles and plural markers (Dulay and Burt 1975), and between Korean- and Spanish-speaking pupils on English article usage. Apparently L₂ acquisition processes involve both transfer and developmental factors. Mulford and Hecht (1979) found, in the phonological development of English by a six-year-old Icelandic child, that the process involved a systematic interaction between transfer and developmental strategies. Hakuta and Cancino (1977) conclude that L₂ acquisition research of grammatical morphemes and patterns reveals an interplay between both strategies.

Fillmore's (1976) longitudinal study of five Spanish-speaking children interacting with five English-speaking peers attempted to isolate specific cognitive and social strategies used in L₂ learning. She found these children used, to varying degrees, three social strategies (stated as maxims):

1. Join a group and act as if you understand what is going on, even if you do not
2. Give the impression – with a few well-chosen words – that you can speak the language
3. Count on your friends to help (e.g. friends used gestures to aid communication)

The cognitive strategies included the following five operational principles:

1. Assume that what people are saying is directly relevant to the situation at hand, or to what they or you are experiencing. Metastrategy: Guess!
2. Get some expressions you understand, and start talking (e.g. Lookit, I wanna play, Beat it).
3. Look for recurring parts in the formulas you know (e.g. How do you do X, I wanna X).
4. Make the most of what you have got (e.g. semantic extension – "sangwish" for food in general, "gotcha" for the verb "kill").
5. Work on big things first; save the details for later (e.g. first produce "how" question, leave out auxiliary "do").

Fillmore (1979:227) summarized her findings by saying that "individual differences among the five children in the study had to do with the interaction between the nature of the task of learning a new language, the strategies that needed to be applied to the task, and the personal characteristics of the individual involved." Nora's behavior reflected her desire to become part of the group that spoke English, while Juan preferred to interact with persons who spoke his language. Nora put to immediate use whatever English forms she had learned without "working out" all the specific grammatical details. Juan, on the other hand, tended to work on one type of construction at a time, not attempting to use the structure until most of the details had been resolved.

Ramírez and Kim (1982) examined individual differences among four Korean children (ages 5, 6, 7, and 11) from the same family learning ESL. The study was longitudinal in nature and included recordings from ten conversational sessions, covering the first nine months of arrival in the United States. The conversations were analyzed according to Dore's (1979) conversational sets framework (requestives, assertives, performatives, etc.), language learning (rehearsal), speech (labeling, self-correcting, repeating, etc.), and communication strategies (interruption, message abandonment, switching to Korean). Differences in the use of various conversational acts as a result of age suggest that, among the three males, the older the child the greater the use of requestives, assertives, regulatives, and expressives (see Table 4). This same pattern (see Table 5) also existed in the areas of ambiguity (conversational acts with possible multiple function), degree of interruption (not waiting for a turn to speak or interrupting a speaker), and message abandonment (not completing a conversational act). The linguistic behavior of the two younger children was relatively similar when compared to the two older brothers. As far as the use of Korean, the younger the child, the greater number of switches to L_1.

CHILDHOOD BILINGUALISM AND CODE SWITCHING

The ability to code swtich (alternate between two languages in and utterance or conversation) is an important developmental aspect of bilingualism. Code switching may occur at the word, phrase, clause, or sentence level. McClure and Wentz (1978) differentiate between complete shifts (code changing) at the level of the sentence, noun phrase, or verb phrase ("*El se va a casa* and I'm going to the movies," "I put the forks *en la mesa*', and code mixing within a constituent ("I put the *tenedores* (forks) on the table," "I want a motorcycle *verde*"). Code switching is governed by functional and grammatical principles (Valdés-Fallis, 1978). Bilingual children acquire code switching rules based on sociolinguistic norms operating within their speech community. Young Mexican American children, according to McClure (1977), tend to code mix more, inserting a single item from one language into the other — English nouns or adjectives used in Spanish utterances — than

Table 4. Major Conversational Acts Performed by Each Child

Conversational Act	M (female 5 years)	K (male 6 years)	H (male 7 years)	T (male 11 years)
Requestives	9.6%	12.9%	22.8%	54.7%
Assertives	15.3	10.7	34.2	39.5
Performatives	13.1	11.4	38.1	37.5
Responsives	15.6	28.1	31.5	24.7
Regulatives	17.0	8.2	23.9	50.9
Expressives	19.1	14.9	31.9	34.0

SOURCE: A. G. Ramírez and B. W. Kim, "The Development of Conversational Abilities in ESL among Korean Children." (Albany: State University of New York, 1982), mimeo.

older children (nine years or older), who switch at the phrase or sentence levels. The switches can serve various situational or stylistic functions (e.g. to resolve ambiguities, for emphasis, for clarification, or as a mode shift—narration to commentary—topic shift, or attention device).

Fantini (1978) examined the bilingual behavior of his two children, Mario and Carla, and addressed the interrelationship of language choice (English, Spanish, code switching) and context (participants—known/unknown, intimate/nonintimate; setting—Bolivia, Mexico, Vermont; and communicative form—joke, song, quotation, etc.). The longitudinal study included data collected from diaries and tape recordings made of the two children (Mario from birth to 9 years and Carla from birth to 5 years). Some of the salient factors—both present and absent—which influenced code choice (English or Spanish) for both Mario and Carla are summarized by Fantini (1978:291):

1.   Clear and consistently differentiated use of codes by the parents

Table 5. Verbal Behavior of Each Child During Conversations

Conversational Aspect	M	K	H	T
Rehearsal Speech	10.6%	18.2%	43.9%	27.3%
Ambiguity	10.8	13.2	29.4	46.6
Interruption	15.0	10.0	25.0	50.0
Mesage Abandonment	13.3	13.3	33.3	40.0
Use of Korean	40.7	37.0	18.5	5.7

SOURCE: A. G. Ramírez and B. W. Kim, "The Development of Conversational Abilities in ESL among Korean Children." (Albany: State University of New York, 1982), mimeo.

2. Overt and covert insistence by their mother on the exclusive use of Spanish
3. Distinctive envrionments in which each code was used
4. The fact that the children were isolated Spanish speakers in an English-speaking milieu, again reinforcing distinctiveness
5. The fact that Spanish was so closely associated with family image and the children's identity

The ability to code switch developed very early – a few days after introduction to English in a nursery school (during the second year). The sorting of the two languages was initially done in relation to persons (caretakers and others) and later with respect to setting (home and other locations). Figure 13 illustrates the two initial stages depicting language choice. As the children developed, additional factors were taken into account for choosing the language in different interactional contexts. Figure 14 presents the interplay of various factors, e.g. characteristics of the interlocutors (degree of familiarity/intimacy, their physical appearance) and of the settings (public locale, home, or Spanish milieu). By age three, "the children were capable of appropriate language use, switching rapidly, and naturally," and by age five, "both behaved like normal children (as perceived by others) – in either of two languages – with the appropriate people, and in the right time and place" (Fantini 1978:292).

BILINGUALISM THROUGH SCHOOLING

The status of the second language (e.g. foreign or second language) can affect the rate of L_2 acquisition. Chun and Politzer (1975) compared first and second language learning among English-speaking in a French/ English bilingual school and among Spanish-speaking pupils in a Spanish/English program. Their analysis of the differences between L_1 (Spanish) and L_2 (English) at the level of comprehension and production of fourteen grammatical categories revealed that by grade three differences between L_1 and L_2 performance were not significant, while differences continued between English and French in grade five. "Balanced" bilingualism, as measured by these instruments, was achieved by grade three among pupils initially dominant in Spanish, and exposed to English in school and their community in California. For those native English-speaking students exposed to French only in the school context and not in the neighborhoods of San Francisco, however, achieving "balanced" bilingualism may require more years of bilingual schooling.

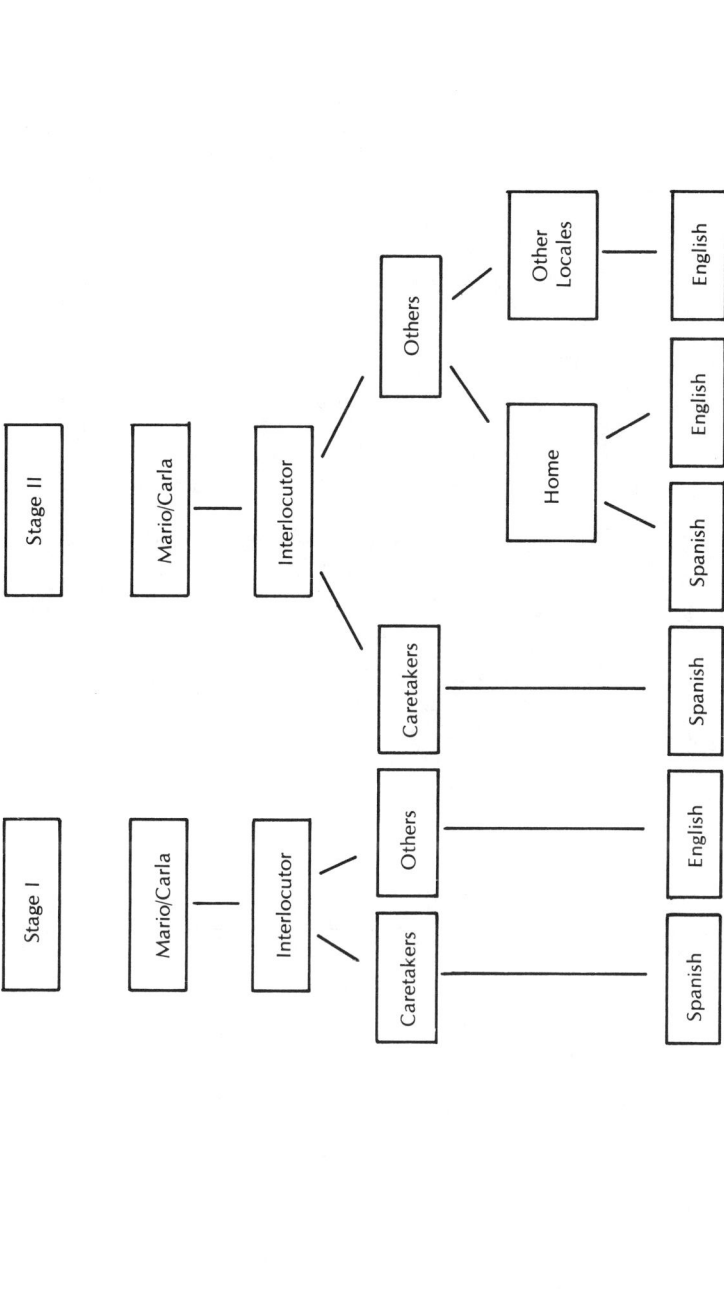

Figure 13. Initial Stages of Language Choice. Reprinted, by permission, from A. E. Fantini, "Bilingual Behavior and Social Cues: Case Studies of Two Bilingual Children." In M. Paradis, ed. *Aspects of Bilingualism* (Columbia, South Carolina: Hornbeam Press, Inc., 1978): 293.

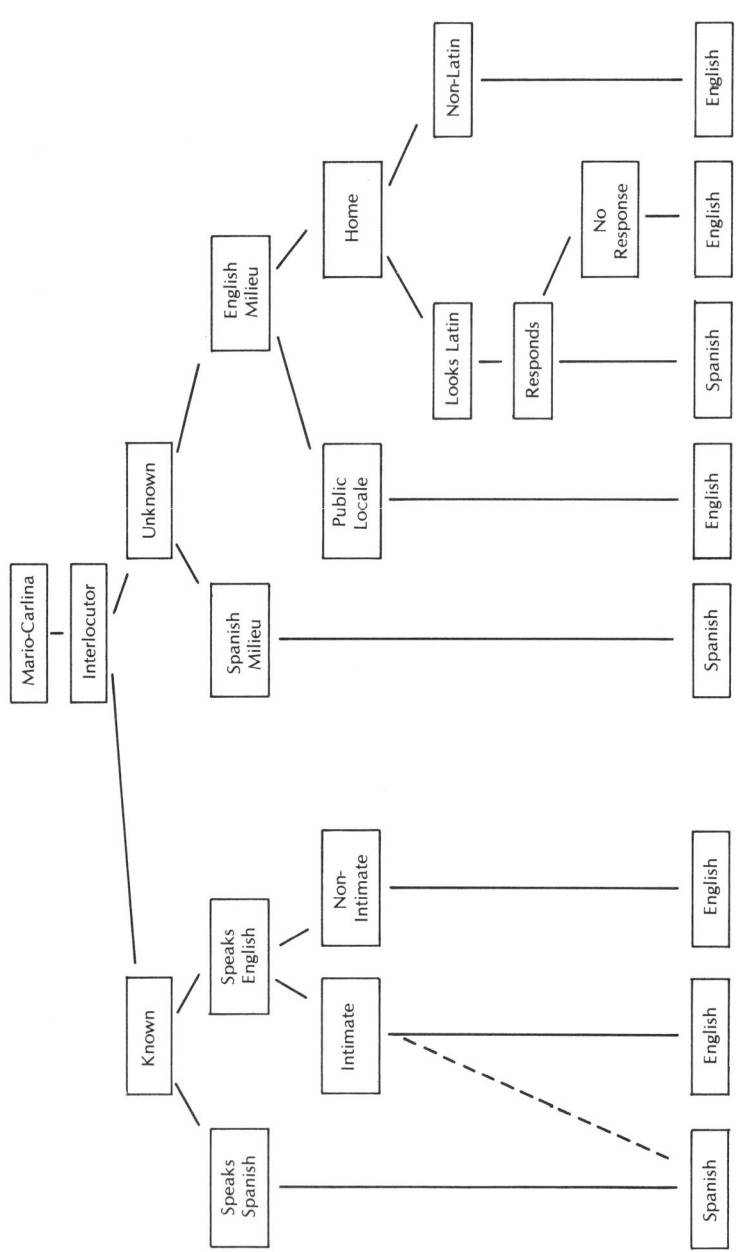

Differences in the development of bilingual proficiency can also be observed within a particular linguistic group. Ramírez and Politzer (1975a, 1975b) studied language development among Spanish/English bilinguals in Texas and California. Some of the pupils in the San Francisco bilingual program achieved "balanced" bilingualism, as measured by two thirty eight-item parallel grammar tests, by grade three. The remaining pupils accomplished the task by grade five. Figure 15 illustrates the development of bilingualism among the students (ten at each level) in kindergarten and grades one, three, and five. Figure 16 depicts the relative degree of balance of these pupils according to performance levels.

Pupils living in a dominant Spanish-speaking environment in a small Texas town near the Mexican border did not exhibit "balanced" bilingualism, as measured by a comparable grammar test, until grade seven. Performance on a thirty two-item, vocabulary-by-domain test consisting of four sections — home, neighborhood, church, and school — each with eight items, varied according to the context. The pupils' performance was similar (balanced) in Spanish and English for the home and neighborhood domains beyond grade one. They were dominant in Spanish in the church domain until grade seven. The only case of dominance in favor of English occurred in the school domain at grade five. Table 6 summarizes the pupils' language dominance according to four grade levels (ten students at each grade equally divided by sex).

Merino (1982) studied the development of English/Spanish bilingualism among pupils in grades K–4 attending a bilingual program in the San Francisco Bay area. Using comprehension and production tests to assess the control of seven grammatical categories (e.g. number, gender, past tense, conditionals), she outlined the order and pace of acquisition for each language. In the Spanish production test, there were significant differences across grades for three categories (tense, conditional, and subjectives). In English production, there were significant differences on six of the categories, all but number. Few significant differences occurred in the comprehension of the two languages (the categories of relatives in English and past tense in Spanish). The acquisition of most categories in English followed a chronological developmental pattern — older pupils performed better than the younger ones. In Spanish, however, the older children tended to perform with less acuracy than younger pupils, particularly in the more complex categories (subjunctives and conditionals). Merino suggests that the older pupils, usually the fourth graders but sometimes third or even second graders, were undergoing a language loss. The loss of Spanish affected the productive use of the more complex categories (conditionals and subjunctives) and

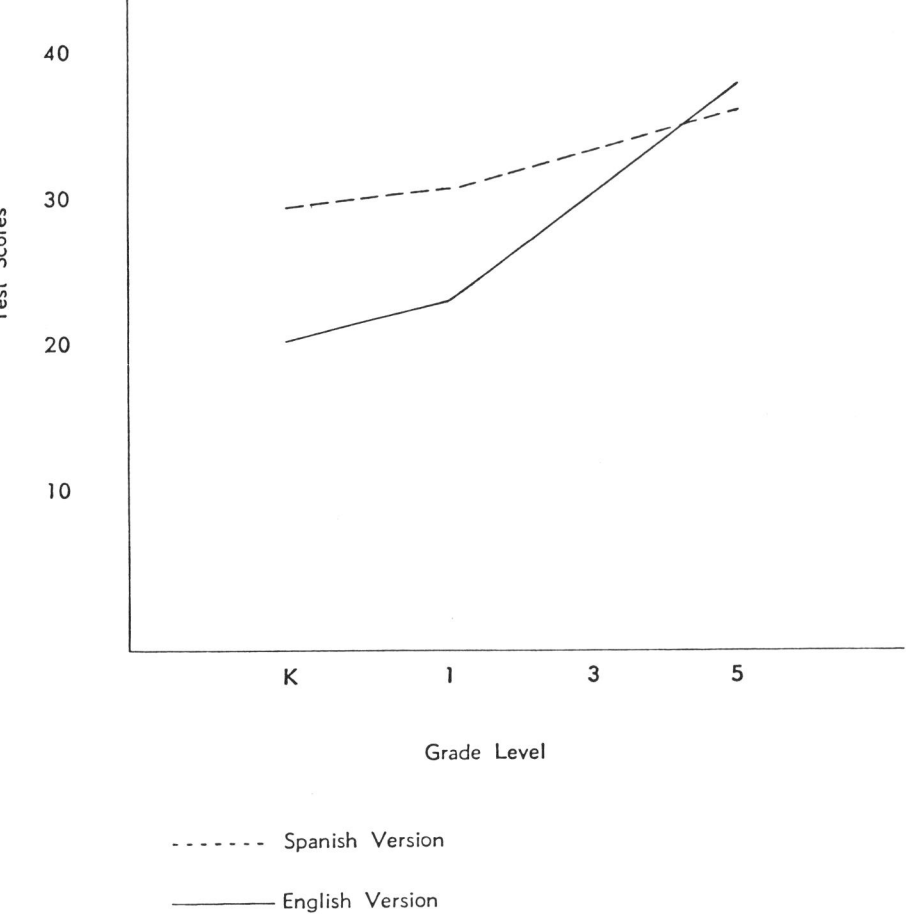

Figure 15. Mean Scores on English and Spanish Versions for Kindergarten and Grades 1, 3, and 5. Reprinted by permission from A. G. Ramíirez and R. L. Politzer, "The Acquisition of English and The Maintenance of Spanish in a Bilingual Education Program" *TESOL Quarterly* 9:2 (June 16, 1975a): 117.

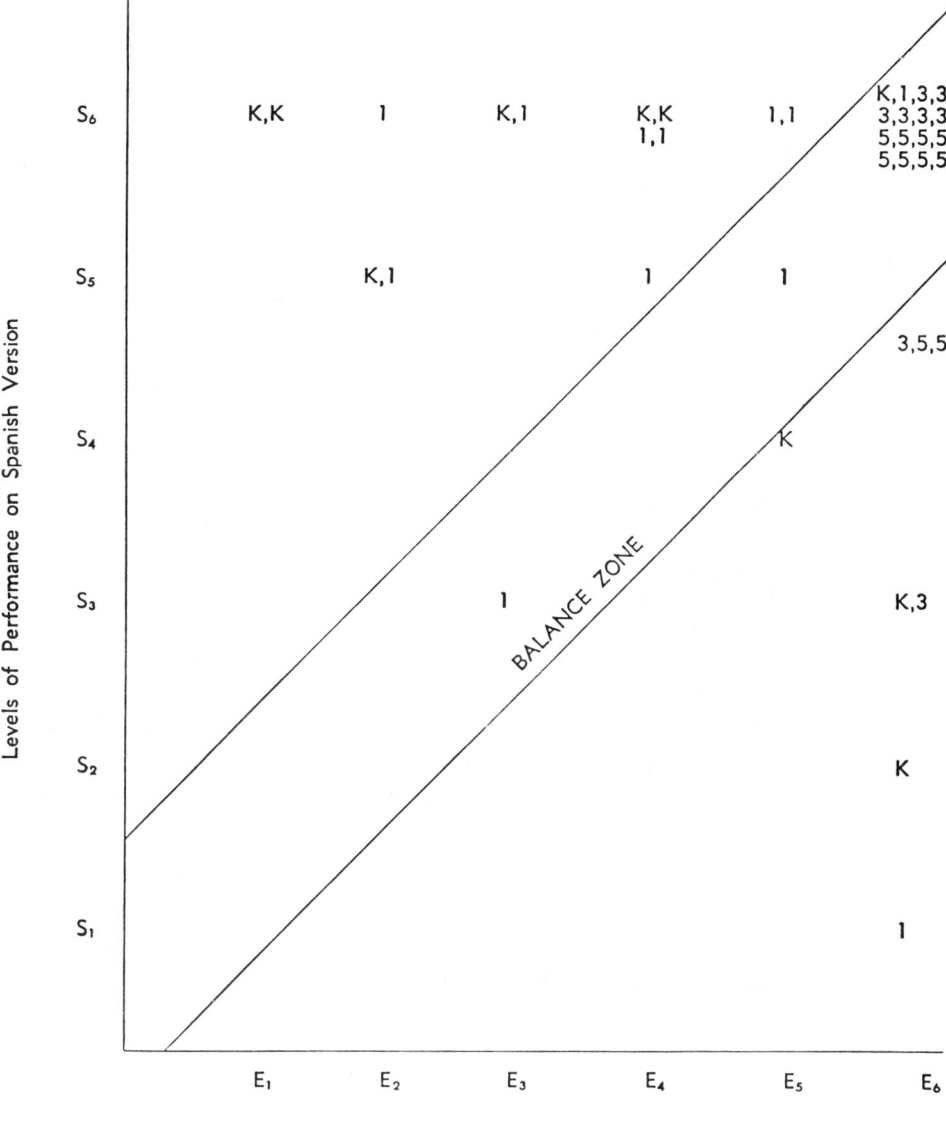

Figure 16. Relative Proficiency on Spanish and English Versions by Performance Levels. Subjects are represented by their grade level. Subjects in the balance zone are equally proficient in English and Spanish. Reprinted by permission from A. G. Ramírez and R. L. Politzer, "The Acquisition of English and The Maintenance of Spanish in a Bilingual Education Program' *TESOL Quarterly* 9:2 (June 16, 1975a): 117.

Table 6. Pupils' Language Dominance According to Domain and Grade

Grade	Home	Domain Neighborhood	Church	School
1	B	B	S	B
3	B	B	S	B
5	B	B	S	E
7	B	B	B	B

B = Balance in both languages
E = English dominance
S = Spanish dominance

SOURCE: A. G. Ramírez and R. L. Politzer, "The Development of Spanish/English Bilingualism in a Dominant Spanish-Speaking Environment," *ATIBOS: Journal of Chicano Research* (Summer 1975b):38.

grammatical accuracy (e.g. wrong word order). No development occurred in use of relatives (Spanish production) and most categories measured through the Spanish comprehension scales.

To what extent the lack of development in Spanish was due to the bilingual program (e.g. materials, teachers) is not clear. The explanation may lie outside the school program. Paulston (1980) argues that bilingual schooling is a "dependent" variable. The development of bilingual proficiency, for example, could depend on the nature of the relationship between the ethnic groups. While the community is 40 percent Spanish-speaking and the school has a 45 percent Hispanic enrollment, these pupils belong to an ethnolinguistic minority group. Spanish has a lower status than English. The bilingual program itself was initiated as a compensatory effort—to develop English language skills utilizing, to a certain extent, the pupils' first language. The development of "balanced" bilingualism was not a major educational goal.

Sancho (1980) noted that for language-minority pupils the type of bilingual program (transitional versus maintenance) was not as important as the child's initial degree of bilingualism from the language-use patterns at home and/or in the community. He conducted a three-year, longitudinal study comparing the effects of a maintenance approach and a transitional bilingual instructional approach on English language development and academic achievement of Spanish/English bilingual children in San Antonio, Texas. Three of the major conclusions are related to the child's degree of bilingualism upon entering school:

1. The effects of either a maintenance or transitional educational treatment are not as significant to student achievement as the

degree of linguistic competence the bilingual child initially brings to the school setting.

2. The degree of proficiency bilingual children bring to the school in both languages seems to have a direct relationship to their academic performance. Students initially identified as balanced bilinguals performed significantly better than students in all other language classifications including the English dominant.

3. The results of study support the hypothesis that the development and maintenance of two languages increases the ability of bilingual children to perform logical operations such as those required in math.

Thus, the school, as an institution using a particular bilingual education model (maintenance or transitional), was not sufficiently powerful to change or alter the ethnolinguistic dimensions of Spanish/English bilingualism in this community. In turn, the child's proficiency in both languages affected academic performance.

For majority schoolchildren, the type of language program greatly affects the degree of bilingualism or fluency in the second language. Tucker (1974) outlines the four major types of programs.

1. Traditional second language program—study of the target language *per se* for x minutes per day, y days per week, beginning at grade level z (e.g. high school German in the United States).

2. Second language plus content—an introduction to the language at an early grade, using the traditional second language approach, followed by the use of the target language at a later grade level to teach a selected content subject such as geography or social studies (e.g. social studies in French in Ontario or mathematics in English in Jordan).

3. Early-immersion programs—*exclusive* use of the target language as medium of instruction at the early grade levels (e.g. kindergarten, grade one) with the introduction of the mother tongue in a language arts class at grade two or three. The mother tongue is used to teach selected content subject so that by the late elementary years the program becomes fully bilingual (e.g. French and English language arts and content subjects taught in both languages in Canadian programs).

4. Late-immersion programs—several years of "traditional" second language study, followed by a year of total immersion (e.g. grade seven or grade eight) in the target language, followed

by a bilingual secondary-school program (e.g. Canadian programs).

In her comparison of the research findings regarding the types of French immersion monograms available in Canada, Swain (1978), and Swain and Lapkin (1982) concluded that the *early* total immersion program produces students with a more nativelike command of French than either late immsion, involving French for half the school day and English for the other half and starting in grade one.

SUMMARY

Language learning among ethnolinguistic minority groups needs to be examined within interethnic contexts. Second language learning can be described as an acculturation process. A person's individual characteristics can interact with social instructional factors, resulting in different outcomes. Gardner's model represents three major categories that can affect second language acquisition: cultural beliefs, individual differences, and second language acquisition context. On the other hand, Clement's model demonstrates the relationship between the "primary motivational process" and one's social milieu. Giles and Byrne believe these two models do not give adequate treatment to other concepts associated with intergroup theory; therefore, two proposals were given outlining the points that must be met if acquisition of nativelike proficiency is to occur, and the reasons for the lack of nativelike proficiency were stated.

Differences in bilingual acquisition are related to learning conditions—simultaneous bilingualism or sequential bilingualism. One major question concerning studies of simultaneous bilingual acquisition regards whether the two languages are acquired as a single system at first and then differentiated, or whether the two languages develop as separate linguistic systems. Various studies seem to indicate that the simultaneous acquisition of two languages does not differ significantly from the acquisition of one language. It has been noticed that children follow three stages of development during the linguistic differentiation period: language cooperation, linguistic interference, and code separation. Others believe bilingual infants use two distinct sets of rules in language production. The following three generalizations, however, were offered to explain the process of simultaneous bilingual acquisition: (1) balanced exposure develops both languages like monolingual speakers, (2) less balanced exposure accounts for more persistent linguistic transfer, and (3) a single language system underlies both languages.

Various scholarly investigations have been devoted to the nature/degree of L_1 interference and L_2 acquisition. Burt and Dulay's study showed that the L_2 acquisition process appeared to be similar to that found among monolingual English-speaking children. Other studies have demonstrated that L_2 acquisition processes involve both transfer and developmental errors. Fillmore attempted to isolate specific cognitive and social strategies used in L_2 learning. She noted three social strategies and five cognitive strategies used by the children she observed. She concluded by saying that "the individual differences among the five children had to do with the interaction between the nature of the task, the strategies that needed to be applied to the task and the personal characteristics of the individual involved" (Fillmore 1979:227). Code switching is an important developmental aspect of bilingualism and is governed by functional and grammatical principles. Code switching rules are acquired by bilingual children from the sociolinguistic norms operating in their speech communities.

Studies examining the development of bilingualism through schooling show that the process can be influenced by a number of factors including the status of the first and second languages (English, French, or Spanish in the United States), geographic/demographic aspects (use of language in the community, proximity of the target language country), and pupils' initial degree of bilingualism ("balance" in both languages, or dominance in the first or second). The type of language program (early/late immersion, traditional second language program) seems to have a significant affect on the degree of bilingualism attained by majority-language children. The development of bilingualism among ethnolinguistic minority children appears to be affected by a number of factors beyond schooling, including macrovariables (interethnic issues) and microvariables (learner characteristics and personality traits).

The subsequent chapter will examine the English as a second language (ESL) component in bilingual programs designed for language-minority children in the United States. It will examine models of second language acquisition and factors that influence the development of oral English proficiency.

SUGGESTED READINGS

García, E. E. *Early Childhood Bilingualism.* Albuquerque: University of New Mexico Press, 1983.

Escobedo, T. H., ed. Early *Childhood Bilingual Education: An Hispanic Perspective.* New York: Teachers College Press, Columbia University, 1983.

Jungo, M. E. *International Bibliography for a Didactics of Early Bilingualism in the Education of Underprivileged Children, Especially Children of Migrant Workers.* Quebec: Presses de l' Universite Laval, 1982.

Mackey, W. F. and T. Andersson, eds. *Bilingualism in Early Childhood.* Rowley, Mass.: Newbury House Publishers, Inc., 1977.

Saunders, G. *Bilingual Children: Guidance for the Family.* Clevedon, England: Multilingual Matters Ltd., 1982.

DEVELOPMENT OF ORAL PROFICIENCY IN ENGLISH AS A SECOND LANGUAGE __

INTRODUCTION

The learning of English as a Second Language (ESL) among language-minority children attending bilingual education programs can be examined with different second language learning models. Personal, instructional, and linguistic factors influence the rate of acquisition and the development of different English language skills. Apparently, many different types of English language skills are needed by students to function effectively in the mainstream classroom.

Different types of bilingual program models will be described and contrasted to illustrate differential effects on the development of oral English skills. For example, the effects of separate language acquisition (SLAC), fused language acquisition (FLAC) and English monolingual (EM) learning situations will be compared, and it will be noted that the SLAC model promotes, among Italian American pupils, more "advanced" bilingual oral skills than the other programs. Other findings include the case of Mexican American children whose spoken English, learned in a three-year bilingual program, was comparable to their peers who had spent an equal amount of time in an English monolingual program. Differences in the development of oral English skills among language-minority children can also exist at the individual level due to the influence of such factors as sex, age of the learner, verbal flexibility, sociability, and activity preferences. These learner differences — social and cognitive skills — can affect the rate and quality of ESL acquisition as much as the type of bilingual/second language program.

MODELS OF SECOND LANGUAGE LEARNING

Various theoretical models have been proposed to explain the influence of a number of factors in the second language learning process. Schumann's (1976) framework includes three areas: (1) initiating factors (affective variables such as degree of acculturation, attitude, motivation, language ego); (2) cognitive processes (imitation, generalization, inference, memory); and (3) linguistic product (aspects of the language learned — morphemes, questions, negatives). Swain's (1977) model extends Schumann's categories by including the role and nature of "input" (interaction with different native speakers and exposure to the language in the classroom as a subject or medium of instruction). The "learning" dimension includes both conscious and unconscious strategies and behaviors. The "learned" category includes communicative proficiency (pragmatics and discourse) along with linguistic competence (morphemes, auxiliaries, relative clauses).

The model proposed by Dulay, Burt, and Krashen (1982) attempts to account for variation in learners' verbal performance by postulating an "internal processing" mechanism which affects the "intake" from the language environment. The interactional dynamics between the learner and the L_2 environment is described in terms of the learner's (1) age, (2) personality characteristics, (3) past language experience, including proficiency in L_1, (4) a socioaffective "filter," (5) a cognitive organizer, which subconsciously processes data the filte allows in and "organizes" the new language system, and (6) a monitor which acts as a conscious linguistic processor on the data accepted by the filter.

Gardner's (1978) social psychological model emphasizes the social milieu affecting L_2 acquisition. This model is particularly meaningful in studying language acquisition among bilinguals, since such factors as community expectation and beliefs about the relative values of languages and bilingualism could be variables affecting learners differentially in acquiring L_2. Beyond the "culture milieu" factors, there are sociological issues affecting L_2 learning among minority groups. Richards (1972) argues that language learning, particularly by immigrants or minority groups, is not so much a question of language teaching methodologies as it is a function of the social structure. He argues that "nobody can be expected to learn the language of a social group if at the same time he is denied the means by which he can become a member of that group." He notes that German Americans, unlike the Puerto Rican immigrants, "do not live in ghettoes," "learn English easily and well," and, "although a certain amount of German interference is present in their English, it results in no obvious social discrimination." (Richards, 1978:15–*16*). The case of the Puerto Ricans illustrates, to a certain extent, the forces of economic and social segregation affecting both the process and the product of language learning. In the Puerto Rican community of New York City, according to Ma and Herasimchuk (1968:644),

> Bilinguals interact and communicate with each other, using both languages, far more frequently than they interact and communicate with members of the surrounding monolingual community. In such a community, speakers generate their own bilingual norms of correctness which may differ from the monolingual norms, particularly when there is a lack of reinforcement for these monolingual norms.

LEARNING ESL IN BILINGUAL SCHOOLS

The learning of a second language is affected by a multitude of factors (Izzo 1981). These factors can be grouped into three broad categories: personal (age, psychological traits, attitudes, and motivation), situational (setting, instructional approaches, and teacher characteristics), and linguistic aspects (differences and similarities between the first and second languages). Brown (1980) and Dulay, Burt, and Krashen (1982) discuss specific processes the learner undergoes in learning a second language. Hatch (1983) describes second language acquisition processes in relation to different dimensions of language — phonology, morphology, lexicon, syntax, and discourse.

Learning spoken English in bilingual schools can also be examined on the basis of individual differences and type of bilingual program. The development of first language abilities, the nature of L_2 instruction — error correction, communicative teaching approaches, interactional opportunities with native speakers — and the type of L_2 inputs are important factors which can affect the rate and quality of ESL oral language development (Krashen 1981).

TYPES OF ENGLISH LANGUAGE PROFICIENCY

The rationale for federally funded bilingual education programs in the United States (Bilingual Education Act of 1968 – Title VII – and Comprehensive Bilingual Education Amendment Act of 1973) rests on the "linguistic mismatch" hypothesis. This assumption is based on the belief that switching between the home language (L_1) and the school language (L_2) results in academic retardation and eventual school failure. Cummins (1980) argues that entry/exit criteria used to judge the extent to which students speak (know) English is based on superficial linguistic factors (e.g. pronunciation, grammar, and vocabulary) which are manifestations of language used in interpersonal communication. This type of language proficiency can also be described along a "context-embedded" and "context-reduced" communication continuum. He points out (Cummins 1981:11)

> that in context-embedded communication the participants can actively negotiate meaning (e.g., providing feedback that the message has not been understood) and the language is supported by a wide range of meaningful paralinguistic (gestures, intonation, etc.) and situational cues; context-reduced communication, on the other hand, relies primarily . . . on linguistic cues to meaning and may, in some cases, involve suspending knowledge of the "real" world in order to interpret (or manipulate) the logic of communication appropriately.

The length of time necessary for language-minority children to achieve age/grade norms in context-reduced aspects of English proficiency may be on the average of five to seven years, while context-embedded communication abilities require approximately two years. Native speakers of English also need more time to develop the language proficiency necessary to deal effectively with context-reduced (academic) situations than with face-to-face context-embedded communication demands.

Wong Fillmore (1982) suggests that the English language proficiency needed by language-minority students to participate effectively in mainstream English classrooms involves a broad range of skills. These skills include the ability to comprehend the instructional language used by teachers (see Figure 17) and the ability to produce appropriate discourse for participating in lessons (see Figure 18).

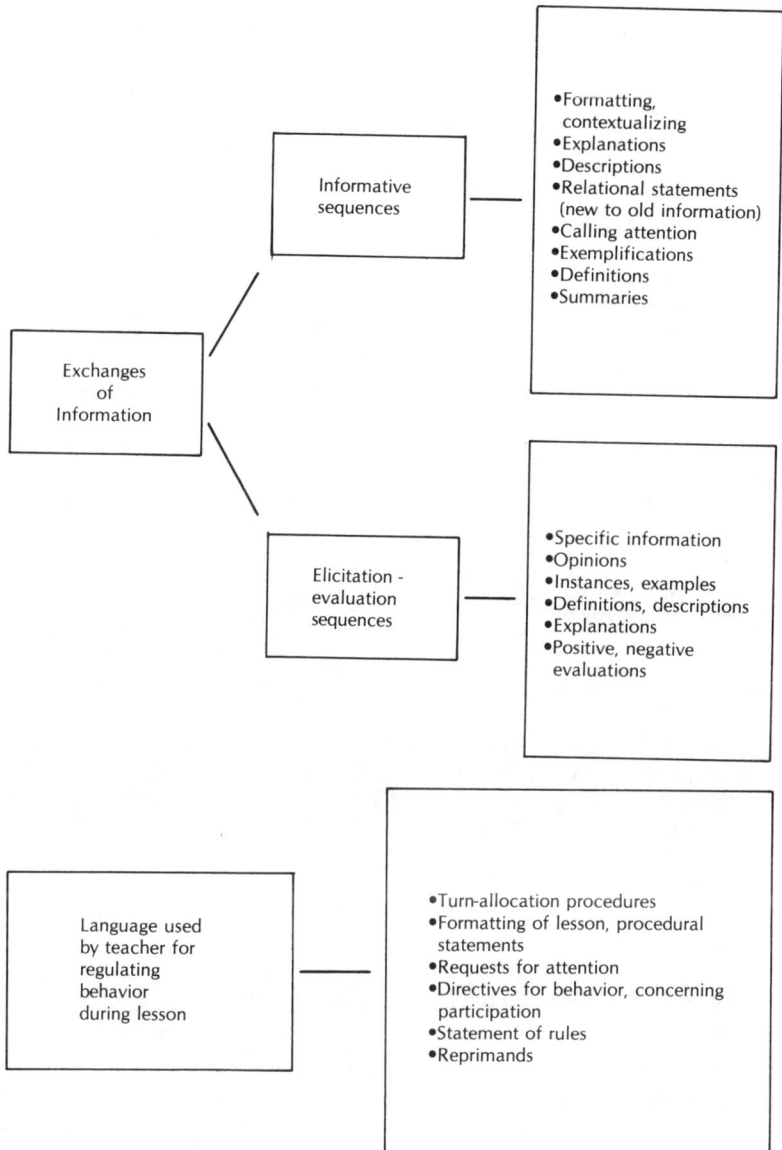

Figure 17. Child's Comprehension of Instructional Language Used by the Teacher in Teaching Lessons. Reprinted, with permission, from L. W. Fillmore, "Language Minority Students and School Participation: What Kind of English is Needed?" *Journal of Education*, 164:2 (1982):150. Copyright by Trustees of Boston University.

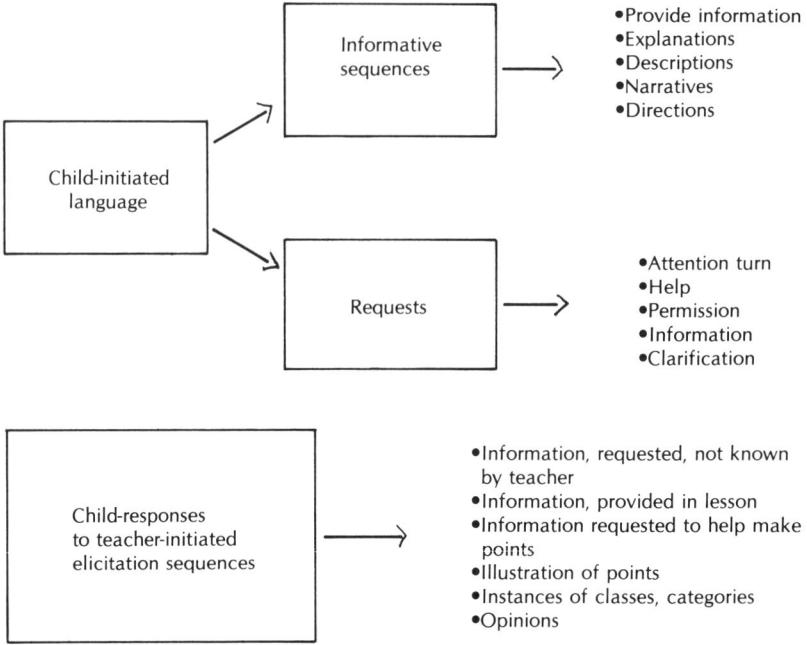

Figure 18. Child's Production of Language Required for Participation in Lessons. Reprinted, with permission, from L. W. Fillmore, "Language Minority Students and School Participation: What Kind of English is Needed?" *Journal of Education*, 164:2 (1982):150. Copyright by Trustees of Boston University.

BILINGUAL PROGRAM MODELS AND ORAL ENGLISH SKILLS

Legarreta (1979) conducted a seven-month longitudinal study to determine the effects of five different program models on the acquisition of English among Spanish-speaking kindergarten children. The five models included two types of English language programs (traditional/regular kindegarten taught in English without a formal ESL component and traditional kindergarten class with an ESL component) and three kinds of bilingual approaches (bilingual with the concurrent translation approach, no ESL component, bilingual with a balanced use of English and Spanish, no ESL component, and bilingual with the concurrent translation approach plus an ESL component). Language proficiency in English and Spanish was measured through the use of four criterion tests:

1. Oral comprehension (Revised Inter-American Oral Language Comprehension Test
2. Naming vocabulary-by-domain (kitchen at home, school classroom, and neighborhood street)
3. Oral producting (story retelling based on a picture book)
4. Communicative competence task based on a two person communication exchange with a screened (hidden) tester.

While the number of subjects in each treatment group was small (not more than thirteen pupils in any one group), the findings are interesting:

1. The three bilingual approaches produced significantly greater gains in English oral comprehension than did the two English treatments
2. The balanced bilingual approach produced the greatest overall gains in English (oral comprehension and communicative competence) and Spanish (communicative competence)
3. ESL training (audiolingual style) produced advances in English listening comprehension but did not increase communicative competence abilities
4. The least effective language program was the traditional all English ("sink" or "swim") immersion approach

Levy (1978) assessed the relative effects of separate language acquisition (SLAC), fused language acquisition (FLAC), and English monolingual (EM) contexts upon English and Italian language development for first and second grade Italian-speaking students. Linguistic behavior was examined in terms of syntactic and vocabulary development in English and Italian, degree of language alternation/mixing, and semantic independence. Students in the SLAC program participated in two separated language learning environments, for example, English in the morning taught by a native English-speaking teacher in an American-like environment and Italian in the afternoon taught by a native-speaking teacher in an Italian-type environment. Pupils in the FLAC program learned in one cultural setting; received instruction from one English/Italian bilingual teacher; and were taught some lessons in English, some in Italian, and others in both English and Italian, using both languages in alternation (code switching/concurrent approach). The conclusions drawn from the study suggest that the separate language acquisition approach promotes greater development of more "advanced" English and Italian oral language skills as compared to the fused bilingual model or the traditional immersion (English monolingual) program. Bilingual instruction, separate or fused, seems to promote first language development (Italian language skills) with at least equal, if not greater, effects on second language (English) development. In the area of language interaction patterns, all three groups demonstrated an increase use of English and a decrease use of Italian among peers in the formal classroom setting. The SLAC group made greater use of mixed language (Italian-English code switching) when interacting with their peers in the Italian classroom cultural area, perhaps reflecting a shift in language dominance. Students from the EM group used as much Italian among their peers as did the pupils from the SLAC group during interaction in the Italian classroom environment.

Ramírez (1974) compared spoken English grammatical patterns between Spanish-speaking Mexican American pupils in grades K–3 of a bilingual (BL) school and a comparable group of students instructed only in English in a traditional school program (ML). The study, cross-sectional in nature, focused on the development of various linguistic dimensions — degree of syntactic complexity (number and type of nominal, adverbial and coordinating sentence combining transformations), type of sentence patterns, and degree of grammaticality and structural explicitness in the constructions. The BL pupils produced a greater number of words in retelling a story based on a film. The BL group also used a greater number of structurally-complete patterns, consisting of T-units — utterances defined as one main clause plus any subordinate clause or nonclausal structure attached to it — as well as a greater number of structurally-incomplete T-units. On the measures related to syntactic complexity — total or mean number of sentence combining transformations (SCT-nominal, adverbial, and coordinate) — and mean number of sentence combining transformations per T-unit, the BL group surpassed the ML group after two years of bilingual schooling (during grade two). Figures 19 to 21 represent the comparative growth patterns for the three indices of syntactic complexity for the BL and ML groups. For both groups, years in school did account for measurable differences in the use of certain syntactic patterns (more nominal constructions and a greater tendency to produce more "surface" explicit T-units and in the production of more grammatical (correct) T-units.

The process by which both groups acquired English over the four years of schooling (grades K–3) was described through a systematic examination and classification of the learners' errors (Politzer and Ramírez 1973). The errors were classified according to Corder's (1973) typology, which includes error type (omission, addition, substitution, word order), language level (vocabulary, morphology, syntax), and error source (interlingual — interference from L_1 — or intralingual — "developmental" or overgeneralization of a rule). A total of 1,055 errors were counted in the

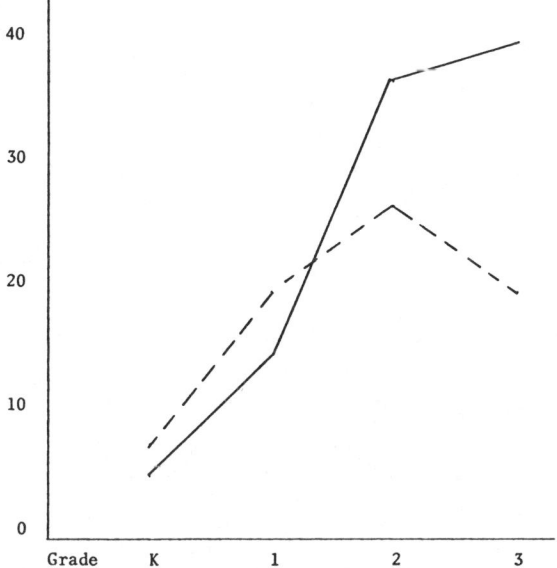

Figure 19. Mean Production of Total SCT as a Function of Grade for Monol-ingually and Biingually-Schooled Spanish-Speaking Children. Reprinted, by per-mission, from A. G. Ramírez. *The Spoken English of Spanish-Speaking Pupils in a Bilingual and Monolingual School Setting: An Analysis of Syntactic Develop-ment (Technical Report No. 40)* Stanford University, Center for Educational Research, *1974: p. 75.*

_____ Bilingually-Schooled Children
-------- Monolingually-Schooled Children

language samples produced by the children, based on a story retelling of a silent movie. The children from the BL group did not differ significantly from those in the ML group with respect to type/frequency of deviations from standard English. Children from the BL group made a total of 525 errors compared to 530 for pupils from the ML group. Most of the errors occurred in the use of the simple past tense (either the morphologically wrong form or the substitution of a perfective progressive or a perfect) and the use of prepositions (wrong use or omission of prepositions before noun phrases). Table 7 shows a general trend toward greater "correctness" in the use of regular (e.g. the addition of -ed, -t, -d, -ad) and irregular past tenses (e.g. go/went, come/came), and of prepositions across the grades. Differences between the two groups were minimal. In the use of preposi-tions, pupils from the BL group performed better than the students from the ML group during the early grades (Kindergarten and grade 1). The ML group, in turn, produced a greater percentage of correct past tenses

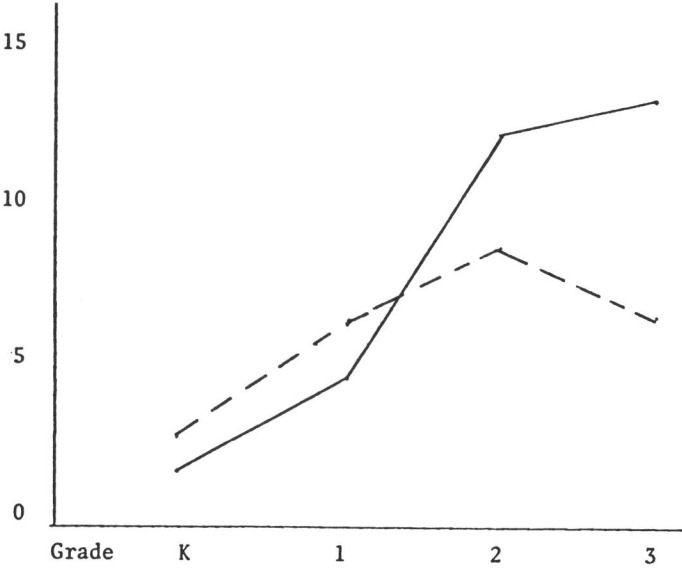

Figure 20. Mean Production of Types of SCT as a Function of grade for Monolingually and Bilingually-Schooled Spanish-Speaking Children. Reprinted, by permission, from A. G. Ramírez. *The Spoken English of Spanish-Speaking Pupils in
a Bilingual and Monolingual School Setting: An Analysis of Syntactic Development (Technical Report No. 40)* Stanford University, Center for Educational
Research, *1974: p. 75.*

_____ Bilingually-Schooled Children
-------- Monolingually-Schooled Children

during the first two years. During grades two and three, the performance
of both groups became more similar. The overall error rate differences
between the two groups are minimal (see Table 8). Pupils from the ML
group have an initial advantage over the BL group in kindergarten,
but, after that, the differences diminish resulting in almost parallel performance by grade three. The lack of significant differences between the
two groups highlights an important educational issue: "the spoken
English of Mexican-American children who had spent approximately
three years in a bilingual program was no worse than that of comparable
Mexican-American children who spent about three years in a monolingual program" (Politzer and Ramírez 1973:60).

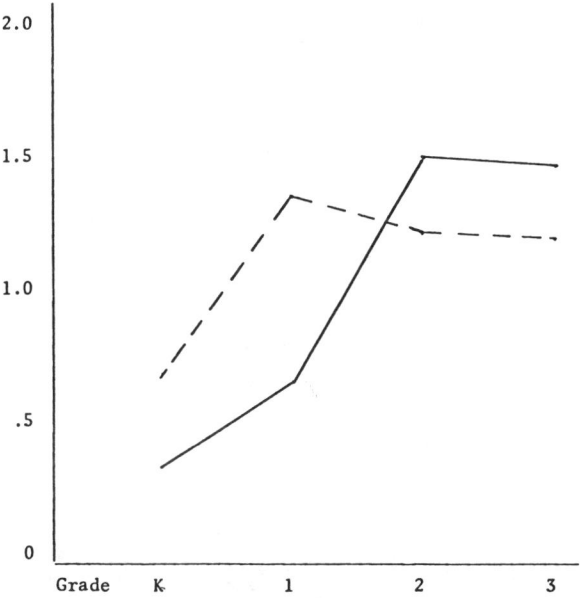

Figure 21. Mean Production of Number of SCT Per T-Unit as a Function of Grade for Monolingually and Bilingually-Schooled Spanish-Speaking Children. Reprinted, by permission, from A. G. Ramírez. *The Spoken English of Spanish-Speaking Pupils in a Bilingual and Monolingual School Setting: An Analysis of Syntactic Development (Technical Report No. 40)* Stanford University, Center for Educational Research, *1974: p. 75.*

_____ Bilingually-Schooled Children
-------- Monolingually-Schooled Children

INDIVIDUAL DIFFERENCES AND ORAL ENGLISH SKILLS

Individual differences among learners affect the rate and quality of second language acquisition. Differences due to sex and age can influence language learning proceses as much as the type of language program. Politzer and Ramírez (1973) noted differences on oral English development due to sex among the pupils reported above, who attended bilingual (BL) and monolingual (ML) elementary schools. Overall, females made a greater use of correct simple past tenses and prepositions than males in either the BL or ML programs (see Table 9). During the first

Table 7. Percentage of Correct Use of Regular and Irregular Past Tenses and Prepositions by Grade Level and Type of School

	Bilingual School			Monolingual School		
Grade	Regular Past	Irregular Past	Prepositions	Regular Past	Irregular Past	Prepositions
K	14	46	75	24	54	56
1	34	49	79	47	63	79
2	51	82	84	63	77	84
3	71	85	91	77	88	95

SOURCE: R. L. Politzer and A. G. Ramírez, "An Error Analysis of the Spoken English of Mexican-American Pupils in a Bilingual and Monolingual School Setting." *Language Learning* 23, no. 1 (1973):39–62.

two years (Kindergarten and grade 1) of bilingual schooling, females surpassed males in correctness on the two measures. Thereafter, in grades two and three, the performance was relatively similar. In the ML group, females employed prepositions to the same degree of correctness as males at all grade levels except in kindergarten. Males made a greater correct use of the past tense than females only at the kindergarten level. On the number of errors per hundred words, females in the BL group made more errors than males at the kindergarten level (see Table 10). In the ML group, males and females had a similar error rate in kindergarten, but, in grades one and four, males tended to produce more ungrammatical features than females.

Table 8. Number of Errors per One Hundred Words by Grade Level and Type of School

	Bilingual School			Monolingual School		
Grade	No. of Errors	No. of Words	Errors/ 100 Words	No. of Errors	No. of Words	Errors/ 100 Words
K	73	903	8.1	67	1243	5.5
1	140	1755	8.0	211	2801	7.5
2	183	3223	5.7	158	2521	6.3
3	129	2987	4.3	94	2339	4.0

SOURCE: R. L. Politzer and A. G. Ramírez, "An Error Analysis of the Spoken English of Mexican-American Pupils in a Bilingual and Monolingual School Setting." *Language Learning* 23, no. 1 (1973):39–62.

Table 9. Percentage of Correct Use of Simple Past Tense and Prepositions by Grade Level, Sex, and Type of School

| | Bilingual School | | | | Monolingual School | | | |
| | Simple Past | | Prepositions | | Simple Past | | Prepositions | |
Grade	Male	Female	Male	Female	Male	Female	Male	Female
K	—	33	—	75	48	28	46	67
1	37	58	73	89	35	79	79	82
2	71	67	87	79	70	68	82	85
3	84	68	92	92	79	87	94	96
$\bar{X}$	48	57	63	84	58	66	75	83

SOURCE: Same as Tables 7 and 8.

In a subsequent study, Ramírez and Politzer (1978) compared the performance on comprehension and production language tasks of two groups of secondary school students, group A_1 (newly arrived junior high and high school students) and group A_2 (students from the same grade range who had been in the United States for one year), with pupils from a bilingual program in Kindergarten, grades one, three, and five. The comprehension (C) and production (P) tasks included fourteen grammatical categories presented in minimal pairs (e.g. affirmative versus negative constructions). Each category was represented by two items and each item was illustrated by two pictures corresponding to the contrast being tested. In general, there was an improvement on CP test scores related to grade level for pupils in the Spanish/English bilingual program. However, there was almost no difference between the scores of the A_1 and A_2 groups, even though the A_2 group had about twelve more months of exposure to English than the A_1 group. The A_1 and A_2 groups performed at about the same level as the third graders. The study "revealed" the superiority of the high school students in the A_1 group (greater memory and a more fully developed conceptual system) who reached, in approximately half a year, the performance level of third graders exposed to English instruction through bilingual schooling since

Table 10. Number of Errors per One Hundred Words by Grade Level, Sex, and Type of School

| | Bilingual School | | Monolingual School | |
| | Errors/100 words | | Errors/100 words | |
Grade	Male	Female	Male	Female
K	4.7	8.4	5.2	5.7
1	8.4	7.0	8.6	5.1
2	5.3	6.2	6.0	6.5
3	3.2	1.3	4.6	2.7

SOURCE: Same as Tables 7 and 8.

kindergarten. Significant differences occurred between the kindergarten and first grade level in eight of the fourteen categories (four in comprehension and six in production); differences between grades one and three included four categories (two in comprehension and three in production); and differences occurred in eight categories (five in comprehension and six in production) for the interval between grades three and five. The grade level contrasts revealed that mastery of some categories (e.g. direct/indirect object reversal) did not occur until the period between grades three and five. At the same time, highly salient, apparently simple categories (singular/plural and present/future) had not been completely mastered by the elementary schoolchildren in the upper grades.

Wong Fillmore and her colleagues at the University of California at Berkeley (1983) have identified differences among ESL learners (Cantonese and Spanish-speaking children) in bilingual and monolingual programs. Sources of variation centered on two major areas: learner characteristics (social and cognitive differences that affect the manner by which L_2 learners approach and handle the activities associated with language learning) and situational characteristics (the features of the instructional setting — "open" or teacher-structured classes — which affect the degree/amount of opportunities L_2 learners find to hear and use the new language). The three-year, longitudinal project focused on the extent learner characteristics (e.g. verbal flexibility, sensitivity to linguistic context, sociability, activity preferences) affected the speed and success in language learning and on the influence of situational variables which can interact with the learner's ability to find situations to use the new language. Based on extensive obervations of children during th first two years of schooling, several findings seemed clear (Fillmore 1983:161–162):

1. "Good" or "poor" language learners cannot be characterized on the basis of one dimension. Learner variables "affect different individuals differently, working in combination with other factors which appear to compensate for, neutralize, or mitigate their effect.

2. The relationship between learner variables — social and cognitive factors — and the speed and success in language learning is not a simple one. Situational characteristics affect the language learning process in significant ways (e.g. "open" classes promote greater individual variation, shy children can do better in highly structured classrooms, and Chinese children are more teacher/adult oriented while Spanish-speaking children tend to be more peer oriented).

3. Considerable differences existed among the children as to how well and how fast they learned English, beyond monolingual or bilingual program considerations.

Only eighteen out of the forty eight subjects (38 percent) observed during the first two years could be characterized "as 'pretty good language learners', comparatively speaking, by virtue of their ability to communicate satisfactorily in English with their teachers, classmates, and members of the research team" (Fillmore 1983:162). Only twelve of the eighteen, however, (or 25 percent of the forty eight subjects) could be classified as "good language learners," and from this group only five (or 10 percent of the total sample) could be described as "fluent" in English. Chamot (1983:3,6) points out the educational implications of these findings for children of limited English proficiency (LEP):

> Excellent language learners able to learn English in about two years represent only about 20–25 percent of the LEP children studied, whereas a large middle group of children (50–55 percent) need at least another year of language support services. Fully 25 percent of the children studied revealed little progress in English acquisition even after three or four years of instruction, and were in need of two or more years' additional bilingual instruction.

SUMMARY

Various models were presented to identify the different factors involved in the second language learning process. Schumann's framework included initiating factors, cognitive processes, and linguistic product. Swain's model included other categories — language "input" and different aspects of language proficiency (linguistic forms and communicative aspects of language). The model proposed by Dulay, Burt, and Krashen attempted to account for in the learner's verbal performance with respect to various factors: age, personality characteristics, past language experience, filter, cognitive organizer, and monitor.

Gardner noted that social factors could also influence the learning process: community expectations, beliefs about values of languages, and degree of bilingualism. Also from a sociological perspective, Richards pointed out that societal stratification could also affect L_2 learning among different ethnolinguistic groups.

The learning of ESL can be described in terms of three broad categories: (1) personal (e.g. age, attitudes, motivation), (2) situational (e.g. setting, instructional approaches), and (3) linguistic aspects (e.g. differences between languages). Cummins has characterized the development of language proficiency in two ways, each type requiring a different amount of learning time: context-reduced proficiency (five to seven years) and context-embedded proficiency (two years).

Legarreta's study of the effects of different types of bilingual education programs on the development of oral English skills indicated that (1) bilingual approaches produced greater English gains, (2) balanced bilingual approaches produced the greatest gains, (3) ESL produced gains in English listening comprehension, and (4) traditional English immersion was least effective. The study by Levy examined the effects of different bilingual instructional models on the development of English and Italian language skills among Italian American pupils. Ramírez compared the syntactic development of spoken English among Mexican American children attending a bilingual program (K-3) and a monolingual English program (K-3), and noted a similar level of proficiency after three years of schooling (grade two).

Individual differences among learners — sex, age, cognitive style, and social skills — have also been found to affect the development of oral language skills. Ramírez and Politzer noted the influence of age on English comprehension and production tests. Fillmore described how differences in social and cognitive skills affected how well and how fast language-minority children learned English *beyond* monolingual and bilingual program considerations. Issues in the development of literary skills — reading and writing abilities — among language-minority children will be discussed in the following chapter.

SUGGESTED READINGS

Alatis, J. E. and K. Twaddell, eds. *English as a Second Language in Bilingual Education.* Washington, D.C.: TESOL, 1976.

Gage, J., ed. *Longitudinal Studies in Second Language Learning and Bilingual Education: A Bibliography.* Rosslyn, Va.: National Clearinghouse for Bilingual Education, 1982.

Krashen, S. S. D. *Principles and Practice in Second Language Acquisition.* New York: Pergamon Institute of English, 1982.

Saville-Troike, M. *Foundations for the Teaching of English as a Second Language: Theory and Method for Multicultural Education.* Englewood Cliffs, N. J.: Prentice-Hall, Inc., 1976.

Stupp, E. G. and J. Gage, eds. *Second Language Learning and Young Children: A Bibliography of Research.* Rosslyn, Va.: National Clearinghouse for Bilingual Education, 1981.

DEVELOPMENT OF LITERACY SKILLS IN ESL _____

INTRODUCTION

Literacy skills involve decoding, interpreting and articulating messages within appropriate sociocultural contexts. Several conclusions have been drawn about the nature of communication through written documents, as well as of some of the distinctions between the communication processes of reading and writing. Within the context of bilingual programs for ethnolinguistic minority groups, literacy concerns usually focus on the language in which reading is taught – the mother tongue or the second language. Issues related to this topic are discussed in the section on literacy and bilingual schooling.

    Literacy development in the bilingual school has generally been directed toward reading as a *product* (e.g. answering multiple-choice comprehension questions) rather than as a *process* (a set of strategies used to comprehend unfamiliar passages, for example). The same finding holds true for the development of writing abilities in a bilingual school context, where product is often stressed over process. Several studies on reading instruction for language-minority pupils have focused on the transferability of reading skills from the native language to L_2 reading.

Teaching reading in the native language, by direct method or concurrently — using both L_1 and L_2, can result in different learner outcomes. Reading ability in the second language can be influenced by many factors, some of which are discussed in the section on reading processes in the second language. Some studies suggest that the competence a language-minority child develops in the second language is partially a function of the type of competence attained in the first language at the time of initial exposure to the second language. Variations in writing due to linguistic-cultural differences in the non-native, English-speaking pupil will be discussed here. Finally, some of the effects of bilingualism on English writing abilities will be described.

CONCEPTS OF LITERACY

From an anthropological perspective, literacy skills involve the decoding, interpretation, and articulation of messages for particular audiences following the appropriate sociocultural norms. Trueba and his associates (1982:23-24) at San Diego State University have studied the functional writing abilities of bilingual secondary students and have reached the following tentative conclusions:

1. Communication through a written document is a process which:
    a. implies the existence of codes and a chain of meaning,
    b. has an underlying structure,
    c. is socioculturally bound and language specific,
    d. is part of a broader system of communication, and
    e. requires specific cognitive skills unique to the articulation in writing.
2. Reading and writing are distinct but closely related communication processes which:
    a. presuppose similar understanding of codes, role relationships, and inferencing of meanings,
    b. contrast in their use of cognitive skills (reading relies more on skills to decipher symbolic meaning while writing stresses the generation of messages),
    c. share levels of asymmetrically correlated performance (good writers read well, not necessarily the other way around),

      d. share formal and informal aspects of the language in contrast with oral and kinesic communication,

      e. presuppose oral language proficiency,

      f. require high degree of skill to fictionalize writer's or reader's role vis-à-vis the role of the audience or audiences,

      g. develop gradually through a long process of acquisition and accumulation of cognitive, cultural, sociolinguistic, and communicative skills, and

      h. require close monitoring, coaching, and rewarding by well-established social mechanisms.

  3. Literacy is of paramount importance in education, upward mobility, and the managing of social, economic, and political information systems in the United States for the ethnolinguistic minority population.

The ability to obtain meaning from a written text is an extremely complex cognitive process, requiring the reader to use available contextual clues and to utilize his competence with the written language variety (cohesive devices, rhetorical structure), as well as to bring to bear his cultural background knowledge of the world (cultural schema). The ability to produce written texts involves, for example, using a number of conventions—spelling, punctuation, paragraph indentation, and following a particular organizational format. Writers must rely on their "context-reduced" communicative proficiency (Cummins 1981) by making use of explicit reference and propositional language linked together on logical grounds, rather than on shared understandings with the reader.

LITERACY AND BILINGUAL SCHOOLING

Literacy concerns in the context of bilingual programs for ethnolinguistic minority groups have centered on the choice of language—mother tongue (L_1) or the second language (L_2)—for teaching reading. The issues include whether or not reading should be taught in the native language (L_1) with students when transferring skills to the second language (L_2), whether students should be immediately immersed in L_2, whether L_1 and L_2 should be a simultaneous process, or whether there is no difference between teaching reading first in L_1 or L_2. Proponents of the L_1 to L_2 method have emphasized attaining literacy in the native language first because the literacy process should occur in the language with which the individual is most familiar.

Reviews of investigations (Engle 1975; Lombardo 1980) in this area suggest that no generalizations are possible due to flaws in research design and/or program implementation. Some studies showed the L_1 approach to reading produced greater gains (e.g. Mexico—Modiano 1968; Philippines—Ramos, 1967; Peru—Wise 1969; and United States, Navajo children in Arizona—Vorih and Rosier 1978—Spanish-speaking pupils in New York City—Ehrlich 1971—Spanish-speaking pupils in San Antonio, Texas—John and Horner 1971), while a comparable number of studies showed the L_2 approach as being more effective (e.g. Canada—Lambert and Tucker 1972; South Africa—Malherbe 1946; United States, English speakers immersed in Spanish—Cohen 1974).

The contradictory nature of the findings could be related to a number of issues—educational/economic factors (e.g. the necessity to learn English as a second language in Ghana or the Philippines since higher education is in English) and social/ethnic factors (e.g. minority students in the United States have to learn English and often put aside their own native language to achieve academically and economically, while middle class, English-speaking children can add a second language without any long-term retardation of first language skills). Studies related to beginning reading approaches have generally been focused on reading as *product* (e.g. examination of reading skills on the basis of students' answers on multiple-choice, comprehension questions) rather than on reading as *process* (e.g. examination of how readers get meaning from a text through the use of the cloze procedure or miscue analysis, or analysis of readers' strategies in comprehending culturally unfamiliar passages).

Theories on reading have influenced the direction of research. A psycholinguistic description of the act of reading as a "sampling, selecting, predicting, comparing and confirming activity," in which the reader makes use of the various cues provided by the text (Goodman 1973), seems to have gained wide-spread acceptance. Similarly, schemata perspectives on reading comprehension has led L_2 researchers to consider the role of cultural background knowledge (cultural schema). Apparently, "based on one's experience of the world in a given culture, one organizes knowledge about the world and uses this knowledge to predict interpretations and relationships regarding new information, events, and experiences" (Tannen 1979:139).

As with reading skills, writing in the context of bilingual schools can be approached as *product* (e.g. the paper the student submits for teacher evaluation) or as process (e.g. the procedures/stages the student followed in composing the final draft). The development of writing abilities among bilingual pupils can be considered from a number of perspectives, using linguistic factors (e.g. the writing systems of the two languages, interference from L_1), cognitive factors (e.g. use of "genre" schemes to direct certain types of writing [Bereiter 1980]), and stages in writing development (e.g. associative, performative, communicative, and epistemic writing [Bereiter 1980]).

BILINGUAL READING APPROACHES

A number of studies in reading instruction for language-minority pupils have focused on the transferability of reading skills from the native language to L_2 (English). At the elementary school level, Canseco (1978) examined the English reading achievement of Spanish-English bilingual students in a Los Angeles elementary school. While she questions the procedure used to determine the pupils' language dominance (joint assessment of teachers and instructional aides), she found that Spanish-dominant pupils, introduced to English reading after the acquisition of decoding skills in Spanish, attained the same level of achievement on English reading tests (CTBS) in a shorter period of time than English-dominant students. For bilinguals, students equally proficient in both languages, the dual reading approach (two hour dual reading program) had positive transfer effects on English skills instead of the expected interference. By the end of the first grade, the bilingual pupils performed as well or better on English reading than their English-dominant peers. In another similar study conducted by Rodríguez-Brown (1979), three reading approaches (reading in L_1, reading in L_1 and L_2, and reading in L_2) for teaching Spanish-English bilingual pupils in grades one and three in Illinois were examined. The students in the third grade instructed in L_1 and L_2 concurrently performed as well as those students taught in L_2 only, and, at the same time, enjoyed a statistically significant gain score on the Spanish reading test. Rodríguez-Brown attributes the lack of achievement in English reading for students in grades one and three, taught to read in L_1, to not only a significantly lower level of English proficiency but to inferior competence in Spanish and cognitive development.

Gunther (1981) also investigated the effects of three reading approaches (native language, direct method, and concurrent) and examined the relationship between sociological, linguistic, and instructional variables on L_1 and L_2 oral language development and reading skills among Spanish-background children, age six, attending thirteen public and private schools in Chicago. Students receiving only English reading instruction attained the highest post-test mean score on the LAS (Language Assessment Scales) measure of oral English proficiency. Students receiving initial reading instruction in Spanish made greater gains in oral English than the group receiving instruction concurrently in English and Spanish. Various explanations are offered to explain these results: learning to read simultaneously in two languages may produce "negative transfer," teaching reading in two languages poses more instructional problems, and the development of L_2 competence is related to proficiency in L_1. In reading achievement, students receiving instruction only in English obtained higher post-test mean scores on the CRS Diagnostic Placement Test than the pupils learning to read concurrently. The group receiving concurrent reading instruction, however, performed better than the other two groups on the Stanford Early School Achievement Test. The group receiving native language reading instruction for seven months made gains on the English post-test measures, suggesting the transfer of skills from L_1 to L_2 reading. Based on these findings, it is difficult to make a definite statement regarding the superiority of one reading approach over the other. Undoubtably, pupil characteristics (e.g. motivation, language attitudes, L_1 proficiency) interact with teaching approaches.

At the secondary level, Meléndez (1980) compared the effects of three instructional modes (monolingual English, bilingual English/Spanish, and monolingual Spanish) on the English reading achievement of limited English-speaking secondary students in grades 7-8 and 8-10. The students who received Spanish reading instruction did better on the English reading achievement test than those taught exclusively in English or through a bilingual approach. For the former students, still two or three years behind the normative population in English reading or language tests, the use of the mother tongue apparently improved reading achievement in both languages, thus promoting biliteracy and a better self-concept.

Studies with other language groups suggest that literacy in L_1 eventually results in improved reading achievement in L_2 (English). The positive effects of this approach may not be immediately apparent and may take between four to five years. Dube and Herbert (1975) report that French-English bilingual pupils in the St. John's Valley bilingual project in Maine performed better (e.g. in English language achievement and math) by grade five than a comparable group of students schooled in L_2 only. The students in the bilingual program were initially instructed in French and then continued one-third of their curriculum in French for five years, thus receiving considerably less instruction in English than the control group.

Rosier's (1977) comparative study of two approaches to introducing reading (direct method — monolingual English and the native language/ bilingual method — initial reading in Navajo and then transfer to English) to Navajo children at Rock Point Community School shows that students receiving at least four years of bilingual schooling scored significantly higher in English reading achievement than pupils instructed exclusively in English. Figure 22 contrasts the results on the Stanford Achievement Test (reading subtests total score) between the Rock Point students and the pupils in the five Bureau of Indian Affairs (BIA) control schools from grades two through six. The results indicate that the difference between the two groups is greater with each additional year after the third grade. The effects of bilingual instruction appear to be cumulative.

A previous study comparing a monolingual English program including English as a second language curricula (TESL) with a Navajo/English bilingual program revealed significant differences at the fifth and sixth grade levels. By the sixth grade, students from the Rock Point program reached an achievement mean score of 6.6, two years higher than that of the control group (4.7). These findings are presented in Figure 23.

READING PROCESSES IN THE SECOND LANGUAGE

Reading abilities in the second language can be influenced by a number of factors (e.g. relative proficiency in L_2, differential productive and receptive reading skills, varying cultural and experiential backgrounds, and variation in learning styles and strategies [Ammon 1983]). Some studies support Cummins' "developmental interdependence" hypothesis (1979), which assumes the competence a language-minority child develops in the second language is partially a function of the type of competence attained in the first language at the time of initial exposure to the second language. Leslie (1977), for example, studied in Canada the reading performance of Cree Indian children in grades one and two. Leslie reports statistically significant correlations between the children's oral language proficiency in Cree and English reading skills (Gates-McGinitie comprehension and Cree, $r = .76$, $p < .001$). Certain aspects of L_1 and L_2 language proficiency are also related to reading abilities in the second language. The ability to interpret and understand the communicative intention of speech acts (relationship

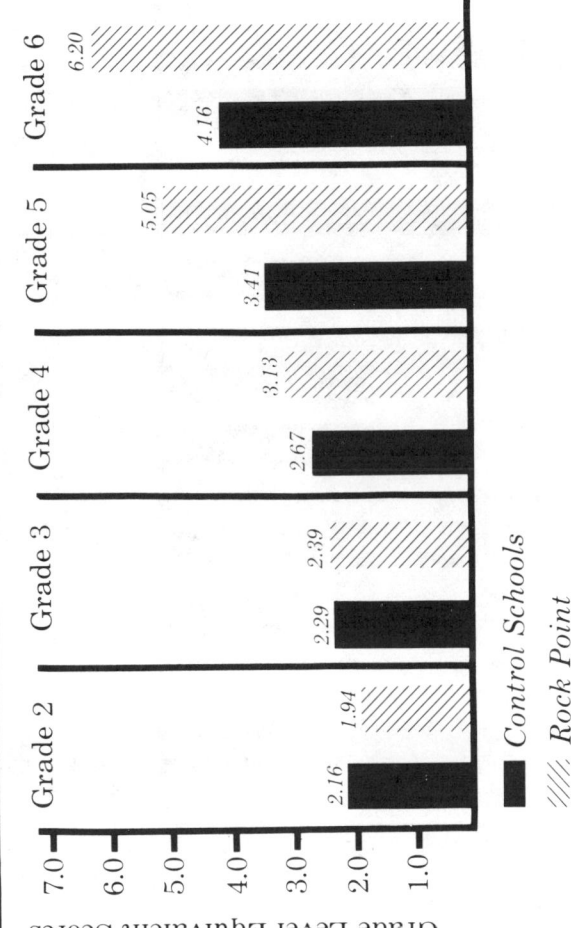

Figure 22. A Comparison of Rock Point Student Achievement with the Achievement of Students in BIA Control Schools in Total Reading. Reprinted by permission, from L. Vorih and P. Rosier, "Rock Point Community School: An Example of a Navajo-English Bilingual Elementary School Program" *TESOL Quarterly*, 12:3 (Sept. 1978): 267.

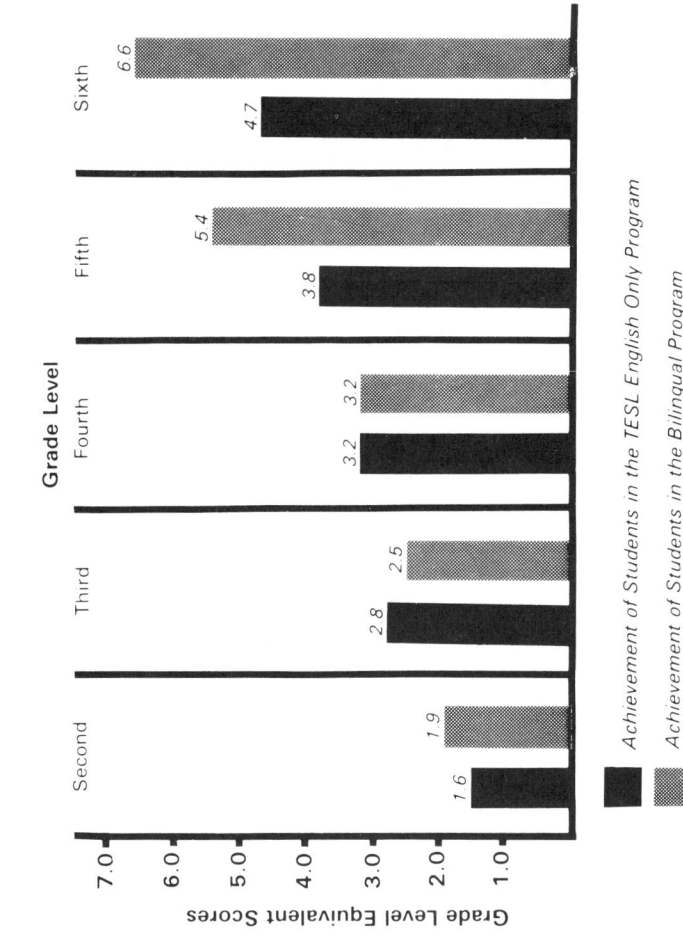

Figure 23. A Comparison of Rock Point Reading Achievement. The Achievement of Students Taught in TESL English Only (1970 and 1972) Compared with the Achievement of Students Taught in the Bilingual Program (1976). Reprinted by permission, from L. Vorih and P. Rosier, "Rock Point Community School: An Example of a Navajo-English Bilingual Elementary School Program" *TESTOL Quarterly,* 12:3 (Sept. 1978): 267.

of language form to function — Sit down/Why don't you sit down/I see that you are not sitting down), defined as an aspect of sociolinguistic competence, appears to be correlated with reading achievement.

Ramírez (1983) found that sociolinguistic competence correlated across languages (English and Spanish, $r = .56$, $p < .01$) for bilingual pupils in grades four and five and was also related to English reading achievement. In one bilingual school in the San Francisco Bay area, sociolinguistic competence in English (direct speech acts, $r = .58$, $p < .05$; indirect speech acts, $r = .59$, $p < .01$) and Spanish (indirect speech acts, $r = .50$, $p < .05$; direct speech acts, $r = .46$, $p < .05$) was related to CTBS English reading scores. Sociolinguistic competence in English (direct speech acts, $r = .46$, $p < .05$) also correlated with CTBS reading achievement in English in another bilingual school in the Lost Angeles area. The significant correlation between sociolinguistic competence (e.g. the ability to interpret a speaker's intentions by listening to items recorded on tape) and reading achievement could be explained by a child's facility in understanding, what Halliday (1973) terms, the "representational" function of language, the communication of information.

Olson (1977) has made a distinction between the logical (ideational) and the interpersonal functions of language. He has noted that the language of prose texts is primarily ideational (specifies the semantic and logical relations between the subject and predicate of a sentence). Fiege-Kollman (1977) noted that fourth and fifth grade Spanish/English pupils made fewer "errors" in oral reading (correction of errors, repetition of correct responses, omission of words, and addition of words) than monolingual readers. The bilingual group had more morphological substitution (e.g. turn as return) and mispronunciation miscues (e.g. eschool for school), suggesting interference from L_1.

Cziko (1978) compared differences among native and non-native speakers of French, focusing on the use of syntactic, semantic, and discourse textual constraints using cloze passages. Three groups of seventh grade students were involved: two English-speaking groups (one "intermediate" group of students that had participated in a year-long French immersion program and one "advanced" group that had received six years of immersion education), and a French control group. The results suggest a development order in the ability of L_2 learners to use contextual constraints. Sensitivity to syntactic constraints develops before sensitivity to both semantic and discourse aspects.

In another study, Cziko (1980) examined differences in L_2 reading strategies due to L_2 competence. Using miscue analysis, he found that the intermediate group of French learners made a significantly lower proportion of deletion and insertion errors than did the advanced group or the native speakers. The intermediate group made a significantly higher proportion of substitution errors that graphically resembled the text than did the French control group. The errors made by the intermediate group suggest a greater reliance on graphic information, while the advanced learners and native speakers used both graphic and contextual information to derive meaning from the text. Sensitivity to contextual information is reflected by fewer errors that violate the syntactic, semantic, or discourse constraints of the text.

González and Elijah (1979) studied the reading behaviors of Spanish/English pupils, grades 2–9, to determine a developmental pattern of language difficulties when reading English. They categorized incorrect responses on cloze items on the basis of illogical errors (substitutions that were syntactically and/or semantically inappropriate), logical errors (meaningful substitutions that were both syntactically and semantically appropriate), interference errors (responses reflecting semantic, lexical, or syntactic interference from Spanish), and other errors (nonsense and partial words, errors in English morphology). Errors resulting from interference were relatively few at any grade level. As reading proficiency increased, the number of illogical errors decreased and logical errors increased, suggesting a greater L_2 competence.

Eaton (1979) investigated the interactions between linguistic factors and cognitive style among Spanish-speaking Mexican American children. Field dependent (FD) and field independent (FI) first grade pupils were asked to read in both English and Spanish. The oral reading behavior was analyzed according to the nine categories set forth in the Reading Miscue Inventory (Goodman and Burke 1972), and a comprehsnsion score was given based on retelling abilities. The results include five major findings:

1. Cognitive style (FD and FI orientation) affected reading behavior in a similar manner across languages. Students in the FI group employed the various cue systems (e.g. graphophonic, syntactic, semantic) to a greater extent than did pupils from the FD group.
2. The reading strategies employed by the bilingual children were similarly applied across languages.
3. The children drew on the same linguistic cue systems in their attempt to reconstruct meaning from print while reading in both languages.
4. The FI readers comprehended more during the reading act than did the FD pupils in both Spanish and English. The FI readers

appear to have understood substantially more while reading in Spanish, while the FD pupils understood slightly more while reading in the second language.

5. Retelling scores were similar across languages. FI readers retold a greater amount of the reading than did FD pupils. Both groups were able to relate more from their reading in Spanish than from English.

Background knowledge (cultural schema) about a topic can also influence L_2 reading abilities. Readers can read faster, recall more information accurately, and make more appropriate inferences from texts that have familiar content than from those for which they do not have background knowledge (Anderson, Spiro, and Anderson 1978; Steffenson, Joag-Dev, and Anderson 1979). Connor (1981) used an interactive research approach with fifth grade bilingual (Spanish/English) pupils to determine the role of background knowledge on reading comprehension in English. She noted the interview method provided a number of insights about reading strategies. Due to the lack of appropriate cultural schemata of Cherokee Indians and Chief Sequoia, bilingual subjects had to rely on the linguistic aspects of the text, and, as a result, made text-bound comments (word-for-word answers) even though they performed well on the standardized reading comprehension questions following the text. Thus, reading assessment procedures (oral interview versus multiple-choice comprehension questions) can distort the degree of comprehension.

Lalas (1982) compared the influence of prior cultural experience on ESL reading for secondary and elementary school Filipino bilingual students living in the Pacific Northwest. The students were asked to read orally a story about an old man, his son and a donkey. Each pupil was then asked a series of questions related to the story. Table 11 contrasts the answers given by the high school pupils and the elementary schoolchildren to key concepts presented in the questions.

The high school students' concept of the farmer, his home, his use of animals, and the type of crops harvested differed from the notions held by the elementary pupils. The high school students maintained the Filipino farming schema (rice fields, nepa huts, the carabao as the beast of burden, and barefooted farmers). The elementary schoolchildren, on the other hand, added or acquired a new set of schema for farming (corn fields, wheat, a cabin or barn, horses and cows, and a moustached farmer wearing a checkered shirt and blue jeans) based on their cultural experiences in the United States. Lalas recommends that ESL reading in-

Table 11. Answers by High School and Elementary Subjects to Key Concepts Presented in the Questions

Key Concepts	High School	Elementary School
1. Farmer	old, old clothes and pants raggedy, old hat, bare footed, no shoes, skinny, torn shirt, torn clothes	moustache, old shoes, old clothes, hat, overalls, jumpsuit, summer shoes, checkered shirt, and blue jeans
2. Home	nips hut, made of bamboo, old hut, not much furniture	wooden, cabin, barn, big house with a barn (one student mentioned hut)
3. Use of animal or machinery	(everybody chose animal) carabao, cows, horse (13 of the 15 subjects mentioned carabao)	(2 of the 15 chose machinery) horse, cow, donkey, (only 4 of the 15 mentioned caraboa)
4. Farmer's garden or field	rice fields, vegetables, fruits (all of the subjects mentioned rice fields)	corn fields, apples, wheat, carrots, cabbages, tomatoes, beans, cantaloupe, rice (only 1 of the 15 mentioned rice)
5. Concept of a donkey	2 subjects equated donkey to a chicken and camel	everybody knew what a donkey is

Source: Reprinted, by permission, from J. W. Lalas, "The Influence of Prior Experience in ESL Reading," *Bilingual Journal* 6, no. 1 (1982):12.

struction should be concerned with schema development along with the improvement of linguistic skills.

DIFFERENCES IN WRITING ABILITIES

Most recent studies on the development of writing abilities in English have focused on the native, English-speaking pupils (e.g. Frederiksen and Dominic 1981; Gregg and Steinberg 1980). Few investigations have examined variation in writing due to linguistic-cultural differences. Several investigations (Johnson 1971; Callary 1971; O'Neill 1972) indicate that high-status socioeconomic groups use more complicated syntactic structures in written work and have a lower incidence of nonstandard features in their speech than do low-status groups. Other studies have found differences in writing abilities due to ethnolinguistic background. In Canada, Braun and Klassen (1973) compared the writing performance of three distinctly different ethnic groups (monolingual, Anglo-Saxon Protestant; bilingual, German Mennonite; bilingual, French Roman Catholic) of pupils in grades four and six in Manitoba schools. The monolingual students showed marked superiority in all indices of language development. The bilingual German (BG) students followed the monolingual pupils in the subordinate clause index and in number of sentence-combining transformations produced. The bilingual French (BF) students ranked lowest in all of the indices. Although the monolingual group showed a higher competence in use of English syntactic structures, it made more grammatical errors than the BG subjects. The BF subjects showed the least syntactic control and also made the most errors. One of the bilingual subgroups (BG, grade six females) surpassed the monolingual group in all the major linguistic indices.

Rodríguez (1974) compared the oral and written English syntax of Mexican American bilingual and Anglo-American monolingual fourth and ninth grade students in Las Vegas, New Mexico. He found that the average clause length of ninth grade bilingual students was shorter than that of the ninth grade monolingual subjects in the written mode. The syntactic maturity measures indicated an increase from fourth to ninth grade, slightly more for the monolingual than the bilingual. There was no difference between the two groups in terms of English syntactic patterns.

Stahl (1977) studied the structure of compositions among Israeli students from European and Mediterranean backgrounds in grades 2, 5, 8, and 11. All the measures showed a developmental trend, in both ethnic groups from the second to the eighth grade. A closer examination, however, revealed a gap between the writing of the culturally privileged European and the disadvantaged Mediterranean. In some cases, the Mediterranean pupils in the fifth grade wrote like the Europeans in the second grade; those in the eighth grade, like the Europeans in the fifth grade; and, in one category (method of arrangement), the Mediterranean group in grade eight wrote like the Europeans in grade two.

Kuhlman (1982) compared the writing abilities of secondary students with different levels of English proficiency (monolingual English speakers, Hispanic pupils fluent in both English and Spanish, and limited English speakers enrolled in bilingual programs). The writing samples were scored according to three assessment procedures: categorical subscales (organization—introduction, body, and conclusion; use of rhetorical devices; syntax; overall format; and fluency), holistic method (each essay scored on a six-point scale according to relative judgements about the whole paper), and state competency scoring (content – nine points; and mechanics – five points; each paper scored twice). The results, contrasting the relative performance of the three groups at the eighth and tenth grade levels, are presented in Table 12. At the eighth grade level, Hispanic pupils fluent in both languages performed better than the limited English pupils (LEP) on the writing sample scored categorically (C), 10.4 to 6.95, and holistically (H), 7.5 to 2.45. Native English speakers in the control group scored higher than the LEP students currently in bilingual programs (C – 11.3 to 6.95; and H – 6.2 to 2.45), while those from the fluent Hispanic group wrote similarly to the control group. Using the state's competency criteria, the Hispanic and control groups attained similar scores (10.1 to 10.6). At the tenth grade level, LEP students in the bilingual program scored higher than their monolingual English-speaking peers using categorical scoring (12.1 to 10.6). Within the bilingual groups, the more fluent bilinguals scored higher than the LEP students (12.5 to 11.7) and, in turn, both groups scored higher than the control group. Using holistic scoring criteria, the control group performed slightly better than the LEP group (4.6 to 4.1). On the competency scores available for the bilingually schooled groups, the more fluent bilinguals obtained an average score of 9.7 (35 percent) compared to the score for LEP pupils of 7.2 (25.7 percent). The findings seem to indicate that the "development" of writing abilities among different ethnolinguistic groups may be greatly influenced by the use of particular assessment criteria. Categorical scoring criteria may be able to differentiate relative writing growth along various traits (e.g. use of dialogue, point of view, tenses, etc.) better than holistic evaluation.

BILINGUALISM AND THE WRITING PROCESS

The effects of bilingualism on English writing abilities has been described from both positive and negative perspectives. Ng (1966), for example, found that English compositions written by bilingual (Chinese/English) fifth grade pupils contained examples of interference from Chinese. He noted "that the highly bilingual subjects displayed four times as many carry-overs of Chinese into English as did the low group" in such areas as grammatical construction, inflections, word order, and literal translations from Chinese (Ng 1966:98). Ney (1977), on the other hand, found that the writing "miscues" of three Hispanic pupils were not

Table 12. Average Scores And Percentages For Categorical Holistic And State Competency Writing Assessment Scales For Eighth And Tenth Graders

Group	Categorical (20 points)	Holistic (12 points)	Competency (28 points)
Eighth Grade (N = 105)	(10.2) 51%	(5.14) 45%	(10.6) 38%
Hispanic (N = 21)	(10.4) 52	(7.5) 62	(10.1) 36
Bilingual (N = 29)	(6.95) 34	(2.45)	- -
Control (N = 55)	(11.3) 56	(6.2) 51	(10.6) 38
Tenth Grade (N = 56)	(11.2) 56	(4.4) 36	- -
Hispanic	-	- -	
Bilingual (N = 20)	(12.1) 60	(4.1) 34	(8.8) 30
Controls (N = 36)	(10.6) 53	(4.6) 38	- -

SOURCE: N. S. Kuhlman, "State Competency Writing Tests: What Do We Learn?" Paper presented at TESOL Annual Conference, Honolulu, 1982.

qualitatively different from their English-speaking peers in Arizona. This study examined writing performance based on the pupils' abilities to combine English sentences (e.g. The man is gone. The man has a broken leg. The man with the broken leg is gone.).

As with reading abilities, the development of writing skills may be affected by nonlinguistic factors. Politzer (1982) found that writing competency among high school Spanish/English bilinguals was related to an acculturation process, based on length of residency in the United States (usually a period of four years). The acculturation process was reflected by increases in field independence and higher self-concept scores. Reading abilities, as well as the numbers of graduation-related competencies passed, were also related to the degree of acculturation, perhaps indicating the acquisition of cultural/academic schemata.

Edelsky (1982) conducted a unique study on the development of writing abilities in the context of a bilingual program for language-minority children. The bilingual program emphasized writing within the whole-language approach to literacy, and literacy in the first language (Spanish) before instruction in the second language (English). The study centered on the relationship between first and second languae writing among pupils in grades 1-3. The main findings included the fact that writing initiated by the children was superior to that assigned by teachers, and that code switching rarely occurred in written texts although prevalent in oral communication. Specific writing strategies support two major perspectives regarding early biliteracy:

1.   What a young writer knows about writing in the first language is used/applied/adapted, and forms the basis for a new

hypothesis for, rather than interfering with, writing in the second language.

2. The application of certain hypotheses/knowledge/processes to L_2 writing interacts with various factors (e.g. the nature of the two writing systems, the writer's proficiency in L_2, the nature of the literacy experience itself—manuscript writing for English and cursive script for Spanish).

SUMMARY

Literary skills, from an anthropological perspective, involve such abilities as decoding, interpretating, and articulating. With respect to bilingual schooling, literary concerns have centered on the choice of L_1 or L_2 to teach reading. Questions such as whether reading should be taught in L_1 with new students transfering skills into L_2 have been considered. Studies regarding this issue appear to be contradictory due to such elements as educational/economic factors and social/ethnic factors.

Reading and writing can be viewed from a product or a process orientation. The development of writing abilities among bilingual pupils can be described from the point of view of linguistic factors, cognitive factors, or stages in writing development.

Different studies have examined the effects of different reading approaches: native language method, direct method, and the concurrent approach. Gunther, for example, found that the concurrent approach produced the least gains in English reading among Spanish-English bilinguals. Studies of other language groups seem to indicate that literacy in L_1 will improve reading in L_2 even though improvements may take four to five years. Reading abilities in the second language can be influenced by many factors. One of these can be explained in terms of Cummins's "developmental interdependence" hypothesis, which assumes that development in L_2 may be a function of proficiency in L_1 among language-minority pupils.

Field dependence and field independence were discussed and studied as factors influencing L_2 reading abilities. Cultural schema may also be an influential factor. Most studies on the development of writing abilities have focused on native speakers. Few investigations have examined variations due to linguistic-cultural differences. Bilingualism can affect English writing abilities in positive and negative terms, depending on the aspects of composition assessed and the evaluation procedures. Writing abilities in English can also be influenced by non-linguistic factors — degree of acculturation — as well as instructional approaches.

SUGGESTED READINGS

Andersson, T. *A Guide to Family Reading in Two Languages: The Preschool Years.* Rosslyn, Va.: National Clearinghouse for Bilingual Education, 1981.

Barnett-Mizrahi, C., ed. *Reading and the Bilingual Learner: A Functional Annotated Bibliography.* Cambridge, Mass.: National Assessment and Dissemination Center, Lesley College, 1979.

Goodman, K., Y. Goodman and B. Flores. *Reading in the Bilingual Classroom: Literacy and Biliteracy.* Rosslyn, Va.: National Clearninghouse for Bilingual Education, 1979.

Krashen, S. D. *Writing: Research, Theory, and Application.* New York: Pergamon Institute of English, 1984.

Simões, A., ed. *The Bilingual Child: Research and Analysis of Existing Educational Themes.* New York: Academic Press, Inc., 1976.

Thonis, E. W. *Teaching Reading to Non-English Speakers.* New York: The Macmillan Company, 1970.

Trueba, H. and B. Blair, eds. *Advances in Second Language Literacy.* San Diego State University, Center for Ethnographic Research, 1983.

Whiteman, M. F., ed. *Variation in Writing: Functional and Linguistic-Cultural Differences.* Hillsdale, New Jersey: Lawrence Erlbaum Associate Publishers, 1981.

Chapter Seven _____

ATTITUDES TOWARD LANGUAGE AND CULTURAL GROUPS _____

INTRODUCTION

Feelings about language — thinking of a language as more pleasant or harsher sounding than another language — and reactions to the use of a particular language variety or dialect in different situations comprise what are generally called language attitudes. At times, conclusions are drawn about a person's competence or social status based on speech. Teachers' language attitudes can affect pupil achievement, particularly in cases where judgments are made with respect to the use of a "standard" or "nonstandard" dialect. The learner's attitudes toward a second language can account for differences in levels of achievement. Language attitudes do exist among people with respect to their own language (intracultural communication) as well as toward other language groups (intercultural communication). Studies of various etholinguistic groups reveal divergent intra- and intergroup differences with respect to language attitudes. Bilingual schooling can have a positive affect on language attitudes and reduce cultural stereotypes. Students who become both bilingual and bicultural can participate in and appreciate two cultural communities.

LANGUAGE ATTITUDES AND CLASSROOM LANGUAGE

Although traditionally the study of attitudes has fallen into the realm of social psychology, attitudes toward language has recently become a topic of sociolinguistic studies. Sociolinguists have adopted the term "language attitudes" (Fishman 1975), which can be defined as evaluative reactions or feelings toward language (e.g. "French is more pleasant to the ear than the hard sounds of German"). Each of the following, could be subsumed under "language attitudes": reactions toward the use of a specific variety of a language under certain circumstances (e.g. emotional responses to hearing someone with a strong Southern accent present the national news on nationwide television), and attitudes toward a language as connoting a specific group affiliation ("Russian is spoken by Communists").

In the classroom, language is used to convey information and, at the same tme, maintain and confirm the social identity and relationship of the participants speaking or writing to one another (Barnes 1973). In most situations, the language variety used for instructional purposes is the formal standard variety. Holmes (1978:135) points out the

> . . . use of a relatively formal code in educational institutions seems to characterize a wide range of speech communities, whether monolingual, bilingual or multilingual . . . There is no convincing evidence to suggest that such instruction cannot be adequately carried out in a nonstandard dialect, a minority group language, or even in a less formal style of a language. The use of formal varieties in the school can be seen then as a reflection of social features of the situation, monolinguistic constraints which in turn reflect the values and beliefs of the society converning education and the ways in which it is appropriately transmitted.

LANGUAGE ATTITUDES OF TEACHERS

A great deal of social information is furnished by features of speech that operate at both a conscious and unconscious level. Speakers, by the way they speak as well as by the specific linguistic items they utilize, communicate rich and varied information about themselves. Likewise, hearers continually draw on the speech of their interlocutor to arrive at conclusions about their social status and about their general competence on a host of dimensions. Hudson (1980:195) refers to this process as "linguistic prejudice," defining it as the "habit of using social signals that speakers send out as sources of information." Peñalosa (1980:181) proposes the term "languagism" to denote "prejudice, discrimination, and oppression against people because of the way they speak," and suggests that language attitudes often function in subtle ways to reinforce established patterns of social control.

Because of the central role played by language in formal schooling, the question of teacher language attitudes and the role they may play as a mediating variable in the learning process, seems particularly worthy of investigation. Hudson mentions two reasons why the language attitudes of teachers may have significant consequences for learning. First, teachers often form their first impressions based on the speech of students. Since first impressions appear to be fairly fixed, the potential for a cycle of self-fulfilling prophecies based on stereotypical judgments derived from children's speech features appears to be a distinct possibility. A second reason for concern is that negative attitudes held by teachers may serve merely to reinforce the negative attitudes already possessed by children toward their own nonstandard varieties (Hudson 1980). The potentially harmful educational consequences of this second concern is evident in a study conducted by Ramírez (1981), in which it was found that the more negative the teacher's attitudes toward the pupil's code switching speech variety, the lower the reading achievement.

The extent to which teachers do, in fact, make evaluative judgments based on the speech of children has been documented in a number of research studies. One study widely cited, conducted by Williams (1976), used dubbed sound tracks over videotaped images of children from different ethnic groups (Anglo, Black, and Mexican American). Although the teachers reacting to these samples were able to determine the ethnicity of the children in the videotape, they were unable to clearly see the lip movements of the children. Consequently, it was possible for the researchers to use the same voices for children from different ethnic backgrounds. Among the findings reported by Williams were that: (1) the speech of Black and Mexican American students was rated as "less standard," and (2) the Mexican American children were rated as "less confident" than the others.

The relative importance teachers place on speech stimuli (as opposed to other stimuli) was investigated by Segligman, Tucker, and Lambert (1972). In this study, teachers evaluated hypothetical pupils based on three types of information: (1) a photo, (2) a recorded sample of speech, and (3) a sample of the child's schoolwork. These three bits of information provided by the researchers were purposely contradictory in terms of the impressions they created regarding the child. It was found that information from the *speech sample* took priority over the other two types of information. In other words, positive impressions based on speech samples overrode negative impressions based on photos or schoolwork, and vice versa. In a second study conducted among Anglo university students, it was found that, in reacting to the speech of Chicanos, speech that sounded more "standardlike" was rated more highly on scales related to success, ability, and social awareness than speech containing certain nonstandard phonological features commonly found in Chicano English (Arthur et al 1974).

A final question related to teacher language attitudes in Southwest bilingual settings is to what extent attitudes vary depending on the ethnicity of the person making the evaluation. Ryan and Carranza (1977), summarizing research related to ingroup and outgroup reactions to Mexican American language varieties, report that (1) both Anglos and Mexican Americans appear to possess an appreciation for the Spanish language, and (2) both ethnic groups downgraded accented English.

LANGUAGE ATTITUDES AND THE LEARNER

The dialect the bilingual child brings to school may not be the "standard" language used by textbooks or by the teacher. A child acquires a particular variety of a language at home. For example, the variety of Spanish spoken at home, marked regionally and socially, is the one the child will learn. If the family also speaks English at home and the variety of English is strongly influenced by Spanish pronunciation or grammar, the child acquires that particular variety. The child may also code switch when using idioms, quoting expressions given in the other language, or in making translations (Huerta 1978). The child may find teachers who disapprove of his nonstandard dialect as well as the use of code switching.

In learning a second language, Richards (1978) notes that individual variables such as age, attitudes, and learning styles account for differences in levels of achievement. The learner may have to adopt various aspects of behavior that characterize the values of the target linguistic group, and the learner's ethnocentric tendencies and attitudes toward this second group will consequently influence his success in learning the language (Lambert et al 1966; Schumann 1978). The language-minority child or adolescent, in turn, may refuse to speak the native language and adopt negative attitudes toward persons speaking it.

In other situations, the stigmatized minority language may serve as a marker for the group identity and may be used to symbolize ethnic solidarity. Giles, Bourkis, and Taylor (1977) suggest that because of a new sense of pride among French Canadians toward their language and culture, some refuse to use English when interacting with English Canadians in Quebec, even though they are fluent in both languages. Cárdenas (1981) notes that in the Southwest, Chicano students tend to favor English for academic and economic reasons, but prefer Spanish for purposes of identity and solidarity.

Bilingual schools can minimize negative attitudes toward the native language among minority children as they learn the second language. At the same time, bilingual schools can help in the development of healthy attitudes toward self-identity and the ability to get along with others. For members of the culturally dominant group, immersion programs in Canada (Swain and Lapkin 1982) and in the United States (Waldman 1975) have fostered less rigid ethnolinguistic stereotypes of target group members.

LANGUAGE ATTITUDES AND ETHNOLINGUISTIC GROUPS

Language attitudes play an important role in multicultural settings. Language is both an instrument of communication and a symbol of the linguistic community. Haugen (1956: 95–96) points out that "whenever languages are in contact, one is likely to find certain prevalent attitudes of *favor* or *disfavor* toward the languages involved" and "these attitudes are directed at the people who use the languages and are therefore intergroup judgments and stereotypes."

Lambert (1960) found that balanced French-English bilinguals were evaluated more favorably when speaking English than when using French. Using the "matched-guise" technique, in which the same bilingual speakers read prose passages in different languages or accents, judges were asked to listen to recordings and then rate the speaker' personalities along different dimensions (e.g. kind-mean, clean-dirty, tall-short, intelligent-not intelligent). English Canadian adult judges rated speakers in their English Canadian (EC) guises as "better looking," "taller," "more ambitious," and as having "more character" than their French Canadian (FC) guises. A comparable group of French Canadian raters made similar judgments of the EC guises, except that FC speakers were evaluated as "kinder" and more "religious." Anisfeld and Lambert (1964) later found that French Canadian children had more favorable evaluations of bilingual speakers speaking French, suggesting developmental changes in self-esteem and social perceptions. Bilingual raters tended to evaluate the speakers more similarly than monolingual subjects, who tended to be more stereotypic in their evaluations.

Ramírez, Arce-Torres, and Politzer (1978) assessed the language attitudes of Mexican American pupils in California at the elementary school level (grades four and five). Using the matched-guise technique, pupils were asked to rate five guises—(1)standard English, (2) Hispanicized English, (3) ungrammatical English, (4) English/Spanish code switching, and (5) standard Mexican Spanish—each spoken by four bilingual adults. Each speech sample was evaluated on its appropriateness and correctness for school and on the speaker's academic potential. The students evaluated standard Spanish and English as equally correct, while the accented (Hispanicized) and ungrammatical English guises were the least correct. Standard English was rated as the most appropriate speech variety for school. The pupils ranked the academic potential of speakers of standard English higher than that of speakers of nonstandard varieties (2 and 3 above) including code switching. The pupils' ranking had a positive relation to their own achievement in English grammar and grade in reading.

In a study of high school Mexican American pupils in Texas and California, Ramírez, Milk, and Sapiens (1984) examined differential reaction to four varieties of Spanish: (1) code switching, (2) ungrammatical Spanish, (3) dialectal Spanish, and (4) standard Mexican Spanish). Pupils also rated their own use and relative proficiency in Spanish. Each tape-recorded language variety was rated in terms of grammaticality, appropriateness and the speaker's likelihood of academic achievement. Standard Mexican Spanish was rated higher than the other three varieties, and the two "nonstandard" varieties were evaluated more favorably than code switching. Judgments about the four varieties were influenced by a number of factors, including language use, location, and sex. The amount of Spanish used affected nearly all the evaluations. The ratings of the nonstandard varieties were affected by the pupils' birthplace, geographic location, and sex. Code switching was rated more favorably by students from Texas living in a code switching environment than by California students born or raised in a predominantly Spanish-speaking environment. Standard Spanish was rated higher by females. The isolation of these factors seems to reveal a complex sociolinguistic picture regarding language attitudes of Spanish/ English bilinguals in the American Southwest.

The attitudes and beliefs about Spanish and English among Puerto Ricans living in the New York City area have been studied by Fishman (1971) through the use of participated observation, self-reports, and recorded conversations. Comparisons between "ordinary" Puerto Ricans and Puerto Rican "intellectuals," consisting of community leaders, artists, and writers, revealed several important differences:

1. The intellectuals claimed to use less Spanish at home with their families and friends than did the ordinary Puerto Ricans. They claimed, however, to use more Spanish in professional context (e.g. work place) than did the other group.
2. The intellectuals had a greater awareness about the varieties of Spanish they used – "*jibaro*," Spanish, "slangy" Spanish, "ordinary" Spanish, "good" Spanish, and "really good" Spanish – in response to situational and contextual features. They also had an awareness of contextual variation in their English – English with or without Spanish phonology.
3. Ordinary Puerto Ricans actually exhibited greater variation in their Spanish than they reported and were aware they lacked this variation in English.
4. Both groups reported they attempted to use the "best" Spanish when speaking to members of other Hispanic groups.
5. The intellectuals felt it was necessary to know Spanish to be Puerto Rican, while the ordinary Puerto Ricans did not necessarily associate language proficiency with ethnicity.
6. The intellectuals were generally dissatisfied with the kind of Spanish used on Spanish radio and television in New York.

These findings illustrate the degree to which members of a subcultural group can differ in their attitudes and use of their own language. Language in this situation can function both as a symbol of ethnicity and solidarity or as a marker of intraethnic conflict, working against the group's ability to meet the linguistic demands of the dominant group.

Closely associated with language attitudes are racial/ethnic attitudes. Kwok (1979) conducted a study among Chinese American children to determine the relationship between language orientation and racial attitudes. Three linguistic groups (monolingual Chinese speakers – MCS, monolingual English speakers – MES, and bilingual English/Chinese speakers – BECS) were identified from pupils in grades K–2. The Kwok found that children learned to differentiate between individuals and groups on the basis of racial/ethnic criteria regardless of language abilities. Perception of racial/ethnic similarity to their mothers was related to language orientation, while perception of racial/ethnic similarity to their fathers and to self was not. Children initially exhibited racial/ethnic awareness (i.e. classify others) before they were able to see racial/ethnic similarities in themselves and in their parents, suggesting a hierarchy in abilities. From an affective perspective, the Chinese American children accepted each other (i.e. were willing to play with children of their own group), but were biased (i.e. negative evaluations of qualities of their own group) toward one another. The MCS group was the most Chinese oriented, and the BECS group was more moderate than the MES group, which tended to be Caucasian oriented or express a neutral position. The development of bilingualism among Chinese American pupils must be considered an important educational goal, since bilingualism seems to be associated with a more balanced (bicultural) approach to ethnicity and race.

LANGUAGE ATTITUDES, CULTURAL STEREOTYPES, AND BILINGUAL SCHOOLING

The effects of bilingual schooling on language attitudes and cultural stereotypes has been examined from different perspectives and contexts. Cohen (1975) found that after three years of bilingual/bicultural schooling, Mexican American children viewed the Mexican culture (cultural items – food, people, words) more positively than did a comparable group of students attending a monolingual program. At the same time, students in the bilingual program rated Anglo culture as positively as did the pupils in the comparison group, suggesting that an appreciation of the minority culture did not result in a loss of esteem for the dominant culture. The parents of the students with two years of bilingual schooling (grades one and two) noted an increase in the use of Spanish among their children, whereas parents of the comparison students reported a general shift to English. School attendance, perhaps reflecting behavioral aspects of attitudes, was significantly higher than among pupils in bilingual programs in grades two and three than among students from the comparison grade levels.

A study by Politzer and Ramírez (1973) of Mexican American and Anglo children in the third grade attempted to determine whether children taking part in a Spanish/English bilingual program had different attitudes towards speakers/language varieties than pupils exposed to monolingual (English) instruction. Pupils reacted to four speech varieties – (1) English with Spanish proper names pronounced in Spanish, (2) English with anglicized Spanish proper names, (3) colloquial Spanish, and (4) Hispanicized English – and rated each speaker on eight characteristics (e.g. nice, handsome, happy, smart). Mexican American children in the bilingual program rated Spanish speakers (guise 3) more favorably (nicer, more handsome, happier, and friendlier) than did similar students attending a monolingual program. Anglos attending the bilingual program, while they favored English speakers (guises 1 and 2) overall, tended to make less pronounced differences between English and Spanish speakers on the individual characteristics than did the comparison Anglo group. Bilingual schooling seems to have promoted a more positive self-concept for the minority children and less rigid ethnolinguistic stereotypes among the Anglo children.

Waldman (1975) investigated the effect of different educational programs on the enhancement of cross-cultural understanding among Anglo schoolchildren. She studied groups of children attending four school programs: second and third grade students in a Spanish immersion program since kindergarten (SIP group); second and third grade students in a Spanish/English bilingual program (a Title VIII, federally funded project); second and third graders from an ethnically mixed school (39 percent Spanish surnamed, 11 percent Spanish speakers, and 43 percent Anglo American); and second and third graders from an ethnically homogeneous English-speaking school. Children from the Spanish immersion program had more positive reactions toward the Mexican American culture and Spanish speakers than children from the other school programs. Children from the SIP program had the same positive attitudes toward Anglo culture and English speakers based on a matched guise instrument and a cross-cultural attitude inventory. Bilingually schooled children reacted more favorably to the Mexican culture and Spanish speakers than did children from the ethnically mixed or ethnically homogeneous schools. Children from the ethnically homogeneous school did not seem to exhibit the typical stereotypic reactions to Spanish speakers (e.g. dirty, lazy, dumb) or negative reactions to the Mexican American culture (e.g. "unhappy" reactions to pictorial stimuli). The degree of intensity of exposure to Spanish and interaction with Spanish speakers (teachers and pupils) did, however, bring about differences in cross-cultural understanding.

In Canada, English speaking children who attended a French immersion program became functionally bilingual by grades five or six. The program did have the effect of highlighting the differences between the students and the French Canadian people, but, at the same time, their feelings toward the French group became more favorable. The students began to think of themselves as both French Canadian and English Canadian in disposition and outlook. Thus, these children became both bilingual and bicultural, being able to participate fully in the two cultural communities (Lambert 1977).

TEACHERS' ATTITUDES TOWARD LANGUAGE VARIETIES

Teachers' attitudes toward varieties of the first or second language may influence the participation of ethnolinguistic minority children in classroom activities, and may eventually lead to low academic achievement. Ramírez, Arce-Torres, and Politzer (1978) noted in their study of language attitudes of Mexican American pupils, previously reported in this chapter, that teachers and pupils had well-defined and similar attitudes toward specific varieties of English found in a Spanish/English environment. Teachers rated standard English higher than nonstandard speech varieties on "correctness" "appropriateness," and "likelihood of achievement in school" dimensions. Spanish/English (code switching) was also rated lower than standard English. Teachers' attitudes regarding the "likelihood of success" of code switching bilingual pupils were directly related to pupils' grades as well as to their relative reading gains, as shown by an objective test. Apparently the teachers' negative attitudes toward code switching and correspondingly strong, positive attitudes toward standard English resulted in low assessment of their pupils' language and academic potential which, in turn, led to low grades in English. Attempts to change teachers' sensitivity toward language differences (i.e. dialects, bilingualism, code switching, etc.) through workshops were not successful. One group of teachers tended to rate code switching even lower than ungrammatical English, while another group of teachers that had participated in a year-long, in-service program ranked code switching bilinguals similarly as speakers of standard English in the area of academic potential. The results suggest that relatively short, in-service workshops may be an unsuitable means for bringing about changes in stereotypic notions about bilingual communicative behavior.

Ramírez and Milk (1982) found that bilingual teachers in the Southwest discriminated among the four varieties (code switching, ungrammatical Spanish, dialectal Spanish, and standard Mexican Spanish) with regard to appropriateness and correctness for classroom use as well as to the speaker's academic potential. Standard Mexican Spanish was rated higher than the other three varieties and the two "nonstandard" Spanish varieties were evaluated more favorably than code switching. The bilingual teachers, unlike the bilingual high school students' ratings reported earlier in this chapter, did discriminate between the two nonstandard varieties of Spanish, reflecting a general teacher orientation to judge language differences in terms of a "standardness" (grammatical) dimension rather than on the basis of meaning or function.

The pedagogical significance of teachers' attitudes toward language varieties used by bilingual pupils can be observed in a number of areas. In terms of achievement in language arts within a bilingual program, Shultz (1975) noted in his study that the variety of Spanish used by the teacher may indeed have affected the students' verbal behavior. Shultz commented that

> The teachers when they used Spanish in the classroom used a more "standard" variety than the one the children were used to. The variety of Spanish spoken in the classroom was not the variety of Spanish the children used at home. This is another reason why the children may not have spoken very much Spanish: they may have been made to feel that somehow the variety of Spanish they spoke was "inferior," and that therefore they shouldn't speak it (Shultz 1975:17).

He also noted that the language used by the teachers conveyed the attitude that English was the "natural" language to use in the classroom, while Spanish was always used in a "marked" way:

> Arithmetic, science and English language arts were all taught in English, and the only subject which was actually taught in Spanish was Spanish language arts. However, even during the Spanish language arts lesson . . . the teachers would frequently revert to English to give directions or to reprimand someone . . . The "hidden agenda" of this classroom, then, was that it was disadvantageous to use Spanish (Shultz 1975:18).

The nature of teachers' attitudes toward the speech of bilingual pupils can also be explored through an examination of the dynamics of classroom discourse. Within the framework of the interactional exchange (Sinclair and Coulthard 1975), consisting of (1) the teacher asking a question, (2) a pupil responding, and (3) the teacher providing evaluative feedback, one can appreciate the kind of language demanded by teachers in different content areas (e.g. Spanish language arts versus social studies). By analyzing the teacher's reaction (evaluation/feedback) to a pupil's response, one can observe the dynamics of language attitudes and how they manifest themselves in the transmission of subject knowledge (Barnes 1969; Stubbs 1976). What counts as "knowledge" — "good" grammar or the correct content? The following examples of two conversations illustrate the questioning behavior of teachers A and B engaged in Spanish reading instruction, each with a group of Spanish-speaking pupils attending an elementary school bilingual program.

TEACHER A

Student 1: . . . interrumpió la garza. (. . . the heron interrupted.)
Teacher: ¿Qué quiere decir eso? Antonia. (What does that mean? Antonia.)
Student 2: es como si, si una maestra está hablando y luego una niña le está hablando—le está interrumpiendo. (It's as if, if a teacher is talking and later a girl is talking to her—she [the girl] is interrupting her.)
Teacher: Ajá. (uh ha.)
Student 3: ¡No! Está metiendo la cuchara. (No! She "is putting in the spoon" ["butting in"—colloquial Spanish].)
Teacher: está metiendo la cuchara—otro modo si—La cuchara quiere decir más o menos . . . , (She "is putting in the spoon" [butting in]—another way yes—the spoon means that more or less.)
Student 3: ¿Qué está interrumpiendo? (What is she interrupting?)

TEACHER B

Teacher: ¿Qué, qué, qué quiere ese [*sic*] garza? Quiere tener las plumas de todos los colores . . . vamos a ver . . . (What, what, what does that heron want? She wants to have her feathers in every color . . . let's see . . .)
Student 1: No quiere ser garza. (She doesn't want to be a heron.)
Teacher: No quiere ser garza, ese garza . . . Alejandro no vamos [*sic*] a seguir—aquí. (She doesn't want to be a heron, that heron . . . Alexander we are not going to continue—here . . . that way.)
Student 1: Así, se di . . . cía . . . (That's the way you would say it . . .)
Student 2: Decía. (Used to say it.)
Student 1: Decía. (Used to say it.)
Teacher: Decía, si. (Used to say it, yes.)

Reprinted by permission from A. G. Ramírez, "Attitudes Toward Speech Variation among Spanish/English Bilingual Pupils: Some Implications for the Teacher and Learner," *Bilingual Education Paper Series*, 2:7 (1979b):16–17 Los Angeles: National Dissemination and Assessment Center, California State University.

Teacher A is primarily concerned with meaning. Student 2 interprets the meaning of "interrumpio la garza" (the heron interrupted) as "como si una maestra está hablando y luego una niña le está . . . interrumpiendo" (if a teacher is talking and later a girl is interrupting her). The teacher acknowledges this interpretation "ajá" (uh ha) and also allows student 3 to explain the meaning metaphorically "está metiendo la cuchara" (butting in) using colloquial Spanish. Teacher B, on the other hand, appears to be more concerned with standard pronunciation — "decía" (used to say it) instead of nonstandard "dicía" — rather than the answer to the question "¿Qué quería la garza?" Interestingly, while the teacher twice produced ungrammatical Spanish "ese garza," (that heron), he agrees with student 2 in not allowing student 1 to pronounce the word "decía" according to his own dialect "dicía." Thus, a teacher's negative attitudes toward the child's native language (nonstandard features) could affect the student's participation in class as well as academic achivement.

SUMMARY

The study of "language attitudes" is generally defined in terms of (1) feelings toward a language, (2) reactions toward language varieties, and (3) attitudes toward a language as a specific cultural marker. Language attitudes can occur at both conscious and unconscious levels. A hearer arrives at conclusions about the interlocuter's social status and general competence by the features of his speech. This process has been called "linguistic prejudice." According to Hudson, teachers' language attitudes can have significant consequences for learning by causing false impressions based on speech and by reinforcing children's negative attitudes toward their own nonstandard varieties. Ramírez noted, for example, that the more negative the teachers attitudes toward code switching among Spanish-English bilinguals, the lower the English reading scores. Other researchers, such as Seligman, Tucker, and Lambert, examined the importance teachers place on speech as opposed to other stimuli.

In addition, the ethnicity of the listener/rater can influence judgments about language. Language attitudes can also influence the learner's success in school as well as learning a second language. Stigmatized minority languages may serve as a marker for group identity and may be used to symbolize ethnic solidarity. Studies of language attitudes among French Canadians and Chicano students in the Southwest serve to illustrate these points.

Studies of language attitudes among French-English Canadian bilinguals, Hispanic American groups, and Chinese American pupils were discussed. Considerable differences can exist within a subcultural group with respect to language. Members of the Puerto Rican community living in the New York City area displayed significantly different attitudes and beliefs about English and Spanish. Bilingualism can foster a more balanced attitude toward ethnicity and race. Bilingual schooling can promote an appreciation of both minority and majority cultures among ethnolinguistic minority groups and improve cross-cultural understanding among members of the culturally dominant group. Cross-cultural understanding is affected by the type of educational program the majority student attends and the degree of exposure to the target language.

Teachers' attitudes toward language varieties may influence student participation and may eventually lead to low academic achievement. For example, teachers' negative attitudes toward Spanish-English code switching pupils and positive attitudes toward "standard" English resulted in a low assessment of pupils' language, reflected in the assignment of lower grades. Teachers' attitudes can also have pedagogical significance. They may influence the degree of students' participation as well as the dynamics of classroom discourse.

SUGGESTED READINGS

Alaud, F. and R. D. Meale, eds. *Cultural Factors in Learning*. Bellingham, Washington: Western Washington State College Press, 1974.

García, R. L. *Teaching in a Pluralistic Society*. New York: Harper and Row, Publishers, 1982.

Giles, H., ed. *Language, Ethnicity and Intergroup Relations*. London: Academic Press, 1977.

Giles, H. and Saint-Jacques, eds. *Language and Ethnic Relations*. Oxford: Permagon Press, 1982.

Kendall, F. E. *Diversity in the Classroom*. New York: Teachers College Press, Columbia University, 1983.

St. Clair, R. N. and H. Giles, eds. *The Social and Psychological Contexts of Language*. Hillsdale, New Jersey: Lawrence Erlbaum Associates Inc., 1980.

Smolicz, J. J. *Culture and Education in a Plural Society*. Camberra: Curriculum Development Centre, 1979.

Chapter Eight _____

TEACHING THE FIRST AND SECOND LANGUAGES

INTRODUCTION

Language teaching in bilingual programs is affected by developments in linguistic theory and language pedagogy. In the area of ESL, research findings have affected language teaching approaches. The characteristics of a successful second language teaching program will be listed here, summarizing the results of studies relevant to language teaching.

Proficiency in the native language should be an important consideration in second language instruction. The language teacher plays a significant role in directing language learning activities in the classroom and implementing a specific approach/method through instructional strategies. The teacher's language proficiency and knowledge about the language affect teaching behaviors, and, in turn, the linguistic input available to the students. Similarly, the teacher's attitude toward the marked or unmarked languages in the bilingual classroom are expressed in classroom behaviors (e.g. the use of particular interactional patterns and use of a language for particular communication functions). This expression can result in greater learning opportunities in one language and inhibit the student who might feel his/her language is relegated to "second place" by use of the other language for more important communicative functions. Several teaching strategies which affect and relate to student language learning will be discussed in the section on teacher-centered activities. Other language learning activities that focus on the student (e.g. various types of peer interactional situations) will also be examined.

DEVELOPMENTS IN LANGUAGE TEACHING

Bilingual programs generally include two components designed to "teach" the pupils' first and second languages. Issues regarding the "teaching" of the two languages have been raised from various perspectives: sociolinguistic considerations (Keller 1982; Valdés, Lozano, and García-Moya 1981), second language acquisition theory (Krashen 1981; Chamot 1981), bilingual education models (Cohen and Laosa 1979; Brisk and Wurzel 1979) and instructional designs (Johnson 1980; Milk 1980; Edelsky and Hudelson 1982).

Current language teaching theory, according to Richards and Rodgers (1982), draws from a number of areas—discourse analysis, ethnography of speaking, speech act theory, sociolinguistics, text linguistics, and presuppositional semantic theory. Specific teaching methodologies include the "silent way," "total physical response," "suggestopedia," "counseling learning," and "communicative language teaching." Curriculum models have been proposed (Urzua 1980) which would allow young learners to develop communicative language skills by interacting at different levels with different groups in environments which provoke thinking, exploration, and problem solving.

ENGLISH AS A SECOND LANGUAGE (ESL) INSTRUCTION

In the area of ESL, Chamot (1981) and Saville-Troike (1982) offer teachers suggestions based on research findings. These suggestions include the use of errors and correction in language development activities which focus more on meaning than on grammatical forms, interaction in small groups and with native English-speaking peers, emphasis on reading and writing activities as soon as pupils are literate in the first language, and L_2 as a medium of instruction as soon as children reach the "linguistic threshold" level needed to relate new labels to known concepts. Krashen (1981:64) claims that any successful second language teaching program will include, at least, the following characteristics:

1. It will supply input in the second language that is, first of all, comprehensible, and, second, interesting and relevant to students. The goal of this input will not be to provide practice on specific points of grammar, but to transmit messages of interest.
2. It will not force students to speak before they are ready and will be tolerant of errors in early speech.
3. It will put grammar in its proper place. Only some adults, and very few children, are able to use conscious grammar rules to increase the grammatical accuracy of their output. Children have very little capacity for conscious language learning and may also have little need for conscious learning, since they can come close to native speaker performance standards using acquisition alone.

PRIMARY LANGUAGE INSTRUCTION

In the area of native language instruction, Legarreta-Marcaida (1981:90) concludes that "there is no magic formula for creating fully bilingual children; but, in all cases, the primary language must be first developed to a high level of proficiency to include literacy." She suggests, for example, that pairing proficient new immigrants with less proficient children is an effective approach to providing meaningful input in a real communication context. The school day could be structured to include communicative language activities — planning field trips, discussing current events inside and outside the school context, and using jokes, riddles, songs, dances, and family stories, as well as members of the community as language resource persons — to offer a great range and variety of primary language input.

EFFECTIVE TEACHING STRATEGIES

Effective language instructional procedures should consider the following principles based on research evidence (*Schooling and*

Language Minority Students: A Theoretical Framework 1981: 192–193):

1. By the age of five or six, all children except those with special learning disabilities have acquired basic interpersonal communicative skills in a variety of the home language.
2. Sociolinguistic factors inside and outside the school influence the language attitudes of both students and teachers. Even though factors exist outside the school, they may be influenced by the school.
3. The amount and quality of primary language use in the home is positively associated with student readiness for the academic demands of schooling and continued primary language development in school.
4. The ability of teachers to speak the primary language of minority-language students is positively related to both primary language development and second language acquisition.
5. The language proficiencies of language-minority students in English and the primary language vary in accordance with a number of factors, such as societal domain, language variety, speech situation, relationship between speakers, and cognitive demands of the task.
6. In the acquisition of a second language, basic interpersonal communicative skills and affective factors are more important than biological maturity, age, or language aptitude.
7. Teachers' knowledge of second language acquisition and first language development processes is positively related to English language acquisition and first language development by language-minority students.
8. Second language acquirers have an innate ability to process "comprehensible language input," to internalize language rules, and to apply those rules to produce an infinite number of appropriate and acceptable utterances.
9. In a natural communication situation, language-minority students will acquire English grammatical structures in a predictable order. Complete mastery of a specific structure, however, is not a prerequisite for the acquisition of later-learned structures, since speech errors are developmental and a natural part of second language acquisition.
10. Programs with informed and involved parents and community members are more likely to reflect community desires and are therefore more likely to achieve programmatic goals.

TEACHER—CENTERED LANGUAGE LEARNING ACTIVITIES

The language teacher plays a significant role in directing language learning activities in the classroom. The directions in language teaching may change to incorporate new curricular developments (e.g. notional/functional syllabus [Chamot 1983]; interactional model of language acquisition [Urzua 1980]), but the teacher must ultimately implement the approach through specific instructional strategies.

Ramírez and Stromquist (1979) conducted a study to examine the ESL methodology used in the context of Spanish/English bilingual schools, and to identify teaching strategies associated with student language learning. The findings revealed that one third of the teachers (N = 18) placed an emphasis on mechanical drills (the teacher modeled English structures and the students repeated the item) and followed a specific sequence for learning language skills (the student should first listen and then speak; reading and writing should not be introduced until the student has attained a certain level of aural-oral proficiency).

Five teaching behaviors were strongly and positively associated with student's language growth in English listening comprehension and oral grammar production. The behaviors included the use of:

1. commands with objects (requiring the student to manipulate concrete objects or visual aids, thus checking the pupil's comprehension);
2. questions with guided responses (asking the student to respond to questions based on information previously presented by the teacher, thus enabling the pupil to utilize the "input" provided in the lesson;
3. explanations of concepts/labels (clarifying to the pupil the meaning of new words using synonyms and antonyms or using Spanish equivalents);
4. correction of grammatical errors (providing the student with the feedback necessary to adjust his/her erroneous hypotheses regarding the use/application of grammatical rules);
5. variation of strategies (utilizing a number of teaching behaviors — modeling, commanding, and questioning — instead of relying on a single teaching strategy).

Teaching behaviors negatively associated with second language growth included the use of:

1. modeling with repetition (asking the student to repeat or imitate a target item-sentence, phrase, or word; or simply direct-

ing the pupil to alter/transform the item or linguistic pattern);
3. linguistic inaccuracies (using confusing and/or inappropriate examples or visual aids while introducing or drilling on specific linguistic items, for example, using two picture contrasts to present superlative adjectives).

In a subsequent study, Hernández (1981) selected the four "highest" and four "lowest" achieving teachers, classified according to teacher effectiveness criteria established by Ramírez and Stromquist (1979) on the basis of student achievement. The two groups of teachers were compared using three levels of classroom discourse:

1. exchange - the minimum unit of interaction involving two or more participants; a turn-taking sequence of interaction, usually consisting of a teacher initiation, a corresponding pupil response, and a subsequent teacher reaction),
2. move - the contribution of one participant to an interactive exchange; the structure consisting of three classes of moves — opening moves initiatory, serving to convey information or solicit a verbal or nonverbal response, answering moves (occurring in relation to opening moves), and a follow-up move serving to accept, modify, or evaluate the previous speaker's contribution.
3. act (the smallest identifiable unit of discourse behavior within the move category, often in the form of an independent clause and serving a specific linguistic function — question, direct, model, feedback, and comment).

In general, the teachers defined the pupil's role as that of respondent, since they controlled the opening and follow-up moves making up the interactional sequences. Teachers initited nearly all of the exchanges with informatives (statements to provide information, grammatical facts, ideas, or opinions) and elicitations (questions, commands, modeled language patterns, or statement/drill needing completion). The discourse patterns for the "high" and "low" teachers differed significantly in the use of four acts within the opening move. Teachers in the "high" group used a greater proportion of explaining, questioning, and commanding acts, while the "low" group tended to use modeling. Pupils, in turn, tended to reflect the teachers' differences in the opening move. Those taught by the "low" teachers tended to repeat more often, while those from the "high" group had more opportunities to reply to questions and react to commands. The two groups of teachers also differed in their reactions (follow-up move) to the pupils' contributions. The effective teachers provided considerably more feedback ("yes," "good," "okay") and reinforcement (repetition, expansion, or overt correction of a response) than the ineffective group.

Apparently, discourse analysis of classroom language offers a viable methodology for investigating teacher-pupil interaction during second language instruction, and particular levels of discourse (exchanges, moves, and acts) can be used to examine the linguistic behavior of teachers as well as the nature of pupils' participation. Discourse analysis can also provide valuable insights about teaching cycles, pupils' language during peer interactions, and quantitative differences between teachers, lessons, or classroom language patterns.

The effect of different teaching strategies in native language reading instruction has been examined by Ramírez (1979c). Bilingual elementary school teachers (N = 18) engaged in Spanish reading instruction were asked to teach two reading lessons, each presented in two, twenty-minute segments. The videotaped lessons were analyzed to identify the teaching behaviors used in the instructional process and, subsequently, to relate those strategies associated with pupils' Spanish reading skills using the Inter-American Pruebe de Lectura — Level II. Five teaching behaviors were strongly and positively associated with student reading achievement in grades one through six, with most pupils in the third grade. The strategies included:

1. decoding reading skills (asking students to identify individual letters and/or sequences of letters, dividing words into syllables, and noting the placement of the accent mark);
2. grammatical/structural analysis (explaining or reviewing Spanish grammatical rules — formation of plurals, verb conjugations, article-noun-verb agreement);
3. reading sentences (asking students to read sentences aloud in order to monitor mastery of reading subskills — decoding, word stress, comprehension);
4. correcting decoding errors (correcting pupil errors in decoding — incorrect syllable stress, and/or syllabication and nonstandard dialect interference);
5. using visuals/chalkboard (using the chalkboard to write words or sentences and thereby emphasizing reading subskills — accent rules, word formation, and word order in sentences).

Teaching behaviors negatively associated with the development of reading skills in the native language included the use of:

1. questions about details from the story (asking questions emphasizing the recall of details — who, what, when, or where);
2. questions related to vocabulary comprehension (asking about words/phrases out of context, particularly through the use of definitions, synonyms, or English equivalents);
3. requests for oral paragraph readings (reading orally entire paragraphs without any focus on reading sub-skills — word/sentence meaning, main idea, cause-effect relationships).

Reading instruction in English as a second language was observed by Ebel (1978), wherein classroom practices among elementary school teachers (N = 25) in grades two through six were assessed. One-third of the reading instructors were native Spanish speakers, and the remaining two-thirds were native speakers of English. Lessons were observed in order to establish the use of the native language, major instructional emphasis, classroom organization, role of teacher aides, cultural awareness activities, and the type of reading/writing activities. The results revealed a number of interesting findings:

1. Silent reading, reading aloud, and writing activities seldom occurred in the lessons.
2. The major emphasis in all classes was on vocabulary meaning, usually discussed orally and without reference to the text.
3. Phonics was used as an aid to solve oral reading problems involving pronunciation miscues.
4. Spanish-speaking teachers tended to be more familiar with the students' home life and, as as result, were able to relate vocabular items to the pupils' personal experiences.
5. The noise level was lower and the incidence of student movement (wiggliness) was less during English reading instruction than during native language lessons and less under English-speaking teachers than with native Spanish-speaking teachers.

In general, the quality of second language literacy experiences for these bilingual pupils was significantly inferior to the type of instruction offered to native English-speaking children. These pupils were "exited" from the reading program with a second grade reading level, even thorugh they were in grade one through six. It is not clear how these pupils would be able to acquire the necessary "context-reduced"/academic language proficiency to function in an all English curriculum in view of "psuedo" second language reading instruction and limited development of first language skills.

STUDENT-CENTERED LANGUAGE LEARNING ACTIVITIES

Recent developments in language teaching emphasize the role of peer interaction (e.g. interethnic tutoring) as a "natural" way of acquiring language, particularly among elementary school children. Johnson (1980) designed a study to monitor the effects of social interaction between pairs of pupils (one limited English-speaking child and one fluent English speaker) on oral English proficiency. The amount of verbal interaction in English between the matched pairs during their free, unstructured time increased with time, though the program lasted only seven weeks. While there was no statistical relationship between the amount of verbal interaction and growth in English, the limited English-speaking pupils (LEP) in the treatment group exhibited greater development in vocabularly comprehension (Peabody Picture Vocabulary Test) than the children in the control group. In another similar study, August (1982) trained LEP Hispanic pupils in the English vocabulary and procedures necessary to teach fluent English-speaking Hispanic pupils (FES) a play activity. During the peer-tutoring sessions the LEP child taught the FES partner the activity in English. The same procedure was followed for limited Spanish-speaking pupils (LSS), who taught in Spanish to the more fluent Spanish-speaking children (FSS) during a game activity. Children in the control group received traditional teacher-centered second language instruction utilizing the Distar Language Program. Verbal interaction during peer tutoring sessions in free play and structured situations were analyzed to determine changes in discourse patterns across the thirty one-hour sessions, and the effects on second language development. LEP pupils interacted more with FES children in the structured situation (two fluent English-speaking children and two bilingual children building a block structure) than did the pupils in the control group. There were significant positive correlations between the amount of verbal interaction in English and development of oral English proficiency. However, training in Spanish did not result in an increase of verbal interaction in Spanish. This situation might have been due to the attitudes and use of Spanish, a marked language both in the school setting and the community.

Edelsky and Hudelson (1982) paired three Anglo first graders with same-sex, Spanish-speaking peers in an effort to study one-to-one verbal interactions during language/play sessions conducted in Spanish biweekly for a period of six months. One of the major purposes of the investigation was to determine what strategies Anglo children might use (e.g. the nature/function of interactions, the type of speech acts utilized) while communicating in a reverse sociolinguistic situation (having to interact with Spanish-speaking schoolchildren in their dominant language). The study was prompted by the fact that English-speaking pupils in bilingual programs do not acquire much Spanish, the second language, except for a few verbal routines, colors, and numbers. Successful language acquisition results from learning to interact/converse in the second language rather than listening to a person (teacher) address a large group (classroom). As Hatch (1978) had pointed out previously, these English-speaking pupils did have the appropriate learning conditions, yet little development occurred in Spanish. The Spanish-speaking children were not able to display their full range of native language abilities (e.g. threatening, planning, directing, informing, etc.) since their English-speaking partners insisted on using English. More importantly, reversing the roles of Chicano and Anglo children in a compensatory bilingual program may not be sufficient to reverse the status of a group and its language. Edelsky and Hudelson (1982:324) explain their findings thus:

> The Anglos helped to teach them that by generally not responding at all to the offerings in Spanish. Learning which was the unmarked language entailed learning which second language it was that learners were expected to acquire. There being no expectations for Spanish language acquisition on the part of either group of children, the Chicanos never played out their potential as teachers of Spanish.

Student-centered reading activities in the native language have had a positive effect on reading abilities and attitudes. Schon, Hopkins, and Davis (1982) found that Hispanic pupils in grades two through four profited in both linguistic and affective domains by being able to read a great variety of books in Spanish during free reading time (sixty minutes per week for a period of eight months). Pupils in the treatment group developed more positive reading attitudes (i.e., Do you like to read? Are most books interesting?) than students in the control group, who had teacher-directed reading instruction using a basal reader. There were no significant differences between the experimental and control groups on any of the three reading measures—comprehension, vocabulary and speed. In Spanish reading the experimental group at level two (grades three and four) performed significantly better than the control group on the three Spanish reading tests. Level one (grade two) students from the experimental group surpassed the control pupils in vocabulary and reading speed in Spanish. Apparently, students who have successful reading experiences in the native language can transfer a number of skills to the second language (Thonis 1981).

TEACHER CHARACTERISTICS AND LANGUAGE TEACHING

Language teaching behaviors seem to be affected by a number of teacher characteristics, ranging from such attributes as proficiency in the language to knowledge about language itself. Merino, Politzer, and Ramírez (1979) found that teachers' Spanish proficiency, consisting of grammatical knowledge, oral and written communicative proficiency, and familiarity with specialized vocabulary, affected pupils' performance on tests. In one of the studies, teachers' performance on the Spanish writing proficiency subtest was significantly correlated with adjusted student gains on the California Test of Basic Skills (CTBS) for English language and reading. Teacher aides who scored high on general Spanish proficiency taught classes that performed significantly better on CTBS Reading in English. For these teachers and aides, a high level of proficiency in Spanish enabled better instruction in English language skills for bilingual children. Teachers' native language proficiency might have resulted in the use of certain teaching strategies which, in turn, promoted greater development of English language skills.

In another study specifically addressing Spanish reading instruction, Ramírez (1979c) noted that performance on the Teachers' Spanish Proficiency Test was strongly related to pupil gains in Spanish reading skills. Five teaching behaviors, described in a previous section of this chapter, along with teachers' proficiency in Spanish, accounted for approximately 70 percent of the observed variance in student reading achievement, based on regression analysis.

A study by Ramírez and Stromquist (1979) supports the claim that teachers' knowledge of applied linguistics in English contributes significantly to student language learning. The teaching of ESL does require some knowledge about language learning processes (e.g., pupils' second language "errors" and learning strategies) and the structure of English (e.g., word formation processes, grammatical patterns). Knowledge of applied linguistics and the use of the five teaching behaviors, previously described in another section in this chapter, accounted for approximately two-thirds of the variation in student achievement in ESL skills (comprehension and production).

Cortéz (1980) found that the teacher's philosophical orientation toward reading affected their teaching methodology, particularly the way they corrected the oral reading of bilingual children in Wales, Spain, and the United States. There were differences between monolingual and bilingual teachers in each region with regard to correcting changes in textual meaning (e.g. reading *house* as *horse*) and in accepting oral reading miscues that did not change meaning (e.g. reading *school* as *eschool*). Analytically trained bilingual teachers favored the approach maintaining that readers must first comprehend the text they read, whether or not there is an exact correlation between what the text says and what the readers actually read. This reading model encourages guessing and emphasizes syntactic aspects of the written text over correct/exact pronunciation of individual words. Synthetic-oriented teachers emphasized decoding as a crucial factor in reading instruction and corrected more nonmeaning change miscues. Monolingual teachers, unable to differentiate between oral miscues due to first language interference or mispronunciation, tended to insist on exact decoding. Bilingual teachers who were knowledgeable about the pupil's first language had a greater tolerance for mispronunciation errors since comprehension and meaning were the crucial components of reading.

Teacher attitudes toward marked and unmarked second languages are reflected through the use of particular language patterns. Hernández (1979) compared English as a second language (ESL) and Spanish as a second language lessons (SSL) taught by a fluent bilingual teacher. The four lessons — two in English and two in Spanish — were analyzed by the ratio of teacher-pupil talk, the number and types of interactional sequences (teacher modeling-pupil repeating, teacher questioning-pupil responding, etc.), and the use of different types of language functions (e.g., reinforcing, translating, managing, structuring), and the amount of language switching to the pupil's native language. The percentage of teacher-to-pupil talk was similar across the two languages: 66.6 percent to 39.4 percent for the SSL lessons and 62.4 to 37.6 percent for the ESL lessons. Modeling (repeating sequence) was the most frequently used exchange in SSL instruction, while questioning-responding and commanding-comprehending cycles were the two most frequently used patterns in ESL lessons. English was used by the teachers in SSL lessons for the purpose of reinforcing, managing, and commanding. English-speaking pupils also used English during the lessons when responding or asking the teacher questions and when talking to other pupils. On the other hand, no Spanish was used either by the teacher or by the pupils during ESL instruction. Using English during the SSL lessons as well as the high incidence of modeling suggests a lack of importance associated with the teaching/learning of the marked language. The teacher demonstrated a more serious effort in teaching ESL lessons – more communicative language activities and no use of Spanish. The teacher's classroom behaviors probably mirrored more general societal attitudes and expectations regarding the importance of learning ESL and SSL.

SUMMARY

The native languge and the second language components in a bilingual program which are designed to develop specific language skills have been influenced by sociolinguistic considerations, second language acquisition theory, bilingual education models, and instructional designs. Current language teaching theory draws from such areas as discourse analyses, ethnography, and text linguistics. Teaching methodologies tend to emphasize the use of language in communication and problem-solving situations.

In the area of ESL instruction, teaching suggestions based on research findings have been offered in a number of areas: (1) the role of errors, (2) the role of correction, (3) interaction in small groups with English-speaking peers, (4) reading and writing activities, and (5) the use of L_2 as a medium of instruction. Krashen has suggested the following characteristics for a successful second language teaching program:

1. Input must be comprehensible, interesting, and relevant
2. Students should speak when they are ready and errors should be tolerated in early speech
3. Grammar should be put in its proper place; children have little capacity for conscious language learning

A variety of language activities has been suggested by Legarreta-Marcaida in the area of native language instruction: (1) pairing proficient new immigrants with less proficient children; (2) using communicative language activities; and (3) using community members as language resource persons.

Effective teaching strategies based on research findings were mentioned. The language teacher plays a significant role in directing language learning activities in the classroom. Activities may incorporate new curricular developments, but the teacher ultimately implements the method via specific teaching strategies. In one study, Ramírez and

Stromquist found five teaching behaviors positively associated with language growth in listening comprehension and oral production in ESL: (1) commands with objects, (2) questions with guided responses, (3) explanations of concepts/labels, (4) correction of grammatical errors, and (5) variation of teaching strategies. Behaviors negatively associated with second language growth included: (1) modeling with repetition, (2) correction of pronunciation, and (3) linguistic inaccuracies.

In another study of the same teachers, Hernández noted the discourse patterns of teachers in the "high" group comprised a greater proportion of explaining, questioning, and commanding. Teachers in the "low" group, however, relied more on repetition. Effective teachers also provided more feedback than those in the ineffective group.

Different teaching strategies and their effectiveness in native language (Spanish) reading instruction were examined. Ramírez found five teaching behaviors strongly and positively associated with student reading achievement, including teacher emphasis on (1) decoding reading skills, (2) grammatical/structural analysis, (3) reading sentences aloud, (4) correcting decoding errors, and (5) using visuals/chalkboard. Negative teaching behaviors included the use of (1) questions asking details from the story, (2) questions related to vocabulary comprehension, and (3) requests for reading paragraphs orally without an emphasis on reading subskills. Reading instruction during ESL lessons needs to be given serious attention since non-native English speakers need to acquire the necessary "context-reduced"/academic language proficiency to function in an all English curriculum.

Student-centered language learning activities emphasize the role of peer interaction. Interethnic tutoring can be used in promoting L_2 development, and individualized reading activities in the native language can have positive effects in reading skills and attitudes toward literacy.

Teacher characteristics can also affect language teaching behaviors. In one study it was noted that teachers and aides with a high level of proficiency in Spanish achieved greater pupil gains in English language skills among bilingual children. In another study, pupil gains in Spanish reading were strongly related to the teacher's proficiency in Spanish. A teacher's knowledge of applied linguistics in English as a second language contributed significantly to language learning. It was also noted that the teacher's philosophical orientation toward reading can influence methodological approaches and, in turn, affect learning outcomes. Moreover, teachers' attitudes toward marked and unmarked languages can result in a differential use of each language during interactional sequences.

Chapter 9 will examine the discourse process in bilingual classrooms—the effect of instructional approaches on teacher-pupil interaction, the influence of classroom structures on language-use patterns, and the identification of effective instructional features in bilingual classrooms.

SUGGESTED READINGS

Dodson, C. J. *Towards Bilingualism: Studies in Language Teaching Methods.* Cardiff, Wales: University of Wales Press, 1968.

Titone, R. *Teaching a Second Language in Multilingual Multicultural Contexts.* Paris: UNESCO, 1977.

Troike, R. C. and N. Modiano, eds. *Proceedings of the First Inter-American Conference on Bilingual Education.* Washington, D.C.: Center for Applied Linguistics, 1975.

Trueba, H. T. and C. Barnett-Mizrahi. *Bilingual/Multicultural Education and the Professional: From Theory to Practice* Rowley, Mass.: Newbury House Publishers, Inc., 1979.

Ventriglia, L. *Conversations of Miguel and Maria: How Children Learn a Second Language.* Reading, Mass.: Addison-Wesley Publishing Company, 1982.

DISCOURSE PROCESSES IN BILINGUAL CLASSROOMS __

INTRODUCTION

Language in bilingual classrooms, as in monolingual classrooms, functions as a system of communication and as a vehicle for learning. Language can be both process and product; the process could involve reading a story in order to write an essay on a certain topic, for example. Classroom language is governed by sociolinguistic rules, many times resulting in a passive role for the student — one who "answers" teachers' questions.

The classroom then, can be seen as a sociolinguistic setting, involving the learning of discourse rules to participate effectively in that context. Different instructional approaches make different linguistic demands on pupils. For example, the language needed to function in a small group (pupil-pupil interaction) is different than that required in a teacher-pupil interaction involving the whole class. Studies of language use in bilingual schools have been conducted from qualitative and quantitative perspectives. A number of quantitative studies examined the use of L_1, L_2, and code switching in teacher-directed lessons and in learning situations wherein the teacher was absent. Many factors seem to influence language choice in the bilingual classroom, and the teacher's language use can greatly influence the language behavior of students. The role of code switching—both intersentential (alternate use of sentences in L_1 and L_2) and intrasentential (switching from L_1 to L_2 within a sentence)—remains controversial. Certain questions will be raised here in conjunction with developing a policy toward code switching. The effect of different classroom group structures on language-use patterns will also be reviewed. Finally, significant instructional features found to be effective in bilingual programs will be described.

LANGUAGE IN THE CLASSROOM

Language enters into the curriculum in two ways: (1) as a system of communication (teachers explaining a lesson or telling students what to do; students asking questions), and (2) as a means of learning (students discussing the meaning of a story; students writing answers to a set of questions after reading a chapter from the history textbook).

Language is both *process* and *product*. In the English class, the desired product may be a persuasive essay on "why women should/shouldn't be drafted"; the process may involve reading magazine articles or discussing the issues in small groups. In the history class, teacher explanation/lecture (oral language) may be used as the process to transmit knowledge about the American Revolution. Writing may be used by the chemistry teacher to assess the students' understanding of scientific phenomena (a description of the results of the laboratory experiment).

Classroom language is not only governed by rules specific to school settings, but it has been described as a highly constrained form of communication. Stubbs (1976:91) notes that "the rules of classroom dialogue are often distinct from conversation between social equals and the pupil often learns, for example, to give short answers to discrete questions and not to initiate discussion: in other words, he often learns a predominantly passive role." An example of the "artificial" nature of classroom dialogue is the characteristic use of questions which are not genuine requests for information. The "unrealness" of the questions arises from the fact that pupils are to answer questions to which the teacher already knows the answers. These "guess-what-I'm-thinking" kinds of questions often function as oral tests assessing the students' knowledge, rather than "real" requests for information (Laswell, 1978).

By studying teacher/pupil verbal interactions, one can analyze how the structure of classroom language constrains or allows students to participate in learning in different ways. The classroom can be seen as a linguistic process, involving the learning of discourse rules (Gage 1974; Mehan 1979) to participate effectively in the question-answer-evaluation cycle.

INSTRUCTIONAL APPROACHES AND LINGUISTIC DEMANDS

Instructional approaches make specific linguistic demands on pupils. The participants in the conversation (teacher-pupil and pupil-pupil), as well as the nature of the group (students in a small group, teacher to individual pupil, and teacher to whole class), affect the type of language (informal, formal) and ordering of thought (inexplicit and explicit). The normal structure of classroom activities allows for teacher-pupil interaction, but does not encourage active pupil-pupil dialogue related to the lesson. The pupil-pupil dialogue, conducted in small groups, would allow for ordering knowledge by means of informal language (exploratory talk) before presenting the knowledge (interpretation of the story or article, description of scientific process, solution to math problem) to the whole class for public (formal) discussion (Barnes 1975).

Stallings and Kaskowitz (1974) found that excessive use of individualized instruction could have negative effects on pupil achievement. They reported negative correlations between the amount of time first and third grade pupils worked alone with achievement measures, while the time that children worked with the teachers in large groups resulted in positive correlations. Cassidy and Vukelich (1977) compared the effects of small, medium, and large group size structures on the listening comprehension abilities of kindergarten children and found significant differences in the receptive language skills among these pupils due to the type of group structure. The teacher's presence or absence also seems to influence the quality of children's talk in classroom settings. Kenefick (1977) observed that children used more varied language functions when the teacher was absent.

LANGUAGE IN BILINGUAL CLASSROOMS

Studies of language use in bilingual schools have been conducted from both quantitative and qualitative approaches. Studies from a quantitative perspective have focused on such aspects as the effects of classroom group structures on language use patterns (Milk 1980), the verbal behaviors of Hispanic teachers and pupils in fifth grade social studies classrooms (Muñoz-Hernández 1980), and the instructional language strategies of bilingual peer tutors (Sapiens 1982). Qualitative studies examining classroom languages have concentrated on the interactive nature of classroom situations from both verbal and nonverbal dimensions (Brause and Mayher 1982) and the cultural dynamics of the teaching/learning process in bilingual contexts (Cazden, Carrasco, and Maldonaldo-Guzmán 1980).

The application of ethnographic/qualitative approaches to the study of linguistic processes in bilingual classroom settings has been advocated by various researchers (Mehan 1977; Tureba 1982). Mehan (1977:87) suggests than an ethnographic approach

> would locate the structure of classroom events and describe what
> students and teachers do and say in each event. Such a description
> would focus on the functions of language used in each situation . . . It
> would also show how students use language for greetings, taking leave,
> joking, insulting and other communicative routines.

Trueba and Wright (1981) discuss a number of issues related to various educational areas where microethnography might prove a valuable research technique. These areas include such topics as teaching styles/cultural congruence, sociocultural rules of interaction, children's social competence, and language use during miscommunication.

Most research on bilingual education has been product oriented. Research findings have been reviewed and presented in various reports. Engle (1975) examined the use of vernacular languages in education for purposes of literacy among minority groups around the world. Paulston (1975) compared the impact of ethnic interrelations (at the societal level) on the achievement of pupils in bilingual schools, especially in Canada and the United States. Cohen and Laosa (1976) contrasted the effects and trends of bilingual schools in different parts of the world according to four approaches (L_1 first, L_2 later; L_2 only; L_1 and L_2 simultaneously; L_2 first and L_1 later) for establishing preliteracy and literacy skills, and three approaches (L_1 only grades one to five; L_2 only grades one to five; L_1 and L_2 simultaneously) for teaching the content areas. Troike (1978) compiled research evidence to demonstrate the effectiveness of bilingual education in the United States. Cummins (1979) advanced the linguistic interdependence hypothesis after studying the research evidence from bilingual programs in different parts of the world. He argues that the cognitive/academic aspects of L_1 and L_2 are interdependent, and that the development of proficiency in L_2 is partially a function of the level of proficiency in L_1 at the time intensive exposure to L_2 is begun.

For the past decade, advocates of bilingual education in the United States have been under pressure to demonstrate that bilingual schooling is an effective alternative to monolingual English language education. The review of research conducted by Zappert and Cruz (1977) is an example of the preoccupation to demonstrate the success of bilingual education in achieving superior outcomes with regard to such variables as oral language development, reading, math, and attitudes. The effectiveness of language use in teaching and the successfulness of specific classroom practices, however, have little or no empirical bases. Gómez (1976) compared the questioning behaviors of first grade bilingual teachers during reading instruction in English and Spanish, but did not relate it to outcome measures. The work by Ramírez and Stromquist (1979) on successful ESL teaching methodology, and Ramírez (1979b) on effective teaching behaviors during Spanish reading instruction represent an effort to relate the language behavior of teachers to pupil achievement.

TEACHER-DIRECTED LESSONS*

A number of studies have been conducted on the uses of language in the Spanish/English bilingual classroom. Most of them have been quantitative in nature and have centered on four major aspects of classroom discourse: (1) amount (percentages) of English and Spanish used during the instructional process, (2) functional uses (e.g. instructing, clarifying, expressing humor) of English, Spanish, and code switching, (3) language use patterns during interaction (teacher-pupil, teacher aid-pupil), and (4) factors which affect language choice (time, teacher's presence, pupils' language proficiency).

Amount of English and Spanish Used During the Instructional Process

Teacher language use was the major focus of a study of five bilingual kindergarten classrooms conducted by Legarreta (1977). The study was concerned with the extent to which two different bilingual

---

*This section is taken from A. G. Ramírez, "Language in Bilingual Classrooms," *NABE Journal*, 4:3 (1980c) 64–73. Used with permission.

education program models — the concurrent model, with the teacher using the two languages interchangeably, and the alternate days approach, with alternating the language from one day to the next — met their stated goal of equal use of both languages in the classroom. A secondary focus of the study was an examination of the various functions used by the teacher in each language (e.g. warning, directing, correcting). Her findings indicate that in classrooms using the concurrent/translation model, English was favored by teachers for all the functions that were examined; whereas with the alternate days model, English was the primary choice for correcting children, and Spanish was used more often for warning and directing. With the concurrent/translation model, teachers used English 70 percent of the time and Spanish only 30 percent of the time, whereas with the alternate days approach, the goal of 50 percent use of each language was maintained.

In a more recent study, Legarreta (1979) compared language use patterns of five program models at the kindergarten level: (1) traditional monolingual instruction with no English as a second language (ESL) training, (2) traditional monolingual instruction with ESL, (3) bilingual instruction using concurrent translation (with no ESL), (4) bilingual instruction using alternate days approach (no ESL), and (5) bilingual instruction using concurrent translation with daily ESL. The results confirmed the earlier findings that balanced language use occurred only with the alternate days approach. The distribution of teacher language choice in the concurrent translation programs was 28 percent Spanish and 72 percent English. The findings relevant to language development were that the bilingual treatments (3, 4, and 5) produced greater gains in English oral comprehension than did the monolingual treatments (1 and 2). While there are some problems with the design of this study, particularly the small sample number for each program model (a total of seventeen classrooms for all five program models) as well as the failure to take the teacher variable into account, the fact that the most positive gains in English oral comprehension were obtained in the bilingual program should be of interest to bilingual educators.

The use of Spanish and English in a secondary American government class in San Jose, California, was investigated by Sapiens (1978). The teacher was bilingual and the students ranged in language proficiency from English dominant to Spanish dominant; six were classified as limited English speaking according to the state's language dominance criteria. The teacher adopted a code-switching strategy in order to teach the course content to a linguistically diverse group of students. The teacher spoke about 80 percent of the time during the fifty-minute period, a figure not unusual for a lecture-type course. The teacher used

Spanish 45 percent of the time and English 55 percent; the students used both languages in the same proportion. In terms of teacher-pupil interactional patterns, the teacher initiated 85 percent of the exchanges; half the exchanges were in Spanish and the other half in English. In the student-initiated exchanges (15 percent), English was used 70 percent of the time as compared to 30 percent in Spanish.

Conversational code switching between speakers, alternation from one language to the other during speaking turns, occurred only 12 percent of the time. Students did switch from English to Spanish twice as often as from Spanish to English. This directional switch was probably due to the number of Spanish-dominant students in the class. An examination of language use in presenting content revealed the following frequency pattern: presentation of basic concepts, four times in Spanish, nineteen in English; expansions, fifty times in Spanish, forty in English. English was used five times more often than Spanish to convey key lesson concepts; however, Spanish was used slightly more often than English to elaborate on the main points of the lesson. Thus, the Spanish-dominant students were given the details (expansions) but were left with deriving for themselves the main points of the lesson. Sapiens concludes that the code-switching strategy was viable to the degree that it helped the teacher "motivate the students and maintain rapport with them" and that "the students understood and/or spoke both languages to varying degrees" (1978:23). Nevertheless, the code-switching strategy favored English for the transmission of basic concepts in the lesson.

Functions of Spanish, English, and Code Switching in the Classroom

Classroom language was analyzed in terms of eight functional categories by Milk (1978), utilizing the same classroom and lesson studied by Sapiens (1978). The eight language function categories, adapted from Sinclair and Coulthard (1975), included:

1. Informatives (to provide information)
2. Elicitations (to request a linguistic response — question, for example)
3. Directives (to request a nonlinguistic response — an imperative, for example)
4. Metastatements (to help students understand the structure of the lesson and the purpose/direction of the dialogue; also included here is the use of summaries and reviews)
5. Expressives (to express solidarity, emotion; to show warmth

and acceptance in the positive vein; to show disagreement, tension, or hostility in the negative sense)

6. Humor expressives (to express humor; to display empathy)
7. Replies (to provide the appropriate response to preceding elicitation)
8. Follow-ups (to acknowledge that the teacher has heard the student's reply; can include an evaluation on the quality of the reply)

Milk was concerned with the functional uses of English and Spanish in a bilingual classroom using the concurrent language approach. He found that only elicitations were carried out equally in both languages. English was used more often for the other functions: informatives, 54 percent; directives, 92 percent; metastatements, 63 percent. Spanish-dominant students were "involved" in the lesson—50 percent of the elicitations (questions) were in Spanish as well as 43 percent of the expressives. Spanish was used equally with English for the purpose of creating humor (sixteen examples for each language). The end result, however, was that the English-dominant students were favored by the functional allocation of language, particularly for information, directions, and the structure of the lesson.

The use of code switching in terms of the teacher asking a question and the pupil replying tended to follow the rule of "answer in the language you're spoken to." Code switching was relatively high for informatives (65 percent) and metastatements (70 percent). Switching was more frequent from Spanish to English for both functions.

The functions of code switching in a bilingual third grade classroom in northern Ohio was investigated by Olmedo-Williams (1979). Tape recordings were made of language behavior during Spanish language arts lessons and English peer teaching sessions (a bilingual child taught English to Spanish monolingual or Spanish-dominant pupils) over a period of four months. The nature of the task (structured reading lesson versus word game) and the presence or absence of the teacher appeared to influence the number and uses of code switching. Code switching was used by the pupils for such functions as: (1) to attract the attention of the listener, (2) to gain the floor, (3) to emphasize or clarify aspects of their communication, (4) to instruct, and (5) to resolve instances of miscommunication or ambiguity.

In examining the choice of language during classroom interaction, Olmedo-Williams notes that "for these bilingual children English seems to be the langugae of 'in-group' relationships, whereas Spanish is the language of more formal relationships, reserved more for child-adult interactions" (1979:26). This pattern does deviate from the norm of using Spanish to create a climate of intimacy or solidarity found among adult Hispanics during in-group interaction (Valdés-Fallis 1978).

Language Use and Classroom Interaction

Townsend (1974) studied the instructional behavior in a bilingual classroom through the use of an observation instrument. His intent was to determine the consistency of interactional patterns of bilingual early childhood teachers while teaching in Spanish and English, and to compare the differences in interactional patterns between males and females and between teachers and assistant teachers working with four-year-old and three-year-old children in San Antonio, Texas.

Significant differences were found in the use of Spanish and English. These differences included more questioning in Spanish, more praising in English, more rejection of student answers in Spanish, and more direction given during English lessons. A greater percentage of student response was recorded during lessons taught in Spanish, but a greater percentage of student-initiated behavior was recorded during English lessons. Significant differences existed between the two languages in sequences, related to reinforcement. The sequence involving a student response followed by teacher acceptance occurred more often in Spanish. The sequence of a student response followed by teacher praise occurred more often in English. There was a greater tendency for the instructors to use English words while teaching in Spanish than to use Spanish words during English lessons, especially among the assistant teachers. The comparison between teachers and assistant teachers produced six significant differences, including more student response for teachers and more "teacher talk" (lecture-type behavior) for assistant teachers.

In a subsequent study, Townsend and Zamora (1975) examined the language of preschool teachers and teacher aides in terms of differences between verbal and nonverbal behavior and different interactional patterns while using Spanish or English. The authors used an observational instrument developed for the previous study which yielded indirect/direct teaching behavior (e.g. accepting pupils' ideas versus lecturing), as well as total ratios of teacher talk, pupil talk, and percent of talk involving a switch from one language to the other. Their analysis found that teachers were more indirect and allowed more student response, while aides both talked more and switched more often from one language to the other. Teachers' overall nonverbal behavior was seemingly more positive than the aides' nonverbal behavior. During Spanish instruction, more questions were asked, there was more student response, more rejection of student answers, and more acceptance of student response. English instruction led to more direction-giving behavior, teacher praise, and use of two or more reinforcing statements. Spanish was apparently used for purposes such as encouraging and accepting pupils' ideas, thus leading to more student involvement in the instructional process and, perhaps, promoting greater achievement.

McLennan (1978) explored the effects of a concurrent model (free alternation of Spanish and English) and an alternate approach (split sessions of each language during the same class period) in five high school bilingual classrooms in the San Francisco area. Students were classified according to language proficiency—English dominant, bilingual, and Spanish dominant. Transcripts were analyzed using Bellack's (1966) pedagogical moves (structuring, soliciting, responding, and reacting). The bilingual group participated equally under both instructional approaches. The English-dominant group participated more in the interactional process under the concurrent approach, while the Spanish-dominant students tended to be more involved under the language alternate model.

Factors Influencing Language Choice in the Classroom

Phillips (1975) reported in her study of code switching in bilingual classrooms (grades K–3) in Los Angeles that the type of language lesson (English or Spanish) and teacher language use greatly influenced the language behavior of pupils. Code switching was more frequent among both teachers and students during Spanish language lessons than during English language sessions. The tendency was to introduce a concept in Spanish and then to elaborate in English. During the English lessons, teachers used only English and expected the students to communicate in English only. She noted in her conclusions that "the contrast between the pattern of teacher code-switching during the language lessons may be signalling to students that English functions more effectively than Spanish for 'important' messages, in the classroom, and that the teacher's language use itself "may be signalling their [negative] attitude toward the functional efficiency of Spanish" (Phillips 1975: 57–58).

The major finding of Shultz's study was that the children's notion of their audience determined which language they used; they used English with those persons proficient in English, and Spanish with those proficient in Spanish. Nearly all the uses of "emotive language," which included "swearing, complaining, lamenting, bragging, insult games," were in Spanish (Shultz 1975:10), even for children who generally preferred to speak English. The English-speaking teachers' ratings of student English proficiency reflected the actual amount of English the children used, although there was great variation in the two teachers' ratings attributable to the different situations in which the children were taped. Here, too, the notion of audience was the critical factor, for the children's choice of language varied according to the language proficiency of their interlocutors. The presence of certain people (e.g. children or teachers who used a lot of English) seemed to demand that the speaker use English. An extracurricular circumstance also heavily influencing language choice was length of time in an English-speaking environment: "children who had been on the mainland longer, and in the bilingual program the longest, . . . spoke English better . . . [and] more often" (Shultz 1975:15). Hence, the two key conditions for choice of English, the language skills of the listener and the length of time the speaker has been in an English-speaking environment, are conducive to more and more use of English. Shultz sees this fact as proof that despite program goals related to Spanish language maintenance, language use tended towards greater amounts of English.

Furthermore, there is a question regarding the varieties of the language used. The Spanish-speaking teachers here used Mexican and Argentinian Spanish, while the children were Puerto Rican. Shultz notes the children may have felt that their Spanish was inferior to that of the teachers, and may thus have preferred to use English. His study thus recognizes an important sociolinguistic dimension, that of variation within a langue (at least for Spanish). Left unanswered is the question of the difference, if any, between the children's English and that of their teachers. Though we cannot insure that classroom studies capture all the subtleties of language, it is still worth asking about the match or mismatch between teacher and student language in the second language as well as the first language in bilingual education.

The study by Bruck and Shultz (1977) utilized ethnographic techniques combined with videotape recordings to determine the context of Spanish and English use in a bilingual program in Illinois. They videotaped their subjects, two first-grade girls, for the total of three school days over the course of seven months. All interactions with the target students were recorded and analyzed in terms of initiator, addressee, seconds of talk in Spanish and English, and context of the situation. Differences in language interactions between the bilingual and the regular classrooms were examined to provide a global view of the child's total school language environment.

Generally, it was clear that both time and teacher made a difference. Children used more English with each other and with the teacher as time progressed. Teacher language dominance also accounted for much of the student language choice, at least in the bilingual classroom: "the teacher's language ability seems to affect the amount of Spanish used among the children" (Bruck and Shultz 1977:73). For example, the arrival of a Spanish-dominant teacher at the end of the year led to more use of Spanish, even though the total use of Spanish never reached the same level as at the beginning of the year.

The type of activity in which the students and teachers were involved also affected the language used, though variations in this area were much greater and fewer clear patterns of language choice appeared. The teacher's addressee was an important factor in teacher language choice, which in turn affected the classroom language environment. In this study, much code switching was attributed to the message being transmitted: directives and comments about appropriateness or correctness took place in English, while Spanish was used to "provide information, facts, opinions, or ideas" (Bruck and Shultz 1977:80). This study, then, advances the understanding of language in the classroom by getting at the functions of comments in different languages. The finding that English often marks off the organizational units of classroom activity shows that the function and intent of classroom language, as well as the amount of talk in one language versus another, need to be considered when describing language use in bilingual classrooms.

In another study utilizing videotaping, Bruck, Shultz, and Rodríguez-Brown (1979) explored language use among three Spanish-speaking children enrolled in the first grade of a half-day bilingual school in a Chicago suburb. One finding, similar to the one reported by Shultz (1975) and Bruck and Shultz (1977), was that the language dominance of the teacher determined the language environment of the classroom: "Language dominance of the teacher affected language use patterns not only in terms of total amount of language used, but also in the ways each language was used" (Bruck et al. 1979:53). A second finding was that the language use patterns changed over the course of the year, and that the transitional goals of the program were being met: "children used less Spanish among themselves at the end of the year than at the beginning" (Bruck et al 1979:54). An analysis of the functional allocation of the languages of the classroom, moreover, showed that English was typically used during transition from one activity to another (i.e. at the beginning and end of lessons), for commenting on what was going on in the classroom, for evaluating student work, and for giving directions. Spanish was primarily used for providing information and transmitting lesson content.

Erickson, Cazden, and Carrasco (1979) have addressed the issue of the social and cultural rules governing interaction in bilingual first grade classrooms in Chicago. Through observation techniques and videotape recordings, one first grade classroom taught by a bilingual Latino teacher was studied in 1978. The following year, four classes were examined; two taught by the Latino teacher and two taught by Anglo teachers. The research addresses three major concerns: (1) the social uses of English and Spanish in pedagogical interaction and in noninstructional situations, (2) the cultural organization of social relationships in routine instructional and noninstructional interaction in the classroom, and (3) the sociolinguistic repertoires of the teachers and selected students. The findings will undoubtably have implications for the training of teachers for bilingual/multicultural settings and for the design of bilingual education programs. The results may indicate that when teachers and students do not share the same sociolinguistic repertoire, pupils' academic performance is affected adversely. The results at this time reveal the strategies teachers and students use to accommodate each other across sociolinguistic repertoires, thus minimizing adverse effects. The analysis of the Anglo and Latino teachers' cultural styles of interaction may provide some guidance to school administrators in making decisions about student placement and teacher assignment. The research may suggest that it may be more beneficial to place Hispanic students with Latino teachers because of their shared avoidance of "audienced" competition.

Zentella (1978) analyzed the code-switching patterns among Puerto Rican teachers and students in two New York City bilingual classrooms, one third grade and one sixth grade. Teachers' code-switching behavior during structured class lessons and other occasions was tape-recorded. Students were recorded while working at their desk during the lessons and at an interview with the researcher. The uses and types of code switching were categorized in terms of format and syntactic constraints, and in relation to pauses preceding the switch. Both teachers switched from one language to the other in response to the language proficiency of the student. English was more predominant than Spanish in both classes. The sixth grade teacher, born and educated in Puerto Rico, switched much less frequently than the third grade teacher who was raised and educated in New York City. Zentella does not address the educational implications of code switching. She does point out that code-switching behavior can vary widely due to such factors as language proficiency, age, sex, and formality of the situation. Though there was a lack of controls to ensure that the same students talked for the same length of time in the classroom setting and during the interview, apparently both third and sixth graders behaved similarly; both groups produced nearly the same percentage of intrasentential switches, but the figure was almost doubled during the interviews. Thus, the full linguistic repertoire and code-switching patterns of bilingual children may not be observed during formal classroom lessons.

CODE SWITCHING IN THE CLASSROOM

The role of code switching in bilingual classrooms remains controversial. Jacobson (1979) favors code switching for pedagogical purposes (e.g. lexical enrichment, conceptual development, capturing the pupil's attention), but he advocates that only intersentential switching (between sentences, each sentence in either L_1 ro L_2) be used. The teacher may accept the intrasentential (the use of both L_1 and L_2 within a sentence) code switching the child brings to class, but the teacher should use full sentences in both languages. González and Maez (1980:133) make the following recommendations:

> . . . the teacher should assure that when the child does engage in intrasentential code-switching, the word switched to English is in his repertoire. In short, the teacher should assure that *the switch is not brought about by a lack of the equivalent word in Spanish*. The ability to code-switch should not be allowed to develop at the expense of Spanish. The child should develop code-switching abilities *in addition to* skills in the two languages. *Inter*sentential code-switching exhibiting (as it does) the child's ability to produce full utterances in both languages, does not pose the same threat to full development of Spanish skills as does *intra*sentential code-switching. If future research reveals that *inter*sentential code-switching leads to *intra*sentential code-switching, our views toward the former will need to be reexamined.

Valdés-Fallis (1978:19) suggests the following questions be considered by Spanish/English teachers in determining their policy toward code switching in the classroom:

1. What is their own attitude toward this mode of speaking? Do they habitually switch, or do they find it distasteful? Do they switch when speaking both languages or only when speaking Spanish?

2. How proficient and confident are they in Spanish? Do they prefer to teach in English and often feel insecure when giving an advanced lesson in Spanish?

3. How proficient are the students in both English and Spanish? If the role of the program is to bring about biliterate bilingualism, is this goal being accomplished, or does most instruction in Spanish get "switched" to English in the course of the lesson? Are the students comfortable in discussing academic subjects in both languages, or do they seem to lack Spanish vocabulary in the higher grades? Has a transition actually been taking place?

4. How prevalent is the use of Spanish in the community? Is it still primarily the home language? What are the attitudes of the community and the parents toward their own code switching?

5. If the community is slowly shifting from English/Spanish bilingualism to English monolingualism, how important is it to provide in the bilingual program a domain in which *only* Spanish is used?

6. If code switching is not considered appropriate in the classroom, is this ban limited to recitations and presentations by both teachers and students, or does it include group work or other in-class peer interaction? Can language use by students *with* students actually be controlled by the teacher?

7. Finally, what is the present overall policy (stated or unstated) for language use in the program?

EFFECTS OF GROUP STRUCTURES

Different classroom participant structures affect language use patterns in a number of ways. Milk (1980) investigated the effect of group size on discourse patterns in two bilingual classrooms. Group settings included the whole class, large groups (eight or more children), small groups (three to seven children), dyads, and the individual student. Some of the questions addressed were regarding the language use patterns of teachers according to group setting, and the relationship between student language proficiency and group setting. The results revealed a number of differences:

Differences between classrooms

There was more talk in classroom P than in classroom Q in all group settings. In classroom P, the highest proportion of talk occurred in the small group settings, whereas in classroom Q the highest proportion occurred in the teacher-directed setting.

Differences among language dominance groups

In classroom P, balanced bilinguals talked the most; in classroom Q, English-dominant students talked the most. In classroom P, Spanish-dominant pupils used their weaker language (English more often in the teacher-directed setting) This usage was not the case for the other two groups.

Differences between group settings

There was more talk in the dominant language in the small group setting than in the large group, but, for the weaker language, there was more talk in the large group than in the small group; there was a higher proportion of academic talk in the small group than in the large group. The range of speech acts for all students was greater during individual work than during teacher-directed instruction.

Differences within classroom P

For both languages there was more talk in the small group than in the large group setting. For balanced bilingual and English-dominant pupils, there was more talk during individual work than during teacher-directed instruction. This fact was true for both languages. The range of speech acts was broader during individual work than during teacher-directed instruction.

Differences between languages

In both classrooms, English was used more often than Spanish. (In classroom P, English was used 20 percent more; in classroom Q it was used 59 percent more.) "Imagining" speech acts were performed only in English in both classrooms. In both classrooms, more "rehearsal speech" occurred in Spanish than in English.

The most significant finding of the study was that the student's weaker language (Spanish in the case of the English dominant; English in the case of the Spanish dominant) was seldom used in the classroom for natural communication. This result was partly caused by grouping strategies which isolated English- and Spanish-dominant students from each other throughout the day.

Enright (1981) compared the patterns of language use in two bilingual kindergarten classrooms, one with a traditional instructional philosophy and the other with an "open" approach. Analysis of the recordings made of three matched pairs of pupils participating in various activities and participant structures in the two classrooms revealed major differences in discourse patterns. Compared to the open classroom, children in the traditional setting exhibited lower rates of verbal participation, made a greater use of Spanish, their primary language, and utilized a narrower range of speech acts, usually only in response to teacher elicitations — informing responses and rehearsal speech acts (repetitions and recitations). The language "rules" for participating in classroom activities also served to extend and/or link the teacher's philosophy of instruction with the student's sociolinguistic environment. Through classroom observations, teacher interviews, and language analysis, Enright (198:212) was able to formulate four sociolinguistic "commandments" for participating in Mrs. Shaw's (traditional) and Mrs. Blake's (open) classrooms (see Table 13).

Enright, Ramírez, and Jacobs (1981–82) found that the teacher's cultural background (United States or Israeli born/educated) influenced the interactional style of children from bilingual and monolingual backgrounds. In addition, the teacher's presence or absence from classroom activities affected the degree of children's participation in the lessons. The Israeli (bilingual) teacher tended to use more "closed," lesson-related questions and directives, and interacted more, both in terms of frequency and range of language functions, with bilingual pupils. The United States (monolingual) teacher, in contrast, provided information along with questions and directives, while interacting with both groups of pupils. As a result, the children interacted differentially with each teacher, varying both their speech functions and degree of involvement. Apparently, the teacher's interactive style was more important than language proficiency, since bilingual pupils used Hebrew only with the "monolingual" United States teacher because she accepted it and incorporated the language as best she could in the lesson.

There were also differences between the monolingual English-speaking pupils and the bilingual Israeli children while conversing in small peer group situations. The bilingual group actively discussed their

Table 13. The Four Commandments for Participating in Mrs. Shaw's and Mrs. Blake's Classrooms

Mrs. Shaw's Commandments	*Mrs. Blake's Commandments*
Full group and Small group P-Structure Commandments	
1. Look at the teacher (without speaking).	1. "Go with what you've got" (1C) It is better to speak and be wrong than not to speak at all.
2. Do not speak unless you are spoken to.	2. If you have something to say, say it. (2C^t) Say what you think. (2C^f) Say what you feel. (2C^k) Say what you know. (2C^w) Say what you want. ("Ask and ye shall receive").
3. Avoid speaking unless it is clearly appropriate.	3. Don't interrupt (including in speaking). (3C) Don't hurt others (including in speaking).
Independent P-Structure Commandment:	
4. *Do, don't talk.*	4. *Work with the group (including in speaking).*
(4A) Don't talk, unless you can do and talk at the same time.	*(4C) Help your friends (including in speaking).*

Reprinted by permission from D. S. Enright, *Student Language Use in Traditional and Open Bilingual Classrooms*. Doctoral Dissertation, Stanford University, 1981: 212.

work projects and talked about other topics, occasionally maintaining two conversations simultaneously. The monolingual United States group tended to remain silent, working to complete the assigned project with little private or social speech.

Peer language situations can provide valuable information about communicative processes in the classroom with the teacher absent. Carrasco, Vera, and Cazden (1981) relied on videotaping to study aspects of bilingual students' communicative competence within a teaching situation. In a multiethnic classroom in San Diego, Veronica, a bilingual, Spanish-dominant child repeating the first grade because of "weak" English skills was asked to teach a lesson to Alberto, a younger, Spanish-dominant first grader. Veronica was first taught a lesson on English spelling in English and then was asked to instruct Alberto. She switched to Spanish first to give the instructions and utilized a number of strategies for communicating the referential information Alberto needed to complete the task and for managing the interpersonal aspects of teaching. The authors suggest that the use of videotape procedures could enable a teacher to compare his/her students' language behavior during peer-peer interaction when no adult (teacher) is present, as well as in dialogues on a one-to-one level with an adult. This information, in turn, could alter a teacher's perception of the communicative abilities of a Spanish-dominant pupil such as Veronica who speaks very little in large group sessions with the teacher present.

Sapiens (1982) compared the instructional language strategies of fluent bilingual and English monolingual Chicano tutors in a peer tutoring situation with partial bilingual Chicano tutees. The high school tutors instructioned the bilingual tuttees almost exclusively in English. The bilingual tutees instructed in this manner showed the most growth on criterion-referenced tests based on three geography lessons. At the same time bilingual tutors received more satisfaction from the tutoring sesions than did the monolingual tutors, suggesting they could be utilized by teachers in working with limited-English-speaking students in regular classrooms. The tutees instructed by bilingual tutors participated more actively in the two-way exchanges (i.e. more soliciting and reacting), resulting in a greater discussion of the meaning and use of geography concepts, resulting in greater learning of the content.

EFFECTIVE INSTRUCTIONAL FEATURES

Effective bilingual instruction shares many of the features of effective monolingual education. Chamot (1982:2) summarizes the main findings of the descriptive study by Tinkunoff (1982), which addressed significant bilingual instructional features:

1. Effective bilingual teachers display active teacher behaviors, spending a large proportion of class time on direct instruction. This includes a focus on academic objectives, a high level of student participation in learning tasks, fairly fast-paced instruction, and immediate and constructive feedback.
2. Academic learning time (ALT), which comprises time allocated to the task, amount of student engagement, and accuracy of student responses, is maintained at a high level.
3. A strong emphasis on the basic skills of reading, language arts, and mathematics accounts for approximately 75 percent of the school day.
4. Effective bilingual teachers are able to use language successfully to mediate instruction in three important ways: they are able to communicate and clarify instruction in both English and the home language; they are sensitive to cultural differences in their linguistic and nonverbal communication with their students; and they work consistently to develop their students' language skills in both languages during the whole school day, not just during language instruction.

SUMMARY

Language in the classroom is both a *process* and a *product*, and it can enter the curriculum in two ways: (1) as a system of communication, and (2) as a means of learning. It is also a highly constrained form of communication differing from language in other social settings. The verbal interactions between teachers and pupils can influence the degree to which language can contrain or allow students to learn in different ways. Instructional approaches make specific linguistic demands on learners. Various aspects of teacher/student interactions affect the type of language used and the learning process.

Studies have found that excessive use of individualized instruction can have negative effects on achievement. Others have noted that the teacher's presence or absence influences the quality of student talk, resulting in the use of different language functions.

Studies of language use in bilingual schools have been conducted from quantitative and qualitative perspectives. The quantitative studies have focused on such aspects as (1) effects of classroom group structures on language use, (2) verbal behaviors of teachers and students, and

(3) instructional language strategies among peer tutors. Qualitative studies have focused on the (1) sociocultural rules of interaction, and (2) cultural aspects of communication or miscommunication.

Most of the studies done on the uses of language in bilingual classrooms have been quantitative in nature. Studies mentioned in this chapter examined the following aspects: (1) amount of English/Spanish used during the instructional process, (2) functions of Spanish, English, and code switching in the classroom, (3) language use and classroom interaction, and (4) factors influencing language choice.

Code switching and the controversies surrounding its use in bilingual classrooms were noted. The effects of group structures (e.g. teacher to whole class, small groups, individual students) on classroom discourse processes were also examined.

Effective instructional strategies in bilingual programs share many of the successful features found in monolingual classrooms. These include (1) a focus on academic objectives and the use of "active" teaching behaviors, (2) an emphasis on academic learning time, (3) an emphasis on basic skills, and (4) an appropriate use of L_1 and L_2 to mediate instruction. The subsequent chapter will examine various immersion programs for language majority students in Canada and in the United States.

SUGGESTED READINGS

Cazden, C. B., V. John, and D. Hymes, *Functions of Language in the Classroom*. New York Teachers College Press, Columbia University, 1972.

Cohen, A. D. *Describing Bilingual Education Classrooms*. Rosslyn, Va.: National Clearninghouse for Bilingual Education, 1980.

Mehan, H. *Learning Lessons*. Cambridge, Mass.: Harvard University Press, 1979.

Trueba, H. T., G. P. Guthrie, and K. H. Au, eds. *Culture and the Bilingual Classroom: Studies in the Classroom Ethnography*. Rowley, Mass.: Newbury House Publishers, Inc., 1981.

Wilkinson, L. C., ed., *Communicating in the Classroom*. New York: Academic Press, Inc., 1982.

Chapter Ten _____

IMMERSION EDUCATION
APPROACHES _____

INTRODUCTION

Immersion in a second language—the teaching of school subjects in L_2 to language-majority children—promotes the development of functional bilingualism and biculturalism. This additive form of bilingualism has a number of cognitive, linguistic, and cultural benefits, with no negative effect on first language skills or intellectual development. Several Canadian French immersion programs will be described here—early total immersion, early partial immersion, and late immersion. These programs are available to English-speaking Canadian pupils who wish to acquire a functional proficiency. The Culver City Spanish Immersion Project, modeled after St. Lambert Project in Montreal, Canada will be discussed. The project is described, noting the details of the students' acquisition of Spanish and the development of their English language skills. The educational consequences of a French immersion program, also modeled after the Canadian early immersion programs and established at the State University of New York at Plattsburgh, are outlined. The results of these projects suggest some of the possibilities immersion education approaches offer for creating bilingual pupils through schooling.

IMMERSION EDUCATION AND ADDITIVE BILINGUALISM

Developing bilingual and bicultural skills among English-speaking children in Canada or the United States can be seen as an "additive" form of bilingualism (Lambert 1980). Immersion in the second language, particularly the teaching of school subjects in L_2, is the principal educational means by which this type of functional bilingualism is promoted.

Immersion education seems to bring positive results in a number of areas for language-majority children. It can promote interethnic skills (Ramirez 1981) as well as a number of cognitive and linguistic benefits (Swain 1978). For these pupils, the second language is added with no negative effect on first language development. Since the child is a member of the dominant social class, he encounters positive attitudes and continued development of his first language from both parents and the community (Lambert 1975). Depending on the type of immersion schooling — early total, early partial, or late immersion — students have the opportunity to acquire high levels of proficiency in the second language. Swain (1981) argues for the need to introduce the second language as soon as possible to allow for the development of basic interpersonal communication skills, since the wider environment does not usually provide this type of "input." Moreover, children have the "motivation" to learn in L_2 and will not suffer a long-term decline in first language skills. Stern (1978) notes that immersion education offers the possibility for creating bilinguals through the school system.

CANADIAN IMMERSION PROGRAMS

French immersion language programs in Canada began as an experiment to counter parental dissatisfaction with conventional second language teaching approaches. Stern (1978:172–173) considers the Canadian experiment "an example of interaction between a language teaching experiment and the development of language teaching policy," which in the course of ten years moved "from a small-scale pilot study in one school to an alternative form of schooling in a number of educational systems across Canada."

The three types of French immersion programs studied and evaluated by the Bilingual Education Project, through funds from the Ministry of Education, Ontario Province, and Office of Research and Development, Ontario Institute for Studies in Education, are described below (Swain 1978; Swain and Lapkin 1982):

1. Early total immersion
   a. Kindergarten and grade one—all instruction in French
   b. Grades two through four—all instruction in French; English language arts introduced for approximately one hour per day during grade two or three
   c. Grade five—60 percent to 80 percent of the instruction conducted in French; language arts are taught in English, and mathematics may be offered in English
   d. Grades seven through eight—half of the curriculum taught in French, the other half in English
   e. High school level—different school subjects available in French or English
2. Early partial immersion
   a. Kindergarten—instruction in English
   b. Grades one through eight—half of the school day in French, the other half in English; French and English language arts, some subjects taught in French (i.e. math and music in grades one and two, science and physical education in grades three through six)
3. Late immersion
   a. Grades six or seven—daily twenty to thirty minute lessons in French
   b. Grade eight—55 percent to 70 percent of the curriculum taught in French
   c. Grades nine and ten—40 percent of the curriculum taught in French, usually history, geography, and French language arts
   d. Grade eleven—25 percent of curriculum in French; usually two school subjects, one being French language arts
   e. Grade twelve—French language arts

The relative effects of the three types of programs are presented in Table 14. In general, immersion education does not have any negative effects on pupils' intellectual growth, and, early total French immersion may even enhance academic achievement. Students in early partial and late immersion programs seem to experience some difficulty relative to their comparison groups (English-educated peers and francophone pupils) in acquiring mathematical and science skills, possibly because of instruction in the weak language (French) and assessment in English or French (Swain and Lapkin 1982). The development of a functional proficiency in French takes time, and, apparently early total immersion programs are more successful in producing English-speaking students with a more nativelike command of French.

CULVER CITY SPANISH IMMERSION PROJECT

The Culver City Spanish Immersion Program in California, a pioneer project in American public school education, was modeled after the St. Lambert French Immersion Program in Montreal, Canada. The program's long range objectives, as stated in 1972, were that (1) monolingual, English-speaking children will acquire nativelike proficiency in speaking, understanding, reading, and writing Spanish; (2) students will make normal progress in achieving the standard objectives of the elementary school curriculum; (3) students will undergo the normal maturation process in their first language — English; and (4) students will develop positive attitudes toward representatives of the Spanish-speaking community while maintaining a positive self-image as representatives of the English-speaking community.

The program has attracted various researchers, principally from UCLA and under the supervision of R. N. Campbell and A. D. Cohen from the ESL section of the English Department, who have carefully evaluated the students' linguistic progress (Flores 1973; Boyd 1974; Cohen 1976; Plann 1976), their progress in nonlinguistic skills (Leback 1974), and their cultural attitudes (Waldman 1975).

Acquisition of Spanish

Among the studies examining the development of Spanish skills, Cohen (1976) analyzed the stability and change of Spanish morphology and use of communication strategies of ten Anglo-American, English-speaking children who had completed four years of Spanish immersion education. Using the Bilingual Syntax Measure to elicit specific structures (e.g. person, gender, and number agreement between articles — nouns and subject-verb) he noted various patterns with respect to the following features from period 1 (June 1974) to period 2 (June 1975):

1. definite articles — 11 percent improvement in the correct use of *el*; stability in the correct use of *los*; a 16 percent "loss" (backsliding) in the correct use of 1a
2. third person present indicative — near stability in the use of the singular form of the third person; in period 1 there was a tendency to use the first person singular form for the third person singular, whereas in period 2 the tendency was to use the second person and third person plural forms; 21 percent increase in the correct use of the third person plural

Table 14. Relative Effects of Three Types of French Immersion Programs on English Canadian Students and Comparisons with English Educated Peers (EEP) and Francophone Pupils (FEP)

Aspect	Early Total Immersion	Early Partial Immersion	Late Immersion
Literacy Skills in L_1 (English)			
Writing	Some difficulty with technical skills — spelling, punctuation, and capitalization — until end of grade 3; comparable to EEP by grade 4	Similar results as with early total immersion pupils	Temporary poor performance at the end of the first year of immersion when compared to the EEP group
Reading	Surpass the performance of EEP by grade 5 on reading comprehension and vocabulary knowledge	Performance not superior to EEP group in different aspects of English language skills after grade 5 or 6	
Oral/Aural Skills in L_1	No apparent lag at any grade level	No apparent lag at any grade level	No apparent lag at any level

Receptive Language Skills in L2 (French) Listening and Reading	Nativelike proficiency levels after six or seven years	Performance of some students in grade 8 resembles the L2 skills of early total immersion	Performance of grade 8 students with one, two, or three years of immersion education is less than students at comparable grade level who have had early immersion schooling
Productive Language Skills in L2 Speaking and Writing	Highly developed communicative language abilities; some problems still with linguistic accuracy; less than native-like proficiency; spoken French judged favorably by francophone adults and children	Pupils at grade 7 non-nativelike proficiency in some areas	Non-nativelike proficiency in a number of areas

Table 14. Relative Effects of Three Types of French Immersion Programs on English Canadian Students and Comparisons with English Educated Peers (EEP) and Francophone Pupils (FEP)

Aspect	Early Total Immersion	Early Partial Immersion	Late Immersion
Achievement in School Subject			
Mathematics	Superior or at least equivalent performance with EEP group in computation and problem solving tasks at grade 5	Equivalent performance or not as well as EEP group on standardized math and science tests	In cases poorer performance than EEP subjects taught in French and tested in English, the results are subject specific and often relate to the student's prior instruction in French as a subject; some students who continue to take course options in French can surpass FEP in such areas as history, geography, etc.
Science and Social Studies	Equivalent performance with EEP group at grade 5	Performance of some pupils in grade 6 as measured through French approximate that of grade 3 and 4 pupils in early total immersion programs	

Social and Psychological Aspects			
School program	More satisfied with program than late immersion pupils; smooth adjustment to the program	More satisfied with program than late immersion pupils; smooth adjustment to the program	Some students would prefer a program with "less" French
Ethnolinguistic attitudes	Less rigid cultural stereotypes than EEP and favor a greater degree of contact with francophones	Less rigid cultural stereotypes than EEP and favor a greater degree of contact with francophones	Less rigid cultural stereotypes than EEP and favor a greater degree of contact with francophones
Identity	Pupils view themselves as English Canadians	Pupils view themselves as English Canadians	Pupils view themselves as English Canadians

SOURCE: M. Swain, "Bilingual Education for the English-Speaking Canadian," in J. E. Alatis, ed., *International Dimensions of Bilingual Education* (Washington, D.C.: Georgetown University Press, 1978), pp. 141–154; and, M. Swain and S. Lapkin, *Evaluating Bilingual Education: A Canadian Case Study* (Clevedon, England: Multilingual Matters, Ltd., 1982).

3. third person singular preterite—stable use at near mastery
    level, although some confusion over regular and irregular past
    forms (*pondio* and *ponio* for *puso* and *tomio* for *tomó*)

With regard to communication strategies, the children made use of
analogy and/or overgeneralized the rule for *that* complement constructions
in Spanish. They also used linguistic features transferred from English and
engaged in semantic avoidance (e.g. bypassed unfamiliar features) or
topic avoidance (e.g. no verbal response to a question/item).

Ramírez (1980a) conducted a cross-sectional study (grades K–4, four
males and four females at each level) to describe developmental trends in
the use of various grammatical features in Spanish, based on the Spanish
Grammar Production Subtest of the Spanish/English Balance Test
developed at Stanford University. Three specific questions were addressed:

1. Differences in the number of correct responses on a Spanish
    grammar test due to grade level and sex
2. Differences in the acquisition of the ten grammatical categories
    on the test due to grade level
3. Types of grammatical errors made on the test items

The number (percentage) of correct responses on the Spanish grammar test are presented in table 13. There appears to be an incremental
pattern in the number of correct answers on the grammar test, ranging
from three in Kindergarten to sixty in grade four. The percentage of correct answers for each grade group (8 students x 20 items = 160 maximum
score) ranges 1.88 percent for kindergarten to 38 percent for the fourth
grade. Significant differences occur between Kindergarten and grade
one ($x^2 = 4.18$, $p = <.05$) and between the second and fourth grades ($x^2
= 6.49$, $p = <.05$). Females respond correctly to more items on the test
than males, except for the third grade group. Overall, the girls' performance (females = 90, males = 56) is superior to that of the boys ($x^2 =
3.32$, $p = <.05$).

To determine the order of acquisition for each of the ten grammatical categories, the number of students correctly completing the two
items for each category was tabulated. The results, presented in table 14,
indicate that different grammatical categories are acquired at different
grade levels. Categories I, II, and IV (plurality and negation) are acquired by some of the students in grade one, followed by category V
(locatives) by grade three, and category III (past tense) and X (comparatives) by grade four. The increase in the number of categories acquired due to grade is also the number of students who successfully complete two items. A ranking of the categories on the basis of number of

Table 13. Number of "Correct" Responses on the Spanish Grammar Production Subtest by Grade and Sex

Sex	Grade					
	K	1	2	3	4	Total
Male (N = 4)	-	5	8	24	19	56
Female (N = 4)	3	16	18	12	41	90
Total	3	21	26	36	60	156
Mean Number Correct	.375	2.625	3.25	4.5	7.5	
Percentage correct	1.88	13	16	22	38	

SOURCE: A. G. Ramírez, "Acquisition of Spanish Grammar by Native English-Speaking Pupils in a Spanish Immersion School Program, Grades K-4." Albany: State University of New York, 1980a, mimeo.

Table 14. Number of Students Completing Each Grammatical Category

Category/Grade level		K (N = 8)	1 (N = 8)	2 (N = 8)	3 (N = 8)	4 (N = 8)	TOTAL
I	Singular to Plural	–	1	1	3	4	9
II	Plural to Singular	–	4	4	6	7	21
III	Present to Past Tense	–	–	–	–	3	3
IV	Affirmative Past to Negative Present	–	1	1	2	3	7
V	Preposition of Location	–	–	–	2	5	7
VI	Interrogatives – Direct to Indirect	–	–	–	–	–	–
VII	Imperatives – Indirect to Direct	–	–	–	–	–	–
VIII	Interrogatives – Direct to Indirect	–	–	–	–	–	–
IX	Imperatives – Direct to Indirect	–	–	–	–	–	–
X	Comparatives	–	–	–	–	1	1
	TOTAL		6	6	13	23	48

SOURCE: A. G. Ramírez, "Acquisition of Spanish Grammar by Native English-Speaking Pupils in a Spanish Immersion School Program, Grades K-4." Albany: State University of New York, 1980a, mimeo.

students producing correct answers yields an order similar to the one established by using grade levels: category II, followed by category I (plurality), then categories IV (negation) and V (locatives) category III (past tense), and then category X (comparatives).

An analysis of fifty errors randomly selected from the pupils' responses on the test items indicates that the acquisition process involves both interlingual and intralingual transfer. Of the seventeen errors classified, eleven could be attributed to intralingual problems (overgeneralization and simplification strategies) and six could be explained in terms of interlingual transfer from English. The fact that many of the errors are due to an incorrect generalization/use of Spanish grammatical rules is not particularly surprising in view of current second language learning theory (Brown 1980; Dulay, Burt, and Krashen 1982). The important consideration is that after four years (pupils in grade four) of immersion education, these pupils seem to have a low linguistic proficiency (grammatical accuracy) in Spanish. The lack of a definite trend of improvement across grades, as well as systematic occurrence of some errors (fossilization) was also noted by Plann (1976). Plann (1979:130-131) makes the following observations:

> The emphasis in the Culver City classrooms has always been on communication, and the children's Spanish, though imperfect, enables them to express themselves and understand their teacher . . . The children's heavy exposure to an ungrammatical form of the target language, namely their peers' classroom dialect of Spanish . . . may be an inevitable by-product of acquiring a second language in an immersion classroom. Perhaps, in the light of limited interaction with native speakers of the target language, the goal of native-like proficiency in an immersion program is an unrealistic one.

Development of English Language Skills

One of the goals of the Culver City Spanish Immersion Program was that English-speaking pupils would maintain normal progress in the development of their first language (English), while instructed primarily in Spanish. Ramírez (1980b) compared the relative development of English writing skills between English-speaking pupils schooled in a Spanish immersion program with those instructed monolingually in an all English school program for grades three and four. Differences between males and females were also examined. The development of English writing skills was examined or both syntactic categories and the types of errors. Students from both programs wrote compositions after attending a bird show in the school auditorium. The written compositions were then analyzed using the "minimal terminal unit" or T-unit (Hunt 1965), defined as one main clause plus any subordinate clause or nonclausal structure (equivalent to a simple or complex sentence, but a compound sentence would be composed of two or more T-units).

The T-unit analysis of the writing sample included five categories: (1) total number of words, (2) total number of T-units, (3) number of incorrect (ungrammatical) T-units, (4) number of correct (grammatical) T-units, and (5) mean number of words T-unit. The first five T-units from each composition were then analyzed for errors in syntax (omission, word order, selection), morphology (word derivation, inflectional endings), and orthography (spelling, capitals) using Corder's (1973) framework. Analysis of variance was used to determine the influence of program, grade, and sex on the five measures.

Sex and program had an effect on four of the measures. Girls produced more words and T-units (correct and incorrect) than boys. Students in the Spanish immersion program produced more words and T-units than those attending the regular school program. Grade did not seem to have a significant effect on the writing development of these students, probably due to the fact that the grade difference involved only one year. O'Donnell, Griffin, and Norris (1967) report significantly greater development between grade five and grade three than between grade seven and grade five for handling syntax in writing. They also reported that the length of T-units was significantly greater in oral language than in written composition for grade three. On the mean number of words per T-unit, the third grade students from the Spanish immersion program produced slightly longer structures ($\bar{x} = 8.3$ words per T-unit) than either the pupils in the English School program ($\bar{x} = 7.1$) or subjects in the O'Donnell, Griffin, and Norris (1967) study ($\bar{x} = 7.67$), selected from white, middle-class families in Murfreesboro, Tennessee. Fourth grade pupils from the Spanish immersion program produced slightly longer T-units ($\bar{x} = 8.1$) than pupils from the English school program ($\bar{x} = 7.2$), and structures of similar length to Hunt's (1965) subjects ($\bar{x} = 8.6$) from the University School of the Florida State University at Tallahassee.

With respect to errors in the T-units, boys in the Spanish immersion program had more problems with spelling than did girls in both grade three and four. Students from the Spanish Immersion program at the third grade level had considerably more problems in orthography than did pupils in the English school program. By the fourth grade, however, orthographic problems were fewer for the Spanish immersion program students, considerably less than the pupils in the English school program. In the areas of syntax and morphology, there appeared to be no significant differences between the two groups of students at either grade three or grade four.

The development of written English skills among the pupils attending the Spanish immersion program did not seem to be affected negatively. As a matter of fact, the writing abilities of the Spanish immersion program students was superior in some areas to those pupils attending the traditional English-only program. Spanish immersion program students produced longer written compositions and used a greater number of syntactic structures. In the process of producing more language, there was a greater opportunity for making more errors. In this respect, Spanish immersion program students produced more "incorrect" T-units; however, an error analysis indicated that most problems with regard to "correctness" were in spelling. By the fourth grade, problems in orthography were reduced and were actually fewer than the ones made by pupils in the English school program. As in other studies examining language development among elementary schoolchildren, girls in both programs were superior to boys in spelling, length of texts, and number of syntactic structures.

PLATTSBURGH FRENCH IMMERSION PROGRAM

The Plattsburgh French Language Immersion Program (FLIP), modeled after the Canadian early immersion program, was established in September, 1976, initially as a full-day kindergarten-first grade class at the laboratory school of the State University College of New York at Plattsburgh. Samuels and Griffore (1979) and Hornby (1980) administered a battery of tests to FLIP children at the end of the first year of immersion and to a comparison group schooled in English. The battery included sections of the Wechsler Intelligence Scale for Children (verbal and nonverbal), English Language Skills, Auditory Discrimination, Wide Range Achievement Test (math, reading, and spelling), Purdue Self Concept Scale, and the Plattsburgh School and Culture Attitude Survey. The results based on analysis of covariance using the pre-posttest scores, revealed no significant differences between the two groups of children on all the measures except the nonverbal performance part of the Wechsler Intelligence Scale. The FLIP pupils performed better in picture arrangement and object assembly than the English control subjects.

In French language development, using the French Comprehension Test (Part I — vocabulary and Part II — phrases) of the Ontario Institute for Studies in Education, the French skills of the FLIP pupils were superior to their English-speaking counterparts studying French as a subject in the traditional classes in Montreal and Ottawa. The FLIP children's proficiency in French was similar to kindergarten and first grade students attending comparable immersion programs in Montreal, Ottawa, and Toronto.

Follow-up studies of FLIP students' performance on the Metropolitan Achievement Test indicate that their achievement was superior to national norms in the total test score as well as in English reading and mathematics subtests (see Table 17). Twenty-five percent of the FLIP students scored in the top 10 percent of the national scores, and 9 percent of the pupils scored in the top 1 percent. In mathematics the results were even more dramatic. On the French language tests, first and second graders performed remarkably well in most areas, and the pupils in grades three, four, and five had reading skills similar to those of English Canadian children in immersion programs (see Table 18).

In the spring of 1981, FLIP students between the ages of eight and ten participated in an exchange program with a class of students from

Table 17. Metropolitan Achievement Test Scores of FLIP Students Compared to National Norms

Percentiles	25%	50%	75%	90%	95%	98%	99%	Spring 1981
Percentages of students in the nation scoring at or above each percentile level (national norms)	75	50	25	10	5	2	1	Expected Percentages
Percentage of FLIP students scoring at or above each percentile level:								
1. Reading	100	81	47	31	22	6	3	Actual FLIP Percentages
2. Mathematics	94	78	56	38	22	22	13	
3. Language	91	44	31	13	3	3	0	
Basic Battery (1, 2, 3)	100	78	44	25	16	13	9	

SOURCE: *Report to Parents of FLIP Students,* ERCD — Campus School, Plattsburgh, N.Y. (1981).

Notre Dame de Pitie School in Quebec City, a francophone school. A report by Randeria and Hornby (1982), based on formal and informal surveys as well as on direct observations of the pupils before and after the exchange program, reveals that:

1. the experience resulted in a marked positive change in the attitude of the FLIP children toward the use of French;
2. the level of French language proficiency did not appear to play

Table 18. Scores of FLIP Students in Grades 1-5 on French Diagnostic Reading Tests (*Tests Diagnostiques De Lecture*) Compared to Canadian Norms for Early French Immersion Classes

Percentiles	25%	50%	75%	90%	95%	98%	99%
Expected Percentages	75	50	25	10	5	2	1
First Grade							
Part 1 — Word Recognition	75	50	17	17	–	–	–
Part II — Word Meaning	100	92	75	67	67	58	58
Part III — Sentence and Short Story Comprehension	83	83	58	50	33	17	17
Second Grade							
Part I — Word blending and grapheme discrimination	88	50	38	25	6	–	–
Part II — Word Meaning	94	88	44	44	31	25	25
Part III — Sentence Completion	88	81	50	44	31	6	6
Part IV — Story Comprehension	81	81	56	44	25	6	6
Grades 3, 4, and 5							
Part IV — Reading Comprehension	88	44	25	6	6	–	–

SOURCE: *Report to Parents of FLIP Students,* ERDC — Campus School, Plattsburgh, N.Y., 1981.

a significant role in the ability to enjoy the experience; and
3. a positive attitude toward the target language and cultural group seems to be more important than second language skills as a predictor of the ability to enjoy and use the language functionally.

SUMMARY

This chapter examined different immersion programs used in Canada and the United States. Immersion programs were noted as producing positive cognitive and linguistic effects among language-majority pupils. The Canadian immersion programs reviewed included (1) early total immersion, (2) early partial immersion, and (3) late immersion. The differential effects of these three types of immersion programs were presented.

The Culver City Spanish immersion program in California was described. The results from various research studies were reviewed. In the case of Spanish acquisition, language learning strategies (e.g. type of errors) and mastery of various grammatical categories were explained. The development of English language skills were examined in terms of the writing abilities of pupils in grades three and four. The effects of the Plattsburgh French immersion program were noted with respect to cognitive, linguistic (English language and French language skills), and affective measures.

The positive results of immersion programs in the United States and Canada offer a number of possibilities for creating functionally proficient bilinguals among majority, English-speaking pupils. In the next chapter, specific cognitive and academic consequences of bilingualism will be discussed.

SUGGESTED READINGS

Carey, S. T. *Bilingualism, Biculturalism and Education.* Edmonton: University of Alberta, 1974.

Lambert, W. E. and G. R. Tucker. *Bilingual Education of Children — The St. Lambert Experiment.* Rowley, Mass.: Newbury House Publishers, Inc., 1972.

Mackey, W. F. *Bilingual Education in a Binational School.* Rowley: Mass.: Newbury House Publishers, Inc., 1972.

Phillips, J. K., ed. *Action for the '80s: A Political, Professional and Public Program for Foreign Language Education,* Skokie, Ill.: National Textbook Company, 1981.

Swain, M., ed. *Bilingual Schooling: Some Experiences in Canada and the United States.* Toronto: Ontario Institute for Studies in Education, 1972.

COGNITIVE AND ACADEMIC ASPECTS OF BILINGUALISM _____

INTRODUCTION

The relationship between bilingualism and cognitive abilities has attracted much scholarly attention since the turn of the century. Much of the early literature on bilingualism was unfavorable, but, upon closer examination, apparently these studies failed to consider a number of factors that influenced the results. More carefully designed studies, particularly those conducted after the 1960s, have noted differential and superior performance by bilinguals in a number of cognitive-linguistic areas. The degree of bilingualism also appears to have an effect on both cognitive and academic performance.

PRE-1960 STUDIES ON BILINGUALISM

The effects of bilingualism on various psychological dimensions have attracted much scholarly attention since the early 1900s. Much of the early literature on bilingualism tended to be unfavorable, often citing a negative impact on intelligence (e.g. Arsenian 1937). Later studies (e.g. Darcy 1963) qualified differences between verbal and nonverbal intelligence, noting that bilinguals suffered from a "language handicap" on verbal measures of intelligence, but not on tests of nonverbal intelligence. Lambert (1977:15) notes that "researchers in the early period generally expected to find all sorts of troubles and usually did: bilingual children, relative to monolinguals, were behind in school, retarded in measured intelligence, and socially adrift." Many of the early studies, however, failed to consider a number of issues:

1. Relative language proficiency among bilinguals
2. Socioeconomic status differences between monolinguals and bilinguals
3. Urban-rural differences between monolinguals and bilinguals (e.g. Welsh-English bilingualism, Jones 1966)
4. Educational opportunities for monolinguals and bilinguals (language-minority group)

COGNITIVE DIFFERENCES BETWEEN MONOLINGUALS AND BILINGUALS

One of the most elaborate studies conducted to investigate the effects of bilingualism on intelligence was carried out in Canada by Peal and Lambert (1962). They set out not only to estimate the differences between monolinguals and bilinguals but to discover the dimensions on which they may differ, hypothesizing that the structure of their intellect may be different.

Subjects were drawn from six French schools in Montreal; all ten-year-olds were tested for degree of bilingualism by means of word association, word detection, picture vocabulary (Peabody) tests, and self-rating scores. A sample of seventy five monolinguals and eighty nine bilinguals, the latter balanced both in oral and in graphic use of their languages, was accepted. These subjects were then rated by socioeconomic status and sorted into seven classes, each including equal numbers of monolinguals and bilinguals; this final sample consisted of 110 subjects.

Data were collected on forty six variables, such as linguistic background, school grade, various verbal and nonverbal I.Q. measures (Lavoie-Laurendeau Group Test of General Intelligence, selected subtests of the Primary Mental Abilities, and Raven's Coloured Progressive Matrices), the linguistic skills of parents, and attitudes of parents and children toward the French and English linguistic communities. The results showed the unequivocal superiority of bilinguals on both verbal and nonverbal tests. In the larger sample (not matched by socioeconomic status), bilinguals performed significantly better on all nineteen intelligence variables, including general achievement in school. In the smaller sample (socioeconomically matched), differences were significant on fifteen variables, and not significant but favoring bilinguals on the remaining four. Bilinguals tended to be in higher grades in school than monolinguals (all were ten years old). Subsequent factor analyses of thirty one intelligence and attitude variables showed differences in the structure of intellect: bilinguals had more diversified patterns of abilities as defined by intelligence variables than monolinguals. The relatively small sample sizes (89 bilinguals and 75 monolinguals) do not allow strong generalizations; however, inspection of the factor matrices suggested to the authors that bilinguals had a more diversified intellectual structure.

The bilinguals' superiority on nonverbal tasks was attributed to their "agility in concept-formation," a consequence of early practice in generalization, that is, thinking without linguistic symbols. Similar reasoning was put forth by Diebold (1968) and Leopold (1949). Thus, bilingualism could be an advantage in abstract thinking (conceptualizing things and events in relation to their general properties rather than relying on their linguistic symbols) and in encouraging mental flexibility (a diversified intellectual structure derived from habitually switching from one language to another). Anisfeld (1964) conducted a follow-up study confirming the 1962 conclusions reached by Peal and Lambert. Other studies, using different approaches and conducted in different settings, seem to confirm the advantages of bilinguals relative to monolingual control groups for such measures as "cognitive flexibility," "divergent thinking," and higher levels of general reasoning and verbal abilities. The major research findings are summarized in Table 19.

LEVELS OF BILINGUALISM AND COGNITIVE PERFORMANCE

Cummins (1978) has suggested that the level of competence attained by bilingual children in both languages can be an intervening variable in the effect of bilingualism on cognitive and academic development. He calls this theory the "threshold hypothesis" and points out that two

Table 19. Comprative Performance of Bilinguals Relative to Monolinguals on Different Cognitive-Linguistic Measures and in Different Settings

Aspect	Setting	Researcher(s)
Greater analytical orientation to sound-meaning relationships and metalinguistic awareness	Israel South Africa Ireland Canada	Ben-Zeev 1972 Ianco-Worral 1972 Cummins 1978 Cummins 1978
Greater sensitivity to linguistic and perceptual feedback cues	Canada United States	Bain 1975; Genesee, Tucker, and Lambert 1975 Ben-Zeev 1975
Higher general reasoning and verbal abilities	France, Germany and Canada Canada Switzerland	Bain and Yu 1978; Cummins and Gulutsan 1974 Balkan 1970
Greater divergent thinking or cognitive flexibility	Canada Singapore	Cummins and Gulutsan 1974; Scott 1973; Torrance, et. al., 1970

thresholds occur in the development of bilingual subjects. If children show a low level of proficiency in both languages, they are at the lower threshold of bilingual competence and the cognitive effects of this situation are negative, especially in terms of achievement. In children who are bilingual but show dominance and nativelike competence in one language, bilingualism will not produce either positive or negative cognitive effects. In contrast, children who have achieved higher levels of competence in both the native and second language will show positive cognitive effects in their learning and academic achievement. Figure 24 illustrates Cummins's threshold hypothesis.

Duncan and De Avila (1979) compared the relative cognitive-perceptual performance of five language groups—proficient bilinguals, partial bilinguals, monolinguals, limited bilinguals, and late language learners—drawn from three Hispanic groups (Mexican American, Puerto Rican American, and Cuban American) in grades one and three. The proficient bilinguals, with high levels of fluency in both English and Spanish, outperformed the four other comparison groups on a neo-Piagetian measure of intellectual development (Cartoon Conservation Scales, De Avila 1977), as well as on two cognitive perceptual components of field dependent/independent cognitive style (Children's Embedded Figures Test and Draw-a-Person Test). The late language learners, those scoring lowest on the Language Assessment Scales used to establish relative proficiency, consistently performed the lowest on all the dependent measures. The "limited" bilingual children did not perform consistently different from the English or Spanish monolingual children. This information suggests that some "deficiencies" among bilinguals are linguistic rather than intellectual, and that a "threshold" level of bilingualism is necessary before a positive relationship between bilingualism and "metacognition" becomes apparent.

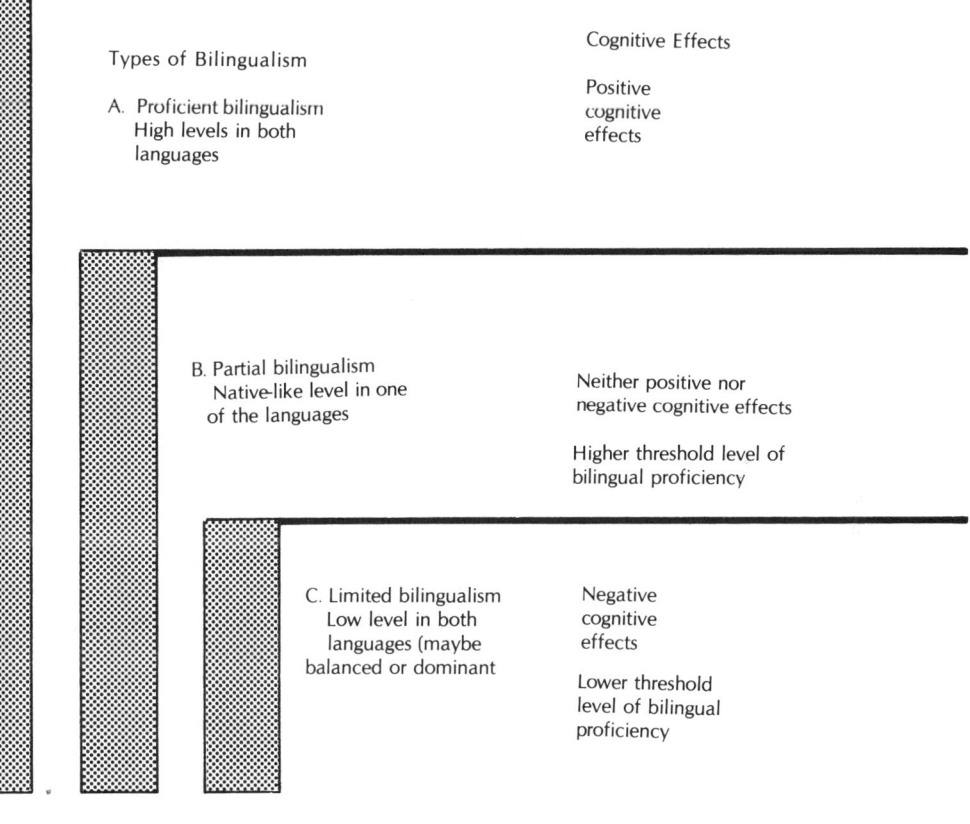

Figure 24. Cognitive Effects of Different Types of Bilingualism. Reprinted with permission from J. Cummins," The Role of Primary Language Development in Promoting Educational Success for Language Minority Student." In *Schooling and Language Minority Students: A Theoretical Framework* (Los Angeles: Evaluation, Dissemination and Assessment Center, California State University, 1981): 39.

In problem-solving abilities in science, Kessler and Quinn (1980) compared monolingual and bilingual pupils—matched on IQ, socioeconomic status, age, grade level, reading scores, and overall grade point average—on hypothesis-generating ability in science and syntactic complexity. Bilinguals were found superior in the quality of hypotheses generated and in scores for written language complexity. In a second study (1981), monolingual pupils were compared to two groups of bilinguals, a group of subtractive bilinguals (nonbalanced bilingualism without schooling in L_1 and a group of additive bilinguals (with the ability to use the two languages successfully in school experiences, particularly developed through at least four years of bilingual schooling—Kindergarten through grade three). The two bilingual groups had greater problem-solving abilities (hypothesis formulation) than the monolingual group, and the additive bilingual, in turn, performed better than the subtractive bilingual pupils.

Díaz (1982) has questioned the validity of Cummins' threshold hypothesis as related to "low" language proficiency and the development of verbal and spacial abilities of kindergarten and first grade Spanish/English children. He argues that a strong relationship between the degree of bilingualism and cognitive abilities exists only before a certain threshold level of proficiency in the second language is achieved.

BILINGUALISM AND ACADEMIC PERFORMANCE

Some of the studies comparing the academic performance of bilinguals and monolinguals have been plagued with the same problems affecting the investigations of the relationship between bilingualism and cognitive abilities. A number of problems stem from the fact that most investigators are educators, less concerned with making contributions to psychology than with solving specific school problems. Sampling bias and a lack of controls were inherent in many of the studies. Many bilingual groups were also members of ethnic minorities, and it was difficult to match them with monolingual groups in educational and sociocultural factors (e.g. Darcy 1963; Jones 1960; Lewis 1960; Macnamara 1966). It was also difficult to assess the academic performance of bilinguals (e.g. math, science, language arts skills) in the minority "weak" language (e.g. Macnamara 1966; Swain and Lapkin 1982).

As a consequence of some of the problems outlined above, the results comparing the performance of bilinguals to monolinguals are mixed. Some studies regard bilingual performance as "inferior," "superior," or not significantly different from that of monolingual controls. For example, Carrow (1957) tested Spanish-English bilinguals against monolinguals in the Southwest and found no differences in oral reading rate, spelling, verbal output, and silent reading comprehension, and vocabulary, although monolinguals were superior in oral reading, listening and speaking vocabulary, and auditory comprehension, reflecting the bilingual's handicap under the time pressure inherent in listening and speech production tasks. Stafford (1968) found no differences in nonverbal problem solving abilities — using geometric figures — between Spanish-English bilinguals and English monolinguals in the Southwest, thus failing to support the notion of bilingualism as a "handicap."

Macnamara (1967) found evidence that Gaelic-English bilinguals in Ireland could perform as well as English monolinguals in computational arithmetic, but not in problem solving involving verbal reasoning. Mosely (1983) conducted a comparative study to examine the academic growth of bilingually instructed Hispanic and non-Hispanic pupils and monolingually (English) instructed counterparts at the fourth and sixth grade levels. After controlling for a number of variables (e.g. socioeconomic status, ethnicity, aptitude, language dominance and use), bilingualism promoted through schooling resulted in greater academic growth (Comprehensive Tests of Basic Skills) in reading vocabulary and mathematical computations at the fourth grade level, and reading comprehension and mathematical concepts at the sixth grade level.

SUMMARY

Most bilingual studies prior to 1960 failed to consider a number of important issues. Peal and Lambert, in a carefully designed study, investigated the effects of bilingualism on intelligence and found that bilinguals demonstrated a superiority over monolinguals in verbal and nonverbal tasks — "agility in concept formation." Other researchers have noted how the level of competence in L_1 and L_2 attained by bilinguals affects cognitive development and academic performance. Cummins' "threshold hypothesis" accounts for the cognitive effects of different types of bilingualism.

Finally, the academic performance of bilinguals and monolinguals was compared. Studies have shown mixed results, partly because of the assessment procedures used. Even though testing problems have plagued this issue, various studies mentioned did find the academic achievement of bilinguals equal to and, at times, superior to their monolingual counterparts.

SUGGESTED READINGS

Albert, M. L. and L. K. Obler. *The Bilingual Brain*. New York: Academic Press, Inc., 1978.

Díaz, R. M. "Thought and Two Languages: The Impact of Bilingualsim on Cognitive Development." In E. W. Gordon, ed., *Review of Research in Education*, vol. 10. Washington, D.C.: American Educational Research Association, 1983, pp. 23–54.

Hornby, P. A. *Bilingualism: Psychological, Social and Educational Implications*. New York: Academic Press, Inc., 1977.

Paradis, M. *Aspects of Bilingualism*. Columbia, S.C.: Hornbean Press, Inc., 1978.

Chapter Twelve _____

BILINGUAL EDUCATION
AND LANGUAGE POLICY ___

INTRODUCTION

There are a number of problems with evaluating and comparing bilingual and monolingual schooling. Bilingual programs can have diverse goals, can serve different student groups (minority and majority children), and are often influenced by "external" factors such as the availability/allocation of funds and degree of parental/community participation. Bilingual education (Title VII) in the United States has gone through various phases since 1968, and today, the challenging possibility exists for creating a language policy which cultivates bilingualism as definitely in the national interest. Bilingual schooling may not be the appropriate educational treatment for all learners, particularly some English-speaking, minority pupils. Decisions regarding the use of a particular type of bilingual program should be based on educational principles, taking into account student input variables and community factors.

RESEARCH IN BILINGUAL EDUCATION

The research evidence regarding the effectiveness of bilingual education appears contradictory. Some differences are due to such factors as the nature of the group being exposed to bilingual education (minority versus majority children), the implicit goals of the program (e.g. assimilation or maintenance of a colonial language), the type of bilingual program (e.g. transitional versus full bilingualism), and the evaluation procedures. Engle (1975), for example, reviewed twenty-four studies which investigated the choice of medium for instruction and concluded that no generalizations were possible given the flaws in research design and/or implementation. She found that while some of the studies showed the L_1 approach to reading produced greater gains (e.g. Modiano 1968; Modiano 1973—Mexico; Ramos et al. 1967—Philippines; Wise 1969—Peru), a comparable number of studies showed the L_2 approach as being more effective (Lambert and Tucker 1972—Canada; Pozzi-Escot 1972—Peru; Malherbe 1946—South Africa).

Although there is a widespread perception that bilingual instruction for minority schoolchildren in the United States is not effective, various well-controlled research studies reviewed by Troike (1978:13) suggest "that a quality bilingual education program can be effective in meeting the goals of equal educational opportunity for minority language children and if a program is not doing so, something is wrong with the program (though the locus of the problem may be external to the instructional program itself)." His review of twelve programs included such sites as San Francisco, California (Chinese/English and Spanish/English), Lafayette Parish, Louisiana (French/English), New York City (Chinese/English and Spanish/English), St. John Valley, Maine (French/English), Rock Point, Arizona (Navajo/English), and Santa Fe, New Mexico (Spanish/English). Cummins (1981) lists successful programs outside the United States which support the bilingual instructional approach for language-minority children—Sodertalje Program for Finnish immigrant children in Sweden, Manitoba-Francophone Project, and the Edmonton Ukrainian-English Bilingual Program.

Chan (1982), coordinator of policy studies at the National Center for Bilingual Research, points out that it is too soon to make definitive judgments about the efficacy of bilingual programs in the United States. There are a number of variables that make it difficult to draw generalizations:

1. Entry-exit criteria vary and are inconsistent. Some programs, for example, only carry through a specified grade level when all students are exited; others might establish a level of achievement to be attained before exiting.
2. Bilingual education programs vary within the classroom. Different teachers will use the native language of students to varying degrees, yet all are supposedly following a bilingual education model.
3. The type of mainstream programs children return to is important as well. Researchers need to assess if students do better or worse in different types of mainstream programs and whether different programs require different levels of English proficiency for student success.
4. Varying school district resources also influence the success of bilingual programs and the success of the transition to mainstream programs.

What counts as "success" is ultimately a philosophical question rather than a technical measurement decision. Should effectiveness be judged only on a linguistic criteria (the degree or pace at which English skills are learned) or evaluated in other areas such as school attendance, self-concept, and native language development?

SUBTRACTIVE AND ADDITIVE FORMS OF BILINGUALISM

Bilingual education for language-minority pupils offers second language development and, at the same time, provides students with the opportunity to acquire subject matter knowledge in the primary language and to stimulate cognitive development. Cummins (1981:44) concludes that research findings "suggest that achievement in English literacy skills is strongly related to the extent of development of L_1 literacy skills." Language-minority children must develop high levels of language proficiency—BICS (basic interperson communication skills) and CALP (cognitive/academic language proficiency)—in both English and the primary language in order to achieve maximum academic benefits from schooling. A high degree of CALP development in the primary language should form the basis for similar proficiency development in L_2 by increasing the range of "comprehension input," and should promote positive adjustment to both majority and minority cultures (*Schooling and Language Minority Students: A Theoretical Framework* 1981: 191–192).

For the ethnolinguistic minority child, however, bilingual education may serve a compensatory function and may result in "subtractive" bilingualism (Lambert 1980). The first language is not developed to the extent that the child can use it to perform cognitive operations. Specifically, this result may mean that some individuals develop less than nativelike CALP in the mother tongue because of the societal status of the home language and insufficicent exposure in the school setting. In certain situations, some individuals experience additional loss of BICS in L_1. In such cases, BICS in L_1 are replaced by BICS in L_2 with no appreciable gains in CALP. Lambert (1980:3) notes that "the hyphenated American child, like the French-Canadian child, embarks on a subtractive bilingual route as soon as he/she enters a school where a high prestige, socially powerful, dominant language like English is introduced either as a language of instruction or as a subject matter."

For the majority children, bilingual education may function as an "enrichment" experience. Lambert (1980:3) describes this process "as an 'additive' form of biingualism, implying that children, with no fear of ethnic/linguistic erosion, can add one or more foreign languages to their accumulating skills and profit immensely — in psychological, social, and even economic domains — from the experience."

BILINGUAL SCHOOLING AND LEGISLATION

Bilingual schooling for students of limited English proficiency has been federally funded since 1968 when Congress established the Bilingual Act, Title VII of the Elementary and Secondary Education Act. The availability of federal funds, also affected a number of states (see Appendixes B and C) who, in turn, revised their statues and allowed the use of languages other than English in school programs.

Arias and Navarro (1981) describe the evolution of Title VII bilingual education in the United States in terms of three major phases:

Phase I, 1968-1974: The Identification of Educational Objectives — Development of programmatic goals regarding the status of the native language (e.g. "maintenance," "transition," "enrichment")

—Development of guidelines for program implementation and evaluation

Phase II, 1974-1979: The capacity building years
—Increase allocation of funds for basic school programs
—Funds for auxiliary services (e.g. material development centers, dissemination and assessment centers, doctoral fellowship programs, and teacher training grant programs)

Phase III, 1978-present: Reflection, deregulation, reauthorization
—Research studies on various aspects of bilingual schooling (e.g. acquisition of English, instructional processes, learner characteristics)
—Evaluation of Title VII projects (i.e. American Institutes for Research, 1978 study; Baker and deKanter of the United States Department of Education, 1982 study)

Bilingual immersion language programs for mainstream Anglo-American children in the United States are available in various languages (French, German, and Spanish and have been described in a number of reports (e.g. Cohen 1976; Hornby 1980; Lambert 1980; Rhodes 1981). The programs appear to be popular in such states as California, Louisiana, Maryland, Massachusetts, Ohio, and Utah. According to Lambert (1980:2-3) immersion education is "an effective means of developing a functionally bilingual citizenry," and "the extent that mainstream children are sensitized to and educated in another language and culture, the better the chances are of developing a fairer, more equitable society" (see Appendix D).

These programs have not been funded nor regulated by federal or state statutes. They have been successful for the most part. The Canadian French immersion programs, according to Swain and Lapkin (1982:85), are successful because of four characteristics:

1. Parental involvement in establishing and insuring the continuation of the immersion program
2. The majority group membership of the participating students and parents
3. Positive attitudes towards French and French Canadians
4. The optional nature of the program

BILINGUAL EDUCATION AND A NATIONAL LANGUAGE POLICY

Bilingual schooling for language-minority children and second language, immersion education efforts for mainstream majority pupils have been separate enterprises in the United States. Since the release of the Presidential Commission on Foreign Language and International Studies report (Perkins, et.al., 1979) increased attention has been directed at the nation's language capabilities. A Joint National Committee on Languages (JNCL) has been established to provide direction in four major areas (Howder 1980:2).

1. Develop professional awareness, especially in the academic community, of the impact of politics on scholastic programs
2. Promote public awareness and information to educate the public about language and area studies
3. Create government awareness to educate legislators about the need for recognition of language needs and the national welfare
4. Encourage union between the language and international studies fields

The 1983 convention theme for the National Association for Bilingual Education was "Bilingualism in the National Interest," emphasizing the nation's need to increase the number of bilingual students in order to promote America's trade, commerce, and international relations. Bilingualism could be developed by two means: educating limited English-speaking pupils in English and the native language, and providing sufficient second/foreign language instruction to English-speaking students.

The importance of a comprehensive language plan is perhaps best represented by the *Sanibel Statement*, drawn initially by a group of educators that met on Sanibel Island, Florida, in September 1981, and prepared a first draft of basic principles for a national (multiple) language policy. The document has undergone various revisions, and it represents a cooperative effort among various organizations: American Association of Colleges for Teacher Education, the American Council on the Teaching of Foreign Languages, the Joint National Committee for Languages, the National Association for Bilingual Education, and Teachers of English to Speakers of Other Languages.

The Sanibel Statement

Whereas the international position of the United States of America necessitates multilingual multicultural awareness in national security, diplomacy and commerce;

Whereas the United States of America occupies a unique international position with special obligations and responsibilities to nurture human understanding in a world characterized by linguistic and cultural differences;

Whereas the United States of America provides education, technical and economic assistance which requires language competence and cultural sensitivity to people and nations throughout the world;

Whereas the United States of America is and has been heavily involved in a world economy dependent upon international trade and commerce as a condition for national economic health, well-being and power;

Whereas the United States of America must increasingly encounter and function within linguistic and culturally different contexts, nationally and internationally;

Whereas the United States of America is and has been, by its history and tradition of openness to immigration, a multilingual multicultural society providing opportunities for a new life as well as refuge from political, religious and economic oppression abroad;

Whereas English is the dominant language of the United States of America, other languages and cultures exist in the land as viable and significant resources deserving respect, preservation and enhancement;

Whereas one's native language is an inherent and intrinsic part of one's self-concept and, therefore, is deserving of the respect of others;

Whereas language and culture, native or otherwise, play crucial roles in human communication and, therefore, are primary means for understanding among human beings;

Whereas intrinsic individual, intellectual, social and economic benefits result from learning other languages and studying other cultures;

Whereas the inadequate utilization of language and cultural resources has the potential to weaken the United States domestically and internationally;

Whereas the United States of America is a signatory to the 1975 *Helsinki Accords*; and

Whereas the United States of America does not have a national multiple language policy:

Now, therefore be it Resolved by this group assembled here at Sanibel Island, Florida, that the United States of America, as a multilingual multicultural society, strive to nurture and advance the human and legal rights of individuals of all languages and cultural backgrounds.

Be it further resolved, that national, state and local governments provide all who reside in the United States of America whose primary language is not English maximum opportunity to learn to function in English, the dominant language of the land.

Be it also resolved, that national, state and local governments provide all who reside in the United States of America, whether they be native or non-native speakers of English, maximum opportunity to learn to function in languages other than English.

Finally, be it resolved, that the Congress and the Executive and Judicial Branches of the United States Government take appropriate action to recognize and promote the principles and resolutions contained in this document; and That State Legislative, Executive and Judicial Bodies exercise their leadership to develop constructive and creative responses to work towards the realization of the principles and resolutions contained in this document.

SOURCE: Reprinted, with permission, TESOL Newsletter, April 1983, p. 4.

Fishman (1981:524–525) reminds us that a national language policy involves a different vision of America.

Languages must be shared as a common good but before they can be shared, they must be saved, loved, treasured. National policy toward this end finally lifts language off of the ethnicity versus anti-ethnicity (lower ethnicity versus higher ethnicity) treadmill and sets them into a new universal orbit in which uniqueness serves not itself but the general good.

A multilingual enrichment policy envisages a multilingual America as being in the public good. We support a multiparty system. We support a multilateral productive machine, i.e., one that operates both in the consumer and in the industrial capacity markets. Our anti-trust laws aim to diversify the economic market place. We can similarly diversify the cultural market place. Other countries do it.

BILINGUAL SCHOOLING AND EDUCATIONAL PRINCIPLES

A final question involves the suitability of bilingual education for all learners — "limited" English-speaking pupils, English-dominant minority children, learning disabled pupils, and slow learners. Within any given student population, differences will exist with regard to a number of learner characteristics. Some students will be gifted; others will possess average academic abilities; and a small number will exhibit learning impairments. Bilingual minority students may be exceptional in many ways, including hearing and visual impairments, communication disorders, and physical handicaps. At present, there apparently is "no consensus on the appropriate treatment of exceptional bilingual children in public school settings" (Ambert and Dew 1982:4). For example, it is not clear on what basis decisions must be made concerning the choice of language for instruction. Ambert (1982:17) argues that the issue of appropriate identification needs to be addressed "prior to the child's referral, evaluation and placement," and that "it is necessary to consider the unique linguistic, cultural, and socioeconomic factors which affect their learning."

English-speaking minority pupils may not be seved adequately by bilingual programs designed for language-minority children with limited English proficiency. For example, English-speaking Hispanic children may need special curriculum and instructional arrangements in light of their special linguistic, cultural, psychological, and socioeconomic characteristics. González (1980) suggests that the special needs of these students could be organized around a set of instructional goals within a comprehensive educational program involving such areas as language development (English langugae skills, Spanish for bilingual pupils), conceptual development in the different subject matters, social arts skills (e.g. interactional skills, leadership training), cultural awareness (e.g. multicultural concepts), and the enhancement of self-concept.

In the case of language-minority (limited English proficient) children, the success of an educational program (e.g. ESL program, transitional or partial bilingual program) may be dependent on such variables as individual student differences and community background factors. This perspective, formulated as the contextual interaction theory, establishes a set of relationships and interactions among a number of variables resulting in differential educational outcomes. The dynamics of the model (Figure 25) can be described as follows:

> . . . community background factors, such as language use patterns in the home and community attitudes towards the student's home language (L_1) and second language (L_2) contribute to student input factors which the child brings to the educational setting. These student input factors, such as L_1 and L_2 proficiency, self-esteem, levels of academic achievement, and motivation to acquire L_2 and maintain L_1, are in constant interaction with instructional treatments, resulting in various cognitive and affective student outcomes. These instructional treatments are primarily determined by such educational input factors as fiscal resources available to the school's staff, knowledge, skills, experiences, expectations, and attitudes, and underlying eduational assumptions or theories (Office of Bilingual Bicultural Education, 1982: p. 4).

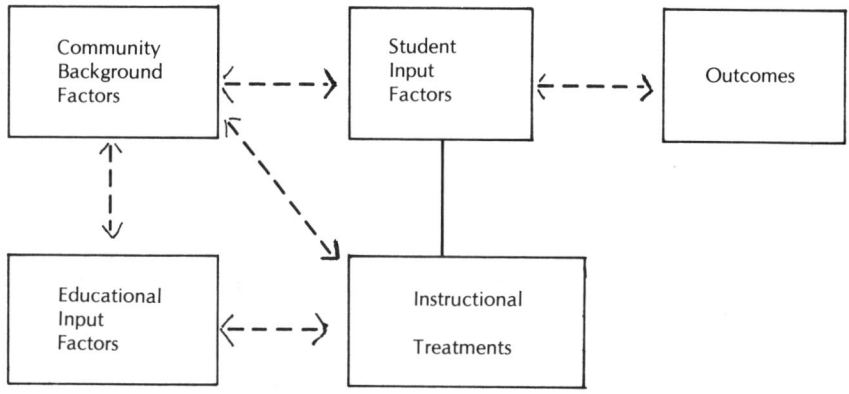

Figure 25. The Interaction Model for Language-Minority Students. From Office of Bilingual Bicultural Education, *Basic Principles for the Education of Language-Minority Students: An Overview*, Sacramento, 1982, p. 4.

The contextual interaction theory is based on the five educational principles supported by research findings and that serve to explain how student input variables interact with instructional treatments and contribute to various educational goals, including the acquisition of English language skills, academic achievement, and positive psychosocial development. The five principles, listed below, are interrelated in nature and should be considered in the design and implementation of instructional programs, including bilingual program models, for language-minority pupils:

1. For bilingual students, the degree to which proficiencies in both L_1 and L_2 are developed is positively associated with academic achievement
2. Language proficiency is the ability to use language for academic purposes and basic communicative tasks
3. For language-minority students, the development of the

primary language skills necessary to complete academic tasks serves as the basis for similar proficiency in English

4. Acquisition of basic communicative competence in a second language is a function of comprehensible second language input and a supportive affective environment

5. The perceived status of students affects the interactions between teachers and students and among students themselves; in turn, student outcomes are affected

Thus, the use of a particular educational treatment – bilingual, ESL, "immersion" in English – may result in differential educational outcomes for a particular group of language-minority students due to differences in community background factors, educational input factors, and student input variables. The choice of a particularly instruction treatment should be based on a series of educational principles.

Bilingual schooling for language-majority pupils is generally viewed as an enriching, optional, educational experience. It does not serve the compensatory function of bilingual education for language-minority children, who may experience a loss of proficiency in the first language through schooling. Majority students in immersion classes are highly motivated and bring positive expectations to the second language experience. Parents and teachers are highly supportive, and children are praised for their growth in the second language. Immersion classes are homogeneous with respect to the students' native language, and students are not expected to perform linguistically at the level/norm of a native speaker. Within this type of educational environment, it may be possible for "below average" majority students to acquire a functional proficiency – speaking and understanding – in the second language (e.g. French) "to the same extent as average and above average students in (a total early immersion) program" (Genesee 1976:23). Bruck (1979) has also noted that English-speaking children with special learning disabilities can progress as well in an early immersion program as they would in a regular monolingual English program. An immersion program may even be the more appropriate way to teach "slow learners" or learning disabled children a second language than the traditional approach (i.e. French as a subject).

SUMMARY

The contradictory research findings regarding bilingual education may be the result of differences in the (1) nature of groups, (2) implicit goals of programs, and (3) evaluation procedures. Various research studies reviewed noted that bilingual education programs can meet the goals of language-minority children; if they do not, this failure may be due to the program, not the concept of bilingual education. At the same time, Chan, from the National Center for Bilingual Research, has pointed out that it may be too soon to make definitive statements about the effectiveness of bilingual programs because (1) entry-exit criteria vary and are inconsistent, (2) programs vary within the classroom, (3) the mainstream program the children return to is important, and (4) school district resources vary.

High levels of language proficiency (BICS and CALP) must be met in both English and the first langugae to achieve maximum academic benefits from schooling; however, for the minority-language children in bilingual programs, education may serve a compensatory function and may result in "subtractive" bilingualism, with less than nativelike CALP in L_1. On the other hand, for the majority children, bilingual education may function as an "enriching" experience.

Three major phases of the evaluation of bilingual education were outlined. It was noted that bilingual immersion programs for English-speaking children exist in various languages. The success of the Canadian French immersion programs was largely due to parental involvement and the optional nature of the program.

Increased attention has been directed to this nation's language capabilities. The Joint National Committee on Languages (JNCL) was established to provide direction for a language policy. The *Sanibel Statement* demonstrates the importance of a comprehensive language plan. In fact, as Fishman points out, a national language policy forces us to view America in a different light. Title VII-type bilingual schooling, however, may not be the appropriate educational treatment for all learners, particularly some English-speaking minority pupils. These pupils, as well as those with learning disabilities, may require different instructional treatments beyond language considerations. The contextual interaction theory is apparently a useful framework for examining interrelationships among the various factors affecting the educational outcomes of language-minority pupils.

SUGGESTED READINGS

Appleton, N. *Cultural Pluralism in Education.* New York: Longman, Inc., 1983.

Baker, K. A. and A. A. de Kanter, *Bilingual Education.* Lexington, Mass.: Lexington Books, 1983.

Epstein, N. *Language, Ethnicity and the Schools.* Washington, D. C.: The George Washington University, Institute for Educational Leadership, 1977.

Greenberg, J., A. Mazzoco, and D. Sauve. *Guide to Current Research.* Rosslyn, Va.: National Clearinghouse for Bilingual Education, 1980.

Leibowitz, A. H. *The Bilingual Education Act: A Legislative Analysis.* Rosslyn, Va.: National Clearinghouse for Bilingual Education, InterAmerica Research Associates, Inc., 1980.

Padilla, R., ed. *Bilingual Education and Public Policy in the United States, Bilingual Education,* vol. 1. Ipsilanti, Mich.: Department of Foreign Languages and Bilingual Studies, Eastern Michigan University, 1979.

Paulston, C. B. *Bilingual Education, Theories and Issues.* Rowley, Mass.: Newbury House Publishers, Inc., 1980.

United States Commission in Civil Rights. *A Better Chance to Learn: Bilingual Education.* Washington, D. C., 1975.

APPENDIXES

APPENDIX A. THE LANGUAGE OF THE SPANISH/ENGLISH BILINGUAL*

The Spanish and English the bilingual child brings to school may not be the "standard" language used in the school's textbooks or by the teacher. A child acquires the particular form of a language he or she hears at home. The variety of Spanish, marked regionally and socially, spoken at home is the one the child will learn. If the family also uses English at home and the variety of English is strongly influenced by Spanish pronunciation or grammar, the child acquires that particular variety of English.

Some children can switch from one language to another when speaking. This ability is known as code switching, which may occur in certain domains only, and is not an example of a speaker confusing his two languages or speaking a random mixture of words with no grammatical base. Code switching is a common phenomenon among Spanish/English bilinguals. It has a significant influence on teachers' expectations and therefore on the learning environment. The teacher in a culturally diverse classroom should understand that code switching is not a random mixing of English and Spanish words and that it may not reflect ignorance of vocabulary in either language. Code switching is a complex process carrying meaning.[1] Recent research suggests that subtle social and psychological factors may be involved.[2] The following sentences are cases in point: "On Sunday voy a ir a rezar." "Don't be a dummy, así no se hace."

Code switching may be used to convey important social information, such as personal feeling, confidentiality, and emphasis: "I would like to eat it, pero es que me hace daño"; "No hombre, I got real sick y me llevaron al hospital." Some things are more readily recalled in one language than the other, perhaps because that language was used in the situation being discussed. Sentences like "Dile a José that we need a ride" and "Estoy con Mónica y Lupe en el drugstore" are examples of this phenomenon. Occasionally there is a slip of the tongue or unfamiliarity with a particular word or expression: "No me dijo, she was desperate, you know." "Cuando van shopping se visten muy bien." You have to realize que no me gusta llegar tarde."

One must remember that words carry culturally specific associations, attitudes, and values, and teachers should appreciate the divergence in their pupils' communicative strategies. Code switching does not mean a child's language is "degenerate" or "structurally underdeveloped." Some form of code switching occurs whenever different language groups come in close, sustained contact.

---

*From A. G. Ramírez, et al. *CERAS Spanish English Balance Tests* Center for Educational Research at Stanford, School of Education, Stanford University, August 1976, Appendix A, pp. 15-28.

---

1. John J. Gumperz and Eduardo Hernández-Chávez, "Bilingualism, Bidialectalism, and Classroom Interaction," in *Functions of Language in the Classroom*, ed. by Courtney Cazden, Vera P. John, and Dell Hymes (New York: Teachers College Press, 1972), p. 98.
2. Ibid., p. 93.

In describing the speech of Spanish/English bilingual pupils with reference to the "standard," one might analyze the differences in terms of the various elements that constitute a language: (1) phonology—the sound system of a language; (2) morphology—the study of the structure of words and their formation; (3) lexicon—the vocabulary or words of a language; and (4) syntax—the way words are related to each other in a sentence or the way they are arranged. Differences or deviations from the "standard" can occur at any one of these four levels of language and may be attributable to one or more of three sources: dialect, interference, or developmental errors.

1. *Dialect.* A "nonstandard" dialect can intrude on the "standard" dialect (of either English or Spanish).
2. *Interference.* One language is intruded in the second (the English in the Spanish, the Spanish in the English)
3. *Development errors.* Children learning a second language may go through developmental stages resembling those characteristic of children learning their first language.

Pinpointing the cause of a deviation inevitably involves guesswork. Deviations may have multiple causes. "They won't have no fun" looks like a negative common in some "nonstandard" English dialects, but it may also reflect the influence of the "standard" Spanish negative (e.g. no-nada, no-ningún). It may also be a developmental error, for with respect to negative quantifiers such as nothing or nobody, the multiple negative can be a simplification occurring in a child's language.[3] Furthermore, what appears to be interference may actually be a dialectical variation: "mi hermana hizo un cake" (my sister made a cake).

The following is two dialogues involving children bilingual in Spanish and English, with an analysis of the deviations from "standard" speech. The first, in Spanish, comes from the home domain; the second, in English, from the school domain. These are not actual conversations, but the dialogues serve to illustrate the interplay of various linguistic features.

Home Domain

Madre:-¿Qué pasa, hijo, no tienes habre?

Ricky:-No mu*n*cho (2),[4], 'amá(2) me duele el est*ógamo*(2).

What's the matter, son, aren't you hungry?

Not very, Mom. I have a stomach ache.

---

3. Paul Kiparski, "Linguistic Universals and Linguistic Change," in *Universals in Linguistic Theory*, ed. by E. Bach and R. T. Harnus (New York: Holt, Rinehart and Winston, 1968), pp. 171-202.

4. Numbers in parentheses refer to the charts and explanation following the dialogues.

Abuelita:-Ricardo, se dice
estómago,
no estógamo(2).

Ricky:-Nada más la carne, ¿O.K.,
'buelita(2)?

Abuelita: — Cristina, el niño quiere
la tetera.

Ricky, one says "estómago"
and not "estógamo."

Only the meat, O.K., Grandma?

Cristine, the baby wants his
bottle.

Cristina:-Hey Ricky, ¿qué te dió la
Patterson para English(5)?

Madre:-¿Les dieron los report
cards ahora?

Cristina:-Yeah, y Ricky flonkeó(7)
dos cursos. Por eso no
tenes(10) hambre, ¿verdad?

Ricky:-Nobody asked you, so keep
out of it, mechuda, it's
just that the vieja Patterson
hates me.

Hey Ricky, what did Mrs.
Patterson give you in English?

Did they give you your report
cards today?

Yeah, and Ricky flunked two
subjects. That's why you're not
hungry, right?

Nobody asked you, so keep
of it, nosy, it's just that
old Patterson hates me.

Abuelita:-Nunca maldigas a tu
maestra. A la maestra se le da el
mismo respeto que a los
padres. Eso es muy importante,
y no estén peleando en la mesa.

Padre:-Ah, pues eso sí que
agarraste(3) buenas marcas(7)
en deportment, ¿pero qué pasó
con tu English(5) y cencia(2)?

Ricky:-She speaks English(5) too
fast, y no la entiendo.

Never curse your teacher. It
is very important that you
respect your teachers as you
do your parents. And don't
fight at the table.

Well, you did get good grades
in deportment, but what
happened with your English
and science?

She speaks English too fast
and I don't understand her.

Padre:-Bueno, parece que también
necesitas más estudio. Ve
ponte a hacer tu homework
'horita(2) mismo. Voy a ir
a l'oficina(1) a hablar con
tu teacher(5) mañana. ¿Por
qué no me dijo tu mayestra(1)
que tenías trouble con tu
English(5) y cencia(2)?

Ricky:-She did, esas eran las
notas en English(5) que
saineabas(7).

Well, it seems that you also
need to study more. Go do
your homework right noiw.
Tomorrow I'm going to go to
the office to talk to your
teacher. Why didn't your
teacher tell me that you were
having trouble with English
and science?

She did. Those were the notes
in English that you signed.

Deviations from "Standard" Spanish

Source	Phonological 1	Morphological 2		Lexical 3	Syntactic 4
		Linguistic Level			
Dialectal	mayestra l'oficina	'amá 'horita 'buelita	estógamo cencia muncho	agarraste	
	5	6		7	8
Interference	English teasher			saineabas marcas flonkeó	
	9	10		11	12
Developmental		tenes			

Explanation of Deviations

1. Epenthesis—the addition of the sound "y" between two vowels: maestra/mayestra.

    The article *le* elides to *l'* before singular nouns that begin with strong vowels: la oficina/l'oficina.

2. Aphaeresis—the omission of an initial sound or syllable: mamá/'amá, ahorita/'horita, abuelita/'buelita.

    Metathesis—transposition of two sounds in a word: estómago/estógamo.

    Monophthongization—reduction of a stressed diphthong into one vowel: ciencia/cencia.

    Archaism—the use of archaic words, phrases, or expressions in present-day Spanish: mucho/muncho.

3. Semantic shift of the verb. The meaning of *agarrar* has been extended beyond its general usage: use of *agarrar* instead of *recibir*.

5. The lack of differentiation in Spanish between the sounds/i/as in "meet" and/I/ as in "bit"; *I*nglish/*E*nglish. Spanish interference in the production of the sound "ch": teacher/teasher.

7. English words integrated into the lexical system of Spanish with the same meaning in English extended into Spanish: signed/saineabas, marks/marcas, flunked/flonkeó.

10. Overgeneralization of a rule—a stage in language acquisition. In this case,

the child treats *tener* as a regular verb without making the necessary alteration in the stem *ten* to *tien*: tienes/tenes.

School Domain

Teacher: Class, turn to page sixty-three and let's talk about the story we read yesterday. Cristina, do you remember what Ann's father is in the story?

Cristina: He is ___(8) postman.

Teacher: He is a postman. Yes, that's right. What do postmen do, Jorge?

Jorge: Post*mans*(10) bring*ed*(10) *cards*(7).

Teacher: Postmen bring letters. Very good. Carlos, was Ann's mother angry with her?

Carlos: No, she ___(12) just worried.

Teacher: Good. She was just worried. Lucy, why is Ann not playing with her friends?

Lucy: *This*(5) is because *he's*(8) thinking what to do with the *yellow*(5) package.

Teacher: Because she's thinking what to do with the yellow package. Very good. Now Cristina, can you tell us what Ann's father is doing on page sixty?

Cristina: The father is put ___(2) on *he*(6) *sh*oes(5).

Teacher: The father is putting on his shoes. Correct. How many of Ann's friends are in her school club, Jorge?

Jorge: *Three*(5) of Ann's friends are *on*(12) the *e*school(5) club.

Teacher: Three of Ann's friends are in the school club. Very good. Carlos, can you tell us why Ann's mother gave Tippy a bath?

Carlos: Because ___(8)is dirty.

Teacher: Because he is dirty. Excellent. What are Jane and Tom doing on page fifty-seven, Lucy?

Lucy: They ___(8) *washing*(7) *the*(6) teeth.

Teacher: They are brushing their teeth. That's right. Cristina, why do people wash dishes?

Cristina: Because *if no*(7), they get dirty.

Teacher: If they don't wash them, they get dirty. Good. Jorge, what must Ann do after school?

Jorge: *She*(5) must do *a*(7) work.

Teacher: She must do work around the house. Good. Carlos, who wants to do the errands for mother?

Carlos: *Nobody no*(4) want__(2) them.

Teacher: Nobody wants to do them. That's right. Lucy, how do we know Ann's brother is sick?

Lucy: They ___(4) going to *operate*(7) him.

Teacher: he is going to have an operation. Excellent. We all did very well today. Well, it's almost time for recess. Put your chairs back in place, please.

Deviations from "Standard" English

Source	Phonological 1	Morphological 2	Lexical 3	Syntactic 4
		Grammatical Level		
Dialectal		The father is put on his shoes. Nobody want them.		Nobody no wants them. They going to operate on him.
Interference	5 *d*is *t*ree jellow *ch*oes *e*school *ch*e	6 They are brushing the teeth. The father is putting on her shoes.	7 cards operate a work They are washing their If no	8 Because is dirty. This is because he's thinking. He is postman. They brushing.
Developmental	9	10 postman Postmen bringed letters.	11	12 No, she just worried. Three of Ann's friends are on the school club.

Explanation of Deviations

2.   Uninflected main verb with *to be*: The father is putting on his shoes./ The father is put on his shoes.
     Incorrect third-person singular verb: Nobody wants them./Nobody want them.

4.   Double negative: Nobody wants them./Nobody no wants them.
     Omission of the verb *to be*: They are going to operate him./They going to operate him.

5.   "th" sound replaced by "d":   this/dis.
     "th" sound replaced by "t":   three/tree.
     "y" sound replaced by "j":   yellow/jellow.
     "sh" sound replaced by "ch": shoes/choes, she/che.
     The "e" sound (with Spanish pronunciation) is placed before a word with an initial "s" followed by a consonant: school/eschool.

6.   In Spanish the definite article is used with parts of the body when the possessor is obvious: They are brushing their teeth./They are brushing the teeth.

Confusion of third-person possessive pronouns (his/her/their are all expressed by "su" in Spanish): The father is putting on his shoes./The father is putting on her shoes.

7. Literal translation from Spanish: cartas/cards, Lo van a operar./They are going to operate him, si no/if no, un trabajo/a work, Se lavan los dientes./They are washing their teeth.

8. Noncorrespondence in the use of articles: El es cartero/He is postman.

Third-person pronoun (because in Spanish the verb is often used without a pronoun, the Spanish speaker has to learn to make the he/she/it distinction): Because he is dirty./Because is dirty. This is because she's thinking./This is because he's thinking.

Omission of auxiliary verb: They are brushing./They brushing.

10. Overgeneralization of pluralization rules: postmans/postmen.

Overgeneralization of past tense rules: bringed/brought.

12. Omission of verb: No. she was just worried./No, she just worried.

Confusion of preposition: in the school club/on the school club.

APPENDIX B. 1981 STATE BILINGUAL EDUCATION LEGISLATION*

Statute Mandates Bilingual Education

Alaska
California
Connecticut
Illinois
Indiana
Iowa
Massachusetts
Michigan
New Jersey
Texas
Virgin Islands
Washington
Wisconsin

State Permits Bilingual Education

American Samoa
Arizona
Colorado
Kansas
Maine
Minnesota
New Hampshire
New Mexico
New York
Oregon
Puerto Rico
South Dakota
Trust Territory of the
  Pacific Islands
Utah

Legislation Under Development

Mariana Islands
Rhode Island

No Statute

Alabama
Arkansas
Delaware
District of Columbia
Florida
Georgia
Hawaii
Idaho
Kentucky
Louisiana
Maryland
Mariana Islands
Mississippi
Missouri
Montana
Nebraska
Nevada
North Carolina
North Dakota
Ohio
Oklahoma
Pennsylvania
Rhode Island
South Carolina
Tennessee
Vermont
Virginia
Wyoming

SOURCE: *NCBE FORUM*, vol. V, no. 6 (June, 1982), p. 5.

APPENDIX C: NEW YORK STATE AID FOR LIMITED ENGLISH PROFICIENT PUPILS*

Part 154 Apportionment for Pupils with Limited English Proficiency is effective as of July 10, 1981, is new subdivision 22 of Section 3602 of the Education Law. The new Regulations are provided below in their entirety:

AMENDMENT TO REGULATIONS OF THE COMMISSIONER OF EDUCATION

Part 154

APPORTIONMENT FOR PUPILS WITH
LIMITED ENGLISH PROFICIENCY

Section 154.1 Scope of Part. The purpose of this Part is to establish standards for the use of funds made available by the Legislature to provide financial assistance to school districts having pupils of limited English proficiency. In accordance with the provisions of this Part, each school district receiving such funds shall provide a program of bilingual education or English as a second language for pupils identified as having limited English proficiency.

154.2 Definitions. (a) Pupils with limited English proficiency shall mean pupils who by reason of foreign birth or ancestry, speak a language other than English, and

(1) either understand and speak little or no English; or

(2) score below the statewide reference point or its equivalent on an English language assessment instrument approved by the commissioner.

(b) English as a second language instruction shall mean an instructional program designed to teach English to pupils with limited English proficiency.

(c) Bilingual education shall mean a program of instruction, designed for pupils with limited English proficiency, in which there is instruction given in English, including English as a second language, and in the native language.

(d) Exceptions. (1) A school district, which is subject to a court order or a party to a pre-existing agreement with an appropriate Federal agency requiring programs substantially equivalent to or in excess of those required under these regulations, will not be required to comply with these regulations and will be eligible for funds under this Part so long as the district is in compliance with the court order or agreement.

(2) For the 1981–82 school year, a program may be approved which is not in full compliance with these regulations so long as the district is providing services to the eligible pupils for whom and is to be paid, pro-

---

*SOURCE: Bureau of Bilingual Education, State Education Department, Albany, New York

vided that such services are determined by the Commissioner to be appropriate services, and provided further that the Commissioner finds that the district will be in full compliance with these regulations by the 1982–83 school year.

154.3 Program requirements. In order to quality for state aid for instruction provided to pupils with limited English proficiency, a school district shall meet the following criteria:

(a) Identification of eligible pupils. To be eligible for the program each pupil shall be identified, by use of an English language assesment instrument approved by the commissioner, as a pupil with limited English proficiency.

(b) Annual evaluation. A pupil's proficiency in the English language shall be measured, at least annually, in order to determine further participation in a program of bilingual education and/or English as a second language. The eligibility of a pupil for such instruction shall continue until such time as the pupil achieves a level of English language skills which will enable the pupil to perform sucessfully in classes in which instruction is given only in English.

(c) Types of programs. (1) Each school district which has an enrollment of twenty or more eligible pupils with limited English proficiency of the same grade level assigned to a building, all of whom have the same native language which is other than English, shall provide such pupils with bilingual education programs, including instruction in English as a second language.

(2) Each school district which has any eligible pupils with limited English proficiency of the same grade level assigned to a building, but which does not have twenty of such pupils with the same native langugae which is other than English, shall provide a program of English as a second language, and may also provide a program of bilingual education to such pupils.

154.4 District plan. Each district which is entitled to funds under this Part shall submit to the department a district plan to meet the educational needs of pupils with limited English proficiency, no later than September 1, 1981, and July 1 of each year thereafter. The plan shall:

(a) specify the instructional services to be provided;
(b) provide for the coordination of local, state, and federal funds;
(c) provide evidence that instruction is provided by personnel holding the appropriate certification; and
(d) provide any other information required by the commissioner relative to the planning, administration, funding, or evaluation of the program.

APPENDIX D: Immersion and Partial Immersion Language Programs in U.S. Elementary Schools, January 1981. Information compiled by the Center for Applied Linguistics Elementary School Foreign Language Project, 3520 Prospect Street, N.W., Washington, D.C. 20007 (202) 298-9292

School District/City	Comments	No. of Schools	No. of Pupils	No. of Teachers	Languages	No. of Aides	Contacts
Alpine (UT) School District	-Started 1979 -Full immersion	1	Grade 1 Combination Grades 2 and 3	2	Spanish	1	Paul Hanson, Principal Cherry Hill Elementary School 250 East 1650 South Orem, Utah 84057 801/225-3387
Chicago (IL) Public Schools	-Magnet School -Four more such schools opening during school year 1979-1980 -Partial immersion	1	450 total		French German Italian Spanish		Edwin Cudecki, Director Bureau of Foreign Languages Chicago Board of Education 228 N. LaSalle Street, Room 858 Chicago, IL 60601 312/641-4048
Cincinati (OH) Public Schools	-Started 1974 -Partial immersion -Maint. biling. ed -Straight immers. in K -Local funding only -artic. w/jr. high, 1979	4 Spanish 3 French 1 German 1 Mid. Sch. --- 9 total	900 Spanish 480 French 580 German 265 Mid. Sch. --- 2225 total	76 (approx. total)	Spanish French German	German - 1 Spanish - 1/2	Mimi Met Bilingual Program Coordinator Cincinnati Public Schools 230 East 9th Street Cincinnati, OH 45202 513/369-4937
Culver City, CA	-Started 1971 -No outside funding -Magnet School	1	149 total	5 (full-time)	Spanish	Some parent volunteers	Eugene Ziff, Principal La Ballona Elementary School 10915 Washington Boulevard Culver City, CA 90230 213/839-4061 Ext.229
Hayward (CA) Unified School District	-Started fall 1975 -Magnet School -Local funds only -Strong parent support (money raisers) -Principal strongly supportive	1	81 total	3	Spanish	Some parent volunteers	Violet Fier, Spanish Coordinator Baywood Elementary School Hayward Unified School District Box 5000 Hayward, CA 94545 415/881-2792
Holliston, MA	-Started 1979 -Full immersion after the St. Lambert model Grades K and 1	1	27 total	1	French	1	James Palladino, Principal Andrews School School Street Holliston, MA 01746 617/429-5211 617/429-1601

APPENDIX D: Immersion and Partial Immersion Language Programs in U.S. Elementary Schools, January 1981. Information compiled by the Center for Applied Linguistics Elementary School Foreign Language Project, 3520 Prospect Street, N.W., Washington, D.C. 20007 (202) 298-9292

School District/City	Comments	No. of Schools	No. of Pupils	No. of Teachers	Languages	No. of Aides	Contacts
Milwaukee (WI) Public Schools	-Started 1977, Magnet Prog. -Begin with kindergarten (4-year olds) -K-12 program (subject content taught in 2nd language in secondary schools) -Full immersion after St. Lambert Model	2 total German K-6 French K-3 Spanish K-1	180 German 130 French 75 Spanish ———— 385 total	16	German French Spanish	10	Helena Anderson Milwaukee Public Schools P.O. Box Drawer 10K Milwaukee, WI 53201 414/475-8305
Montgomery County (MD) Public Schools	-French started 1974 -Small outside funding -Articulation with junior high: one subject course immersion pupils	1 French	160 French	6 French	French	1 position (college volunteers, occasionally parents), high school interns	Gabriel Jacobs, Principal Four Corners Elementary School 325 University Boulevard West Silver Spring, MD 20901 301/593-1125
	-Spanish immersion	1 Spanish	42 Spanish	2 Spanish	Spanish		Louise Rosenberg, Principal Rock Creek Forest Elementary School 8330 Grubb Road Chevy Chase, MD 301/589-0005
Pittsburgh (PA) Public Schools	-Magnet Program -Started 1979 in grades 1 and 2 -Grade 3 added in fall 1980	3 total	52 German 51 Spanish 60 French ———— 163 total	2 German 2 Spanish 2 French ———— 6 total	German Spanish French		Leonard E. Glassner Supervisory Instructional Specialist Pittsburgh Board of Education 341 S. Bellefield Avenue Pittsburgh, PA 15213 412/622-3958
Plattsburg, NY	-Started 1976 -Full immersion after the St. Lambert model and emphasizing open-education principles	1	70 total	4	French	(occasionally college student/parent) 1 volunteer, 4 hours/day	Khorshed Randeria, Head Teacher Sibley Laboratory School French Language Immersion Program (FLIP) Plattsburgh State University College Plattsburgh, NY 12901 518/564-3031

School District/City	Comments	No. of Schools	No. of Pupils	No. of Teachers	Languages	No. of Aides	Contacts
San Diego (CA) City Schools	-Title VII funded -Different program models in different schools	5 (includes one junior high school)	850 total	35 total	French Spanish	35 (native speakers)	Harold B. Wingard Curriculum Specialist, Foreign Language Education San Diego City Schools 4100 Normal Street San Diego, CA 92103 714/293-8440
Tulsa (OK) Public Schools	-Starting Fall 1981) -Kindergarten immersion	1		1			Patricia Buckley Foreign Language Instructional Assistant Tulsa Public Schools P.O. Box #45208 Tulsa, OK 74145
Washington, D.C.	-Started 1966 -independent school -Double immersion, 1/2 time each English/French, English/Spanish, throughout elementary -Nursery through grade 12: Subjects through two working languages. -Pupils 85 nationalities; staff 35 nationalities	1	530	60 full-time equivalents	French Spanish		Dorothy Bruchholz Goodrran, Director Washington International School 3100 Macomb Street, N.W Washington, D.C. 20008 202/244-0959
Woodburn, OR	-Trilingual district Russian/Spanish/English -"Old Believer" Russian population -Spanish population -ESL in grade 1, decrease native language gradually until junior high	2			Russian Spanish		Ruthann Audritsh Curriculum Director 965 North Boones Ferry Road Woodburn, OR 97071 503/981-9555

APPENDIX E. HIGHLIGHTS OF BILINGUAL PROGRAMS

St. John Valley Program Shows Impact*

One of the longest sustained records of impact in the U.S. belong to the St. John Valley Bilingual Program in Maine. Begun in 1970-71 in a French-speaking area in which students had a long history of achieving below grade level, the program has brought students up to near – or in most cases, *above* – grade level in every one of the past eight years of its operation.

In 1969, the last year before the program started, 80 percent of 4th and 5th graders scored below grade level on the SAT language subtest, and the percentage of students falling below grade level in arithmetic was 80 percent or more in each of several years. In grades 3-6, the mean on the SAT was below grade level for all but one subtest in one grade. By the sixth grade, the median score in science was 1.5 years below grade level.

Now in its eighth year of operation, the program has been implemented in grades K-11 in three school districts located in Frenchville-St. Agatha, Madawaska, and Van Buren, Maine. Figures for 1974-75 show that students in the Title VII – funded program achieved *average or above average stanines in all subject areas* on the Metropolitan Achievement Test in grades 1-4. The progress has continued at the secondary level as well, with project students scoring at the 4-6 stanine range in reading, math, and language arts on the SRA Achievement Test. Title VII students averaged .5 to 1.0 years above students in regular classes on the SRA in grades 2-4.

An attitude survey of sixth graders in Madawaska in 1977 showed nearly twice as many students in the bilingual in the Title VII-funded program (33%) strongly agreed with the statement "I feel proud to be French speaking," though attitudes toward school showed little difference. Seventh-graders, however, showed no attitude difference toward language. School drop-out rates in the St. John Valley have long been negligible, so that program effect in this aspect is not significant.

Spotlight on a Navajo Bilingual Bicultural Education Program by Benny Hale, Title VII Director, Pine Hill Schools*

The Pine Hill Schools, situated in Northwestern New Mexico, are run by a five-member school board that serves the Ramah Navajo Reservation which has a population of approximately 1800.

The Title VII Program consists of a teacher training component, a student activities component, media support services, and a parent and community par-

*SOURCE: *NCBE FORUM*, vol. 1, issue 6 (August, 1978), p. 2.

*SOURCE: *NCBE FORUM*, vol. 1, issue 6 (August, 1978), p. 3.

tlcipation component. The program has helped to provide bilingual education to a school population composed of 95 percent Navajo students. In addition, it has helped train teachers and teacher's aides and now has seven individuals who have been certified through the on-site Teacher Training Program.

As part of the latter component, the elementary school has a classroom called

The second broad objective was to retain and reinforce Navajo cultural parents (paid with Title VII and Title IV-A money) who teach Navajo children about their traditions, in particular Navajo Culture, Navajo Arts and Crafts, and other Native American cultural traditions. Kindergarten through sixth grade students come to the PT/RR classroom three hours each week. The students engage in a great variety of activities. Their arts and crafts projects include rug weaving, sandpainting, beading, pottery, sash belt weaving, etc.

Navajo science explores beliefs and traditions regading, for example weather, animals, plants, insects, astronomy, and nature in general.

Navjo math lessons cover the Navajo method of counting and measurement and explore the different geometric figures and symbols embodied in Navajo rug weaving. (Note: Navajo language arts and literacy are taught within the K–6 classrooms).

Navajo values are discussed in class, and both material and behavioral values are covered. Values tie into traditional uses of natural resources and both are interrelated in class work. For example, upper level students study the controversy surrounding the operation of the Black Mesa coal mine, and the Four Corners power plants.

The PT/RR classroom is directed by a bilingual teaching professional who coordinates the K–6 instruction and also provides training for the parent teachers in classroom observation and management, Navajo literacy, and instructional methodology.

The creation of the parent-teacher classroom was a response to the needs of individual students and families, and a realization that Navajo culture must be a part of the Navajo child's education if our children were to build a strong self-image and a sense of pride in their Navajo ways.

To meet these needs, two broad objectives were set for the PT/RR. The first was to involve the community, especially parents, in the education of their chldren and to create a dynamic school/parent/student relationship. In addition to the full-time parent-teachers, community members are regularly brought into the PT/RR classroom to work with the students as "cultural consultants."

The second broad objective was to retain and reinforce Navajo cultural values, beliefs and traditions by the teaching of Navajo history, law and government, religion, economics, arts and crafts, etc. To meet this objective, the Pine Hill Bilingual/Bicultural Education Model was designed over several years. That curriculum model is currently being implemented, and the Parent Teacher Resource Room is a vital component of its implementation.

Although the PT/RR component is just ending its second year of operation, we feel it has already shown considerable success. With continued improvement we expect it will be one of the twin pillars of education for Ramah's children, a combination of "the best elements of our Navajo traditions. . . with the best of the Anglo world. . . We want to surpass 'traditional' Anglo American schooling. . . (through) a school which will help us create new cultural patterns based on the finest things we have to offer the humanistic quality of our traditional ways." (from the Goals of the Ramah Navajo School Board).

Study of Bilingual Education in Colorado, by Ross P. Goldsmith*

At the request of the Colorado Department of Education's Bilingual Education Unit, an evaluation was conducted of programs in grades K–3 funded during the 1979–80 school year under the state's Bilingual Bilcultural Education Act. This is the third in a series of such studies. The evaluation attempted to determine the extent to which students did better in the bilingual program than they would have done without it.

Forty of the 43 Colorado school districts with bilingual programs participated in the study. Approximately 10,000 students were in these programs, with an almost even ratio of linguistically different and nonlinguistically different students.

The report focuses on the success of the programs in:

• Improving performance in comprehension, reading, writing, and speaking the English language.
• Improving school attendance and reducing the drop-out rate.
• Developing some positive self-concepts and attitudes.
• Increasing parental involvement in the school program.

Methodology

The general design of this study was to compare how well students did in the program with an estimate of how well they would have been expected to do without the program. Since no control groups are available for this sort of comparison, a norm-referenced evaluation design was employed, using pre-test scores of participating students to generate expected post-test scores against which to compare actual post-test scores.

Gains of three normal curve equivalents (NCEs) between pre- and post-test scores was the criterion used to determine the program's success. This standard has been used extensively in other evaluations of programs designed to improve the academic skills of low-achieving students.

The implicit assumption of the evaluation model and decision criteria employed is that no gains would be made by the participating students were it not for the bilingual program itself. Yet, there is a large body of literature that suggests that Mexican American students (most minority language students in the Colorado program are Mexican American) in traditional academic programs lose

*SOURCE: *NCBE FORUM*, vol. 5, no. 7 (July/August, 1982), pp. 2–3).

ground over time when compared with their Anglo peers. Thus it can be argued that programs that prevent Mexican American students from falling further behind, even though the students evidence no gains, might be judged effective in reversing historical patterns of Mexican American student achievement.

Findings

Improved performance in comprehension, reading, writing, and speaking the English language. Overall, 87 percent of the programs that reported grade levels showed gains or maintenance of achievement for linguistically different students (LDS), while 89 percent reported gains or maintenance of academic achievement for non-linguistically different students (NLDS).

The results were also broken down by grade. It was found that 75 percent of the schools reporting kindergarten data showed substantial gains in excess of seven NCEs for both linguistically and non-linguistically different students. All the programs reporting pre- and post-test data for both groups were successful in showing exemplary improvement (a gain of seven or more NCEs), good improvement (between three and seven NCEs), or at least a constant level of achievement.

In the first grade, all but one program (96 percent) reported gains or no change for both LDS and NLDS. In the second grade, 79 percent of the projects reporting data for LDS showed gains or no change, compared with 75 percent for NLDS. More specifically, 27 percent of the programs reporting showed that their LDS gained at least seven NCEs with 25 percent reporting comparable gains for their NLDS.

In the third grade, 84 percent of the programs reporting indicated significant gains or no change for LDS in the program and 93 percent reported the same for NLDS. Thirteen percent of the third grade programs reported gains in excess of seven NCEs for LDS and 21 percent reported such gains for NLDS. Gains of at least three NCEs were reported by 39 percent of the projects for both LDS and NLDS.

Improved school attendance. In all the programs, linguistically different students attended school between 90 and 95 percent of all possible days during the 1979-80 school year. Non-linguistically different students evidenced slightly higher attendance at some grade levels than did LDS, although overall attendance rates fell within the same general range (91 to 95 percent). There is a general trend toward increased attendance rates for both groups (kindergarten through grade three).

Development of a positive self-concept and attitude. This objective is the most difficult to measure accurately and to interpret meaningfully. Of the six schools that made attempts to measure the self-concept and attitudes of program participants, all reported that their students displayed positive self-concepts and attitudes.

Improved parental involvement in the school programs. Two sets of data regarding parental involvement were reported: the first pertaining to the parent advisory councils and the second reflecting general activities by parents. There has been a generally improving trend in parental participation both areas over the three years that these studies have been conducted.

A wide variety of parental activities was reported. These range from volunteer service such as serving as aides in the classroom to fund-raising activities.

Conclusions

Overall, the bilingual programs in Colorado have been successful in improving the English language skills of participating linguistically different students. Equally important, the English langugae skills of the non-linguistically different students in the bilingual programs have improved as well.

It should be remembered that since the classroom is only one of several factors that contribute to student learning, even dramatic improvements in the effectiveness of an educational program produce relatively modest achievement gains. Nonetheless, when judged against what can reasonably be expected from educational programs, Colorado bilingual programs, on the whole, have been quite effective.

San Diego Demonstration Project*

San Diego's Title VII Bilingual Demonstration Project has offered bilingual education programs in six schools to both limited-English-proficient (LEP) children and fluent English speakers over the last seven years. The program was inspired by the language immersion programs conducted in Montreal, Canada. Students who participated in the San Diego project for six years, according to evaluations conducted for the school district, equalled or surpassed the established norms for reading, mathematics, and oral language development in both English and Spanish.

The San Diego program has covered the elementary years, from preschool through grade six. Some 60 percent of the participating students are Spanish speaking and limited in English proficiency; the remaining 40 percent are fluent English speakers. The project seeks to make the LEP students functionally bilingual in English and Spanish, while bringing these students to the same level of academic achievement as their monolingual English-speaking peers. A bilingual capability at similar levels is the goal for non-Spanish-speaking students as well. Participation in the program is voluntary because the pattern of language and academic instruction requires a long-term commitment.

LEP students are initially taught in Spanish, with the goal of increasing primary language skills. English is gradually introduced, beginning with 20-minute daily sessions at the preschool level and ending with an equal division between English and Spanish by the fourth grade. Students fluent in English are not taught Spanish as an academic subject. Instead, Spanish is used as the medium of instruction for all other subjects.

*SOURCE: *NCBE FORUM*, vol. 5, no. 9 (October, 1982), pp. 1, 3, 6.

Staff development in the program centers around preservice and inservice workshops. In-depth assistance is offered in the project's philosophy, instructional methodology, and evaluation procedures.

Instructional materials for the program have come primarily from the Title VII Spanish Curricula Development Center in Miami, Florida for the lower grades. The San Diego program tested new materials for the upper elementary levels as they were developed by the center. The staff of the program have developed their own materials when other appropriate publications could not be found.

Parental involvement has been encouraged through special workshops and a volunteer program. Participation in the administration of the program occurs through the Parent Advisory Committee.

The project is the subject of an independent evaluation each year. A longitudinal survey showed the following comparisons in achievement between students in the program and their non-participating peers:

• LEP students entering in kindergarten achieved grade level oral proficiency in English within three years; those entering in first grade too four years. Non-Spanish speakers achieved oral proficiency in Spanish by grades one through five if they entered in kindergarten, within two years if they entered in first grade.

• English reading levels went from one year below norm in the second grade to eight months below level in fifth grade for kindergarten entrants. First grade entrants were one year above grade level in English reading by sixth grade.

• Spanish reading levels remained five months below norm for kindergarten entrants through the fifth grade. First grade entrants had similar scores until grade six, when they jumped two years above grade level.

• Scores in English mathematics were one month below average by the end of fifth grade for kindergarten entrants; one year above grade level by the end of sixth grade for first grade entrants. Spanish math scores were two months above the norm by the end of fifth grade for kindergarten entrants; 1.3 years above the norm by the end of the sixth grade for first grade entrants.

APPENDIX F. STUDENTS' OPINIONS OF BILINGUAL EDUCATION*

"What Bilingual Education Has Meant To Me"*

by José Céspedes, Age 13, Eleanor Roosevelt Junior High School, Grade 8, New York, New York

Three years go I came from Dominican Republic to the United States for the first time. As you might suspect, I did not speak a world of English, and it was very hard for me to adjust to a new environment. I was not able to communicate with the people working in a supermarket or a grocery store, if there were no Spanish-speaking people around. I had trouble making friends with people who did not speak Spanish, and even those who spoke Spanish gave me a little trouble. When I spoke to them in Spanish, they would answer me in English, I felt I did not belong to their group, I felt like a stranger.

Now in school things are very different. The first day I went to school I felt uncomfortable and nervous because I thought that everybody in the class was going to be speaking English, and that I was not going to be able to understand a word. But what a surprise! Nothing of that came true. I was put into a bilingual program in which I was able to take subject classes in Spanish while at the same time learning English. I felt comfortable in those Spanish classes because I was able to communicate with the teachers and my classmates who spoke Spanish. I also felt comfortable in my English class because I found that I was not the only one who did not speak English; my classmates did not either.

But beyond feeling comfortable, I felt enouraged to learn more English each and every day. I did not fall behind in any subject because I was able to understand and to do my work in my original language. At the same time I felt the necessity to learn English in order to succeed in school and make more friends.

I am very grateful to the bilingual program. It not only helped me to adjust to a new environment where my original language was not spoken, but it also made me feel comfortable. It made me feel at home. The bilingual program helped me to learn a new language without forgetting my original one. Thanks to the bilingual program for helping me to succeed in school, for helping me to have more friends, and for helping me not to forget my roots.

"What Bilingual Education Has Meant To Me"*

by David Vázquez, Age 18, Berrien Springs High School, Grade 12, Berrien Springs, Michigan

I am a Cuban refugee who one year ago arrived in this country. Here I have found protection, affection, a home, food and most of all, liberty—a thing I ignored for seventeen years.

*Source: *NABE News*, Vol. 5, No. 4 (March, 1982), pp. 1, 5.

When I first arrived in the United States I thought I was in a fantasy world. Everything was so new, so different and especially, I thought, oversized. I remember how flustered I felt, for instance, when I went into the grocery store and could not communicate. I had many comical experiences in those early days, but I am grateful because now I can appreciate even more the value of Bilingual Education.

Once in this country I felt the desire to proceed with my education. But when school started I was worried; I wondered if I would understand my teachers or my schoolmates. I felt at a loss. But when my situation seemed hopeless, I heard a comforting voice that spoke to me in my own language, it was the bilingual teacher who would help, not only me, but also other foreign-born students like myself.

After six months of school, I can appreciate better the advantages of being an American. This is due to the fact that now I am understanding something about the lifestyle and the culture of this country, also about the historical influences that have shaped it into its present greatness.

What Bilingual Education Means to the Nation*

Bilingual education means that a person knows two languages. Knowing two languages makes it easier for anyone to communicate. It is also a good thing to have for the future when more and more jobs are available for bilingual persons. Having learned two languages gives a person a better understanding of problems all over the world.

If you go to other places and you can speak another language, you are more capable of understanding what is said to you. You can solve problems in minutes that normally would take a person who doesn't know the language days.

This nation needs capable people—bilingual people to work in different positions of the government. This nation needs leaders that are able to speak in many languages. This nation needs leaders that can understand other cultures and at the same time be able to go along with it.

Bilingual education can teach you all that the United States is a nation that gives you opportunities. A person can take the opportunity but also be able to be proud of having a heritage. I used to be ashamed of speaking Spanish until our teacher read an article about Chang-Díaz, the first and only Latino astronaut in the history of America in the Space Program. That article gave me a desire to become someone important. Ever since that day I have decided to be proud of my Nicaraguan heritage.

Bilingual education means more opportunities, a wider world to the citizens of this nation.

Axel Rodríguez
Wisconsin Avenue School
Milwukee, WI
Grade 5

*Source: *NABE News*, vol. 6, no. 4 (March, 1983), p. 3.

What Bilingual Education Has Meant to the Nation*

Last year, I stepped off the plane and found myself in the United States. I had come to a totally new world. Everything seemed so unfamiliar. Everybody was speaking a language that I could not understand. Even the sky looked different. It was snowy, cloudy, and as unclear as my future.

People like me come from all over the world. We speak different languages. We also have various cultural backgrounds. However, we have one problem in common — adapting to a new environment. We are totally unaccustomed to the American way of life. We find it hard to understand the Americans. In the other hand, the Americans think of us as isolated, inactive people.

It looks like we are separated by a river. The water is icy, and the current is too strong for us. Trying to swim across by ourselves would be too risky. Some of us might "drown." In fact, we often become frustrated and hopeless. Most of us back up, stay apart, and avoid every contact with the outer world.

The bilingual program has been established to serve as a bridge over which new people, mostly children, will cross to join the rest of the country. It is the gateway to your future. We quickly learn how Americans live and work. In turn, we help our parents to become familiar with new social system. We will become more and more active. Eventually, we will be to take our places as members of the whole nation.

In addition, the bilingual program has an effect on the native-born Americans. They will have a chance to know the new settlers better, thus gradually giving up all misconceptions.

Last but not least, the children who benefit from bilingual education will grow up having special advantages — being able to speak two languages fluently. Imagine how easily international affairs could be settled, and how profitably the commercial enterprise could be expanded if such persons were available for the United States government and business.

Bilingual education is truly bringing the new-comers into the mainstream of the nation. It is helping to unite people while encouraging each individual to retain his uniqueness. The united body of the people will help build the United States into an even stronger country.

Anh Tuan Nguyen
Gallagher Junior High School
Cleveland, OH
Grade 9

*Source: *NABE News*, vol. 6, no. 4 (March, 1983), p. 3.

APPENDIX G. Guidelines for the Preparation and Certification of
Teachers of Bilingual-Bicultural Education*

This statement, designed primarily to apply to teachers of bilingual-bicultural education in the United States of America, is intended to assist teacher certification agencies and educational institutions in the establishment of certification standards for bilingual-bicultural education teachers, and in the design and evaluation of bilingual-bicultural teacher education programs. The statement (1) describes the personal qualities and minimum professional competencies necessary for the successful teacher and (2) sets forth the guidelines considered essential in designing teacher training programs in bilingual-bicultural education. It should be noted that the competencies set forth herein apply only to the certification of bilingual-bicultural teachers, and not *all* teachers in bilingual-bicultural programs, which may also include English-medium teachers. Such teachers, however, should have as many of these competencies as possible.

Introduction

Bilingual-bicultural education has become one of the most significant and widespread movements in American education in the twentieth century. Not since the Renaissance has there been such a general acceptance of the idea that the goals of education might best be served by offering instruction in the native language of the learner. The passage of the Bilingual Education Act of 1968 helped bring about a major change in our educational philosophy, from a rejection or disparagement of other languages to a respect for their validity and their value as mediums for learning. The cultures of their speakers have come to be recognized as forming a valuable part of our national heritage, and as occupying an important place in our pluralistic society.

Today, state after state is adopting legislation supporting or mandating bilingual-bicultural education. Recent court decisions, including the *Lau vs. Nichols* decision by the Supreme Court, are giving added impetus to this movement. In order to meet the urgent need for competent teachers trained to teach in bilingual-bicultural programs, colleges and universities are rapidly instituting teacher training programs, and state departments of education are moving to prepare or approve credentials in this field. These developments have created a need for a set of guidelines which could help bring about comparability in training programs, and provide a basis for certification requirements which would assure high standards of quality for teachers in this field. The following guidelines represent an attempt to meet this need.

Because of the great variation in educational institutions which might undertake to prepare teachers for bilingual-bicultural education programs, these guidelines do not attempt to work out a set curriculum or to recommend a

*Source: Center for Applied Linguistics, Washington, D.C., 1974.

specific series of course titles. It is not only useful but urgent, however, to formulate the principles upon which such a program of teacher preparation should rest.

Accordingly, the guidelines emphasize personal qualities, attitudes, skills, experience, and knowledge rather than courses and credit hours. The manner of the formulation owes much to the documents from different states that were consulted and it represents the consensus of a number of leaders in the field, drawn from all levels of instruction and supervision, and representing a broad range of experience and points of view.

Although these guidelines are intended to be applicable primarily to teachers at the preservice level, they will also apply to teachers at the inservice level. One cardinal principle must be rigidly observed throughout, namely that the teacher of bilingual-bicultural education should have the same quality academic preparation as teachers of other subjects at comparable levels.

Personal Qualities

The teacher of bilingual-bicultural education should have the following qualifications:

1. A thorough knowledge of the philosophy and theory concerning bilingual-bicultrual education and its application.
2. A genuine and sincere interest in the education of children regardless of their linguistic and cultural background, and personal qualities which contribute to success as a classroom teacher.
3. A thorough knowledge of and proficiency in the child's home language and the ability to teach content through it; an understanding of the nature of the language the child brings with him and the ability to utilize it as a positive tool in his teaching.
4. Cultural awareness and sensitivity and a thorough knowledge of the cultures reflected in the two languages involved.
5. The proper professional and academic preparation obtained from a well-designed teacher training program in bilingual-bicultural education.

The guidelines which follow are designed to meet thse necessary qualifications and describe the various academic areas considered essential in teacher training programs in bilingual-bicultural education.

I. Language Proficiency

The teacher should demonstrate the ability to:

1. Communicate effectively, both in speaking and understanding, in the

languages and within the cultures of both the home and school. The ability will include adequate control of pronunciation, grammar, vocabulary, and regional, stylistic, and nonverbal variants appropriate to the communication context.

2. Carry out instruction in all areas of the curriculum using a standard variety of both languages.

II. Linguistics

The teacher should demonstrate the ability to:

1. Recognize and accept the language variety of the home and a standard variety as valid systems of communication, each with its own legitimate functions.
2. Understand basic concepts regarding the nature of language.
3. Understand the nature of bilingualism and the process of becoming bilingual.
4. Understand basic concepts regarding the natural effects of contacts between languages and the implications of this information for the instructional program.
5. Identify and understand regional, social, and developmental varieties in the child's language(s) at the phonological, grammatical, and lexical levels.
6. Identify and understand structural differences between the child's first and second languages, recognizing areas of potential interference and positive transfer.
7. Develop curricular activities to deal with areas of interference.
8. Understand theories of first and second language learning, differences between child and adult language learning, and their implications for the classroom.

III. Culture

The teacher should demonstrate the ability to:

1. Respond positively to the diversity of behavior involved in cross-cultural environments.
2. Develop awareness in the learner of the value of cultural diversity.
3. Prepare and assist children to interact successfully in a cross-cultural setting.
4. Recognize and accept different patterns of child development within and between cultures in order to formulate realistic objectives.
5. Assist children to maintain and extend identification with and pride in the mother culture.

6. Understand, appreciate and incorporate into activities, materials and other aspects of the instructional environment:
    a. The culture and history of the group's ancestry.
    b. Contributions of group to history and culture of the United States.
    c. Contemporary life style(s) of the group.
7. Recognize both the similarities and differences between Anglo-American and other cultures and both the potential conflicts and opportunities they may create for children.
8. Know the effects of cultural and socio-economic variables on the student's learning styles (cognitive and affective) and on the student's general level of development and socialization.
9. Use current research regarding the education of children in the U.S. from diverse linguistic and cultural backgrounds.
10. Understand the effects of socio-economic and cultural factors on the learner and the educational program.
11. Recognize differences in social structure, including familial organizations and patterns of authority, and their significance for the program.

IV. Instructional Methods

This component should enable teachers to assist students in achieving their full academic potential in the home language and culture as well as in English. To this end, the teacher is expected to demonstrate the following competencies:

1. Assist children to maintain and extend command of the mother tongue and the second language in listening, speaking, reading, and writing.
2. Apply teaching strategies appropriate to distinct learning modes and developmental levels, including preschool, taking into consideration how differences in culture affect these and other learning variables.
3. Organize, plan, and teach specific lessons in the required curriculum areas, using the appropriate terminology in the learner's language(s) and observing the local district curriculum guidelines. Basic elements and methodologies best suited to the teaching of reading and language arts, mathematics, social studies, and science, as a minimum, must be identified and applied in the learner's language(s).
4. Utilize innovative techniques effectively and appropriately in the learner's language(s) in the various content areas, namely:
    a. Formulation of realistic performance objectives and their assessment.
    b. Inquiry/discovery strategies.
    c. Individualized instruction.
    d. Learning centers.
    e. Uses of media and audio-visual materials.
    f. Systems approaches to the teaching of reading and mathematic skills.
    g. Team teaching and cross grouping.
    h. Interaction analysis.

5. Develop an awareness of the way in which learner's culture should permeate significant areas of the curriculum.
6. Utilize first and/or second-langugae techniques in accordance with the learner's needs at various stages of the learning process.
7. Utilize effective classroom management techniques, for optimal learning in specific situations.
8. Work effectively with paraprofessionals, and other adults.
9. Identify and utilize available community resources in and outside the classroom.

V. Curriculum Utilization and Adaptation

The teacher should demonstrate the ability to:

1. Identify current biases and deficiencies in existing curriculum and in both commercial and teacher-prepared materials of instruction. Materials should be evaluated in accordance with the following criteria:
    a. Suitability to student's language proficiencies and cultural experiences.
    b. Provision and respect for linguistic and cultural diversity.
    c. Objectives, scope, and sequence of the materials in terms of content areas.
    d. Student's reaction to materials.
2. Acquire, evaluate, adapt, and develop materials appropriate to the bilingual-bicultural classroom.

VI. Assessment

General

The teacher should demonstrate the ability to:

1. Recognize potential linguistic and cultural biases of existing assessment instruments and procedures when prescribing a program for the learner.
2. Utilize continuous assessment as part of the learning process.
3. Interpret diagnostic data for the purpose of prescribing instructional programs for the individual.
4. Use assessment data as basis for program planning and implementation.

Language

The teacher should demonstrate the ability to:

1. Determine language dominance of the learner in various domains of language use – oral and written.
2. Use assessment results to determine teaching strategies for each learner.
3. Identify areas of proficiency (oral and written: vocabulary, syntax, phonology) in the learner's first and second language.
4. Assess maintenance and extension levels of the learner's language(s).

Content

The teacher should demonstrate the ability to:

1. Evaluate growth using teacher-prepared as well as standard instruments, in cognitive skills and knowledge of content areas utilizing the language of the home.
2. Assess accuracy and relevance of materials utilized in the classroom.
3. Prepare tests to evaluate achievement of proposed objectives of instruction.

Self

The teacher should demonstrate the ability to identify and apply procedures for the assessment of:

1. Own strengths and weaknesses as a bilingual teacher.
2. Own value system as it relates to the leraner, his behavior, and his background.
3. The effectiveness of own teaching strategies.

VII. School-Community Relations

Current trends in education have specifically identified the significant role of the community in the educational process. The knowledge that the community has goals and expectations creates for the schools the need to include, integrate, and enhance those expectations in the regular school program.

Bilingual education offers distinct opportunities to bridge the structural and cultural gap between school and community. The school with a bilingual-bicultural education program should serve as a catalyst for the integration of diverse cultures within the community.

The teacher should demonstrate the following competencies:

1. Develop basic awareness concerning the importance of parental and community involvement for facilitating the learner's sucessful integration to his school environment.
2. Acquire skills to facilitate basic contacts and interaction between the learner's family and school personnel.
3. Demonstrate leadership in establishing home/community exchange of sociocultural information which can enrich the learner's instructional activities.
4. Acquire and develop skills in collecting culturally relevant information and materials characteristic of both the historical and current lifestyles of the learner's culture(s) that can serve both for curriculum contents and for instructional activities.
5. Acquire a knowledge of the patterns of child rearing represented in the families of the learners so at to better understand the background of the learners' behaviors in the classroom.
6. To act as facilitator for enhancing the parents' roles, functions and responsibilities in the school and community.
7. Serve as a facilitator for the exchange of information and views concerning the rationale, goals, and procedures for the instructional programs of the school.
8. To plan for and provide the direct participation of the learner's family in the regular instructional programs and activities.

VIII. Supervised Teaching

Because of the great disparity between theory presented in the context of a college environment and practical teaching realities in a bilingual-bicultural classroom setting, it is essential that a portion of every teacher's training experience include on-site supervised teaching experience in a bilingual-bicultural program. To the extent possible, relevant competencies should be demonstrated in the direct context of such a classroom setting.

REFERENCES _____

Agrawal, K. C. "The 'Short Tests of Linguistics Skills' and Their Calibration." *TESOL Quarterly*, 13:2 (June 1979), 185-208.

Ambert, A. N. "The Identification of LEP Children With Special Needs" *Bilingual Journal*, 6:1 (Fall 1982), 17-22.

— — — and Dew, N. *Special Education for Exceptional Bilingual Students; a handbook for educators*. The University of Wisconsin - Milwaukee, Midwest National Origin Desegregation Assistance Center, 1982.

Ammon, M. S. "Assessing Reading Comprehension: Issues in Development." Paper Presented at AERA annual conference, Montreal, April 1983.

Anderson, R. D., Spiro, R. J. and Anderson, M. C. Schematha as Scaffolding for the Representation of Information in Connected Discourse. *American Educational Research Journal*, 15 (1978), 443-440.

Anisfeld, E. A Comparison of the Cognitive Functioning of Monolinguals and Bilinguals. Unpublished Ph.D. dissertation, McGill University, 1964.

— — —and Lambert, W. "Evaluative Reactions of Bilingual and Monolingual Children to Spoken Languages" *Journal of Abnormal and Social Psychology*, 69 (1964), 89-97.

Arias, M. B. and Navarro, R. "Title VII, Bilingual Education: Developing Issues of Diversity and Equity." Stanford University Institute for Research on Educational Finance and Governance, Autumn 1981.

Arsenian, S. *Bilingualism and Mental Development*. New York Teachers College, Columbia University, 1937.

Arthur, B. *et. al.*, Evaluation Reactions of College Students to Dialect Differences in the English of Mexican Americans. *Language and Speech*, 17 (1974), 255–270.

August, D. L. *The Effects of Peer Tutoring on the Second Language Acquisition of Hispanic Elementary School Children*. Stanford University Doctoral Dissertation, 1982.

Austin, J. *How to do Things with Words*. London: Oxford University Press, 1962.

Bain, B. C. Toward an Integration of Piaget and Vygotsky: Bilingual Considerations. *Linguistics: An International Review*, 160 (1975), 5–20.

– – – and Yu, A. "Toward an Integration of Piaget and Vygotsky: A Cross-Cultural Replication (France, Germany, Canada) Concerning Cognitive Consequences of Bilinguality." In Paradis, M. *Aspects of Bilingualism*. Columbia, South Carolina: Hornbean Press, Inc. 1978, 113–126.

Balkan, L. *Les Effets du Bilinguisme Francais-anglais sur les Aptitudes Intellectuelles*. Bruxelles: Oimon, 1970.

Barnes, D. "Language in the Secondary Classroom," in Douglas Barnes, J. Britton, H. Rosen and the L.A.T.E. *Language, the Learner, and the School*. Harmondsworth, England: Penguin Books, 1969.

– – –. *Language in the Classroom*. Bletchley, England: The Open University Press, 1973.

– – –. *From Communication to Curriculum*. Harmonsworth, England: Penguin Books, 1975.

– – – and Todd, F. *Communication and Learning in Small Groups*. London: Rutledge and Kegan, Paul, 1977.

Beardsmore, H.B. *Bilingualism: Basic Principles*. Clevedon, England: Multilingual Matters, 1982.

Bellack, A. et. al. *The Language of the Classroom*. New York: Teachers College Press, Columbia University, 1966.

Ben-Zeev, S. *The Influence of Bilingualism on Cognitive Development and Cognitive Strategy*. Ph.D. Dissertation. Department of Human Development, University of Chicago, 1972.

– – –. *The Effect of Spanish-English Bilingualism in Children from Less Privileged Neighborhoods on Cognitive Development and Cognitive Strategy*. Bilingual Education Service, Arlington Heights, Illinois, 1975.

– – –. "Mechanisms by Which Childhood Bilingualism Affects Understanding of Language and Cognitive Students." In Hornby, P.A. ed. *Bilingualism Psychological, Social and Educational Implications*. New York: Academic Press, Inc., 1977, 29–56.

Bereiter, C. "Development in Writing" In Gregg L. W. and Steinberg, E. R. *Cognitive Processes in Writing*. Hillsdale, New Jersey: Lawrence Erlbaum Associates, Inc., 1980, 73–93.

Bergman, C.R. "Interference vs Independent Development in Input Bilingualism." In G.D. Keller, R.V. Teschner and S. Viera, eds. *Bilingualism in the Bicentennial and Beyond*. New York: Bilingual Press/Editorial Bilingüe. 1976, 88–96.

Bilingual-Bicultural Education and English as a Second Language Education: A Framework for Elementary and Secondary Schools. Sacramento: California State Department of Education, 1974.

Bordie, J. B. "Language Tests and Linguistically Different Learners: The Sad State of the Art." *Elementary English* 47 (1970), 814–828.

Boyd, P. The Acquisition of Spanish as a Second Language by Anglo Children in the Third Year of an Immersion Program. Unpublished M.A. Thesis, UCLA, 1974.

Braun, C. and Klassen, B. "A Transformational Analysis of Written Syntactic Structures of Children Representing Varying Ethno-Linguistic Communities." *Research in the Teaching of English*, 7:3 (Winter 1973), 312–323.

Brause, R.S. and Mayher, J.S. "Teachers, Students, and Classroom Organization." *Research in the Teaching of English*. 16:2 (May 1982), 131–148.

Briere, E. "Are We Really Measuring Proficiency with our Language Tests?" *Foreign Language Annals*, 4 (1971), 385–391.

– – –. "Testing Communicative Language Proficiency," *Occasional Papers on Linguistics*, 6 (Department of Linguistics, Southern Illinois University at Carbondale), 1979, 254–275.

Brisk, M. and Wurzel, J. "An Integrated Bilingual Curriculum Model." *NABE Journal*, 3:2 (Winter 1979), 39–51.

Brown, H.D. *Principles of Language Learning and Teaching.* Englewood Cliffs, New Jersey: Prentice-Hall, Inc., 1980.

Brown, M.E. and Zirkel, P.A. "Emerging Instrumentation for Assessing Language Dominance" *Occasional Papers on Linguistics*, no. 1, Carbondale, Illinois: Southern Illinois University, Department of Linguistics, 1977, 202–225.

Bruck, M. "Problems in Early French Immersion Programs." In B. Mlacak and E. Isabelle, eds., *So You Want Your Child to Learn French.* Ottawa, Ontario: Canadian Parents for French, 1979, 42–47.

– – – and Shultz, J. "An Ethnographic Analysis of the Language Use Patterns of Bilingually Schooled Children." *Working Papers on Bilingualism/ Travaux de Recherches sur le bilinguisme*, 13 (1977), 49–91.

– – –, Shultz, J., and Rodríguez-Brown, F.V. Assessing Language Use in Bilingual Classrooms: An Ethnographic Analysis. *Bilingual Education Series: 6.* Arlington, Virginia: Center for Applied Linguistics, 1979.

Callary, R.E. *Syntactical Correlates of Social Stratification.* Baton Rouge: Louisiana A. & M. University, 1971.

Canale, M. "From Communicative Competence to Communicative Language Pedagogy." In J. Richard and R. Schmidt, eds. *Language and Communication.* New York: Longman, 1981.

– – – and Swain, M. "Theoretical Bases of Communicative Approaches to Second Language Teaching and Testing." *Applied Linguistics*, 1 (Spring 1980), 1–47.

Canseco, J. H. *English Reading Achievement in a Bilingual School.* Rosslyn, Virginia: National Clearinghouse for Bilingual Education, 1978.

Cárdenas, A.A.G. *Mexican American and Anglo American Attitudes Toward Spanish and English as a Function of Social Factors in South Texas.* Doctoral Dissertation, University of Texas at Austin, 1981.

Carrasco, R. L., Vera, A., Cazen, C. B. "Aspects of Bilingual Students' Communicative Competence in the Classroom: A Case Study." In R. Duran, Ed. *Latino Language and Communicative Behavior Discourse Processes: Advances in Research and Theory,* vol. 4. Norwood, N.J.: Ablex Publishers, 1981, 237-249.

Carrow, M.A. "Linguistic Functioning of Bilingual and Monolingual Children." *Journal of Speech and Hearing Disorders,* 22 (1957), 371-380.

Carrow, E. "Comprehension of English and Spanish by Preschool Mexican-American Children." *Modern Language Journal,* 50:5 (May 1971), 299-306.

Cassidy, A. and Vukelich, C. "The Effects of Groups Size on Kindergarten Children's Listening Comprehension Performance." *Psychology in the Schools* 14:4 (1977), 449-455.

Cazden, C. B. et. al. "Language Assessment: Where, What and How," *Anthropology & Education Quarterly,* 8:2 (May 1977), 83-94.

– – – et. al. "The Contribution of Ethnographic Research to Bicultural Bilingual Education." In J.E. Alatis, ed. *Current Issues in Bilingual Education,* Washington, D.C. Georgetown University Press, 1980, 64-80.

Chamot, A.U. "Applications of Second Language Acquisition Research to Bilingual Classroom." *NCBE Focus,* No. 8 September 1981.

– – –. "Effective Schools - Effective Bilingual Education." *NCBE Forum* 5:10. (November/December 1982), 2.

– – –. "Findings in Current Bilingual Education Research." *NCBE Forum* 6:2 (March/April 1983), 2-3, 6.

Chan, K. Testimoney at the Special Seminar on "Effectiveness of Bilingual Education: Policy Implications of Recent Research." American Psychological Association, Washington, D.C. August 1982 Meeting. *NCBE Forumn* 5:9 (October 1982), 1,3.

Chun, J.A. and Politzer, R.L. *A Study of Language Acquisition in Two Bilingual Schools.* Stanford University, School of Education, 1975.

Clement, R. "Ethnicity, Contact, and Communicative Competence in a Second Language." In Giles, H., Robinson, W.P., and Smith P.M., eds. *Language: Social Psychological Perspective.* Oxford: Pergamon, 1980.

Cohen, A.D. "The Culver City Spanish Immersion Program: The First Two Years". *Modern Language Journal,* 58 (1974), 95-103.

– – –. *A Sociolinguistic Approach to Bilingual Education.* Rowley, Mass.: Newbury House Publishers, Inc., 1975.

– – –. "The Acquisition of Spanish Grammar Through Immersion: Some Findings After Four Years." *The Canadian Modern Language Review,* 32:5 (May 1976), 562-574.

– – –. "The Case for Partial or Total Immersion." In A. Simões, ed. *The Bilingual Child.* New York: Academic Press., 1976, 65-89.

— — — and Laosa, L.M. "Second Language Instruction: Some Research Considerations." *Journal of Curriculum Studies*, 8:2 (1976), 149-165.
— — — and Swain M. "Bilingual Education: The 'Immersion' Model in the North
American Context." *TESOL Quarterly*, 10 (1976) 45-53.
— — — and Laosa, L.M. "Second Language Instruction: Some Research Con-
siderations." In H. T. Trueba and C. Barnett-Mizrahi, eds. *Bilingual
Multicultural Education and the Professional - From Theory to Practice.*
Rowley, Mass.: Newbury House Publishers, Inc. 1979, 74-88.
Conklin, N. F. and Lourie, M.A. *A Host of Tongues: Language Communities
in the United States.* New York: The Free Press, 1983.
Connor, U. "The Role of Cultural Background Knowledge in ESL Learners'
Reading Comprehension." Paper Presented at the Georgetown University
Roundtable on Languages and Linguistics, Washington, D.C., March
1981.
Cooper, R. L. "An Elaborated Language Testing Model." *Language Learning*
3 (1968), 57-72.
— — — . "Testing." In R.C. Lugton, ed. *Preparing the EFL Teacher*, No. 7. Phila-
delphia: The Center for Curriculum Development, Inc., 1970.
Corder, S. P. *Introducing Applied Linguistics.* Harmondsworth, England: Pen-
guin Books, Inc., 1973.
Corrigan, A. and Upshur, J.A. "Test Method and Linguistic Factors in Foreign
Language Tests." Paper presented at the TESOL Convention. Mexico
City, 1978.
Cortéz, J. *Miscue Corrections by Bilingual and Monolingual Teachers When
Teaching Bilingual Children to Read: A Comparative Survey in Wales,
Spain, and Regions of the United States.* Doctoral Dissertation. Uni-
versity of Washington. Seattle, Washington, 1980.
Cummins, J. "Bilingualism and the Development of Metalinguistic Awareness."
Journal of Cross-Cultural Psychology, 9: 2 (1978) 131-149.
— — — . "Linguistic Interdfependence and the Educational Development of Bi-
lingual Children." *Review of Educational Research*, 49:2 (Spring 1979),
222-251.
— — — . "The Entry and Exit Fallacy in Bilingual Education." *NABE Journal*,
4:3 (Spring 1980), 25-59.
— — — . "The Role of Primary Language Development in Promoting Educational
Success for Language Minority Students." In *Schooling and Language
Minority Students; A Theoretical Framework.* Los Angeles: Evaluation
Dissemination and Assessment Center, California State University, Los
Angeles, 1981, 3-49.
— — — and Gulutsan, M. "Some Effects of Bilingualism on Cognitive Func-
tioning." In *Bilingualism, Biculturalism and Education*, Carey, T., ed. Al-
berta, Canada: University of Alberta, Edmonton, 1974, 129-137.
Cziko, G. A. "Differences in First and Second Language Reading. The Use of
Snytactic, Semantic, and Discourse Constraints." *Canadian Modern Language Review*, 34:2 (February 1978), 473-489.

— — —. "Language Competence and Reading Strategies: A Comparison of First and Second Language Oral Reading Errors." *Language Learning*, 30:1 (June 1980), 101–116.

Darcy, N.T. "Bilingualism and the Measurement of Intelligence: Review of a Decade of Research." *Journal of Genetic Psychology*, 103 (1963), 259–282.

Dato, D.P. *American Children's Acquisition of Spanish Syntax in the Madrid Environment*. Preliminary Edition, HEW Fund Rep/3036, 1970 (ERIC ED 053-631).

Davies, A. "Language Testing" *Language Teaching and Linguistics Abstracts*, *11 (1978), 145*–159, 215–231.

Day, C. E. "Assessing Communication Competence: Integrative Testing of Second Language Learners," in *Communication Assessment of the Bilingual Bicultural Child*. Baltimore: University Park Press, 180, 179–197.

De Avila, E. A. *Cartoon Conservation Scales, Level I and Level II*. Larkspur, Ca.: De Avila, Duncan and Associates, 1977.

Díaz, R.M. *The Impact of Second Language Learning on the Development of Verbal and Spatial Abilities*. Doctoral Dissertation, Yale University, 1982.

Diebold, A.R., Jr. "The Consequences of Early Bilingualism in Cognitive Development and Personality Formation." In Norbeck, E. *et. al.*, eds., *The Study of Personality: An Interdisciplinary Appraisal*: New York: Holt, Reinhard and Winston, Inc. 1968, 218–245.

Dore, J. "Conversation and Preschool Language Development." In Fletcher, P. and Garman, H. eds. *Language Acquisition*. London: Cambridge University Press, 1979, 337–361.

Dube, N.C. and G. Herbert, *St. John Valley Five-Year Evaluation Report 1970–1975*. Washington, D.C.: U.S. Department of H. E. W., 1975.

Dulay, H. and Burt, M. "Errors and Strategies in Child Second Language Acquisition" *TESOL Quarterly*, 8:2 (1974), 129–135.

— — — and Burt, M. "Creative Construction in Second Language Learning and Teaching." In *New Directions in Second Language Learning, Teaching, and Bilingual Education*, M. Burt and H. Dulay, eds. Washington, D.C.: TESOL, 1975, 21–32.

— — —. Burt M. and Krashen, S. *Language Two*. New York: Oxford University Press, 1982.

Duncan, S.E. and De Avila, E.A. "Bilingualism and Cognition: Some Recent Findings." *NABE Journal*, 4:1 (Fall 1979), 15–50.

Eaton, A. J. *A Psycholinguistic Analysis of the Oral Reading Miscues of Selected Field Dependent and Field Independent Native Spanish-speaking Mexican American First Grade Children."* Doctoral Dissertation at University of Texas, Austin 1979.

Ebel, C.S. *An Examination of Theory and Practice in Teaching Reading to Limited English Speakers in the Elementary Grades*. Doctoral dissertation, Temple University, 1978.

Edelsky, C. "Writing in a Bilingual Program: The Relation of L_1 and L_2 Texts." *TESOL Quarterly* 16:2 (June 1982), 211–228.

– – – and Hudelson, S. "The Reversing the Roles of Chicano and Anglo Children in a Bilingual Classroom: On the Communicative Competence of the Helper." In J. A. Fishman and G. D. Keller, eds. *Bilingual Education for Hispanic Students in the United States*. New York: Teachers College, Columbia University, 1982, 303-325.

Education for a Global Perspective: A Plan For New York State. Albany: The State Education Department, 1982.

Ehrlich, A. "Bilingual Teaching and Beginning School Success." 1971 (ERIC - ED 057279).

Engle, P.L. "Language Medium in Early School Years for Minority Language Groups." *Review of Educational Research*, 45 (Spring 1975), 284-310.

– – –. *The Use of Vernacular Languages in Education*. Arlington, Virginia: Center for Applied Linguistics, 1975.

Enright, D.S. *Student Language Use in Traditional and Open Bilingual Classrooms*. Doctoral Dissertation. Stanford University, 1981.

– – –. Ramírez, A.G. and Jacobs, J. "Language Use in an English/Hebrew-Bilingual Preschool Classroom." *NABE Journal*. 6:2-3 (Winter/Spring 1982-82), 69-88.

Erickson, F. Cazden, C.B. and Carrasco, R. "Social and Cultural Interaction in Classrooms of Bilingual Children." Paper Presented at Teaching as a Linguistic Process - Mid-Project Research Report, Washington, D.C.: National Institute of Education, 1979.

Ervin-Tripp, S. "Is Second Language Learning Like the First?" *TESOL Quarterly*, 8:2 (1974), 111-127.

Fantini, A.E. "Bilingual Behavior" and Social Cues: Case Studies of Two Bilingual Children." In Paradis, M., ed. *Aspects of Bilingualism*. Columbia, South Carolina: Hornbean Press, Inc. 1978, 283-301.

Ferguson, C.A. "Diglossia," *WORD*, 15 (1959), 325-340.

– – –. Houghton, C. and Wells, M.H. "Bilingual Education: an International Perspective." In B. Spolsky and R. Cooper, eds. *Frontiers of Bilingual Education*. Rowley, Mass.: Newbury House Publishers, Inc., 1977, 159-1974.

Fiege-Kollman, L. "Reading in a Second Language." *Occasional Papers on Linguistics*, no. 1. Carbondale: Southern Illinois University, 1977, 40-52.

Fillmore, L. Wong. *The Second Time Around: Cognitive and Social Strategies in Second Language Acquisition*, Doctoral dissertation, Stanford University, 1976.

– – –. "Individual Differences in Second Language Acquisition." In Fillmore, C.J., Kempler, D., and Wang, W., eds. *Individual Differences in Language Ability and Language Behavior*. New York: Academic Press, 1979, 202-228.

– – –. "Language Minority Students and School Participation. What Kind of English is Needed?" *Journal of Education*, 164:2 (Spring 1982), 143-156.

– – –. "The Language Learner as an Individual: Implications of Research on Individual Differences for the ESL Teacher." In Clark, M.A. and Handscombe, J. eds. *ON TESOL '82 Pacific Perspectives on Language Learning and Teaching.* Washington, D.C.: TESOL, 1983, 157-1974.

Fishman, J.A. "Language Maintenance and Language Shift as Fields of Inquiry." *Linguistics,* 9 (1964), 32-70.

— — —. *Language Loyalty in the United States.* The Hague: Mouton, 1966.

— — —. "Bilingualism, With and Without Diglossia: Diglossia With and Without Bilingualism." *Journal of Social Issues,* 23:2 (1967), 29-38.

— — —. "Attitudes and Beliefs About Spanish and English Among Puerto Ricans" *Viewpoints* (Bulletin of the School of Education, Indiana University), 47:2 (March 1971), 51-72.

— — —. "Language Attitudes." *International Journal of the Sociology of Language,* 1:3 (1975), 1-14.

— — —. *Bilingual Education: An International Sociological Perspective.* Rowley, Mass., Newbury House, 1976.

— — —. "Language policy: past, present and future." In *Language in the U.S.A.* by Ferguson, C.A. and Heath, S.B. New York: Cambridge University Press, 1981, 516-526.

— — —. "Sociolinguistic Foundations of Bilingual Education" *Bilingual Review,* 9:1 (January - April 1982). 1-35.

— — —. "Bilingualism and Biculturalism as Individual and Societal Phenomena." In J.A. Fishman and G. D. Keller, eds. *Bilingual Education for Hispanic Students in the United States.* New York: Teachers College Press, Columbia University, 1982, 23-36.

— — — and Lovas, J. "Bilingual Education in Sociolinguistic Perspective." *TESOL Quarterly,* 4:3 (1970), 215-222.

Flavell, J.H. *et. al. The Development of Role Taking and Communication Skills in Children,* New York: John Wiley, Inc., 1968.

Flores, M. An Early Stage in the Acquisition of Spanish Morphology by a Group of English-speaking Children. Unpublished M.A. Thesis, UCLA, 1973.

Frederiksen, C.H. and Dominic, J.F., eds. *Writing: Process, Development and Communication,* (Volume 2). Hillsdale, New Jersey: Lawrence Erlbaum Associates, Publishers, 1981.

Gage, N.L., ed. *Teaching as a Linguistic Process in a Cultural Setting.* (National Conference on Studies in Teaching, No. 5). Washington, D.C. National Institute of Education, 1974.

García, R.L. *Teaching in a Pluralistic Society.* New York: Harper and Row, Publishers, 1982.

Gardner, R.C. "Social Psychological Aspects of Second Language Acquisition." (Research Bulletin No. 445). London, Canada: University of Western Ontario. Department of Psychology, 1978.

— — —. "Social Psychological Aspects of Second Language Acquisition." In Giles, H. and St. Clair, R.N., eds. *Language and Social Psychology.* Oxford: Blackwells, 1979.

Genesee, F. "The Role of Intelligence in Second Language Learning." *Language Learning,* 26 (1976), 267-280.

– – –. Tucker, G.R. and Lambert, W.E. "Communication Skills of Bilingual Children." *Child Development*, 46 (1975), 1010-1014.

Giles, H. and Powesland, P. F. *Speech, Style and Social Evaluation*. New York: Academic Press, 1975.

– – –. Bourkis, R. and Taylor, D. "Towards a Theory of Language in Ethnic Group Relations." In *Language Ethnicity and Intergroup Relations*, ed. H. Giles. London: Academic Press, 1977.

– – – and Byrne, J.L. "An Intergroup Approach to Second Language Acquisition." *Journal of Multilingual and Multicultural Development*. 3:1 (1982), 17-40.

Gómez, G. *Questioning Behaviors of First-Grade Bilingual Teachers During Reading Instruction: English Versus Spanish*. Doctoral Dissertation, The University of Texas at Austin, 1976.

González, E. and Lezama, J. "The Dual Language Model: A Practical Approach to Bilingual Education." In Alatis, J. and Twaddell, K., eds., *English as a Second Language in Bilingual Education*. Washington, D.C.: TESOL, 1976, 105-12.

González, G. and Maez, F.L. "To Switch or Not to Switch: The Role of Code-Switch- in the Elementary Bilingual Classroom." In Padilla R. V., ed. *Theory in Bilingual Education*. Ypsilanti, Michigan: Eastern Michigan University, Department of Foreign Languages and Bilingual Studies, 1980, 125-135.

González, G. A. "The Non-Spanish Speaking Hispanic Child: Curriculum Concerns, Supervisory Initiative" In. A. Valverde, R. Castro-Feinberg and E. Marquez, eds. *Educating English-Speaking Hispanics* Alexandria, Virginia, Association for Supervision and Curriculum Development. 1980, 1-14.

Gonzalez, P. and Elijah, D. "Error Patterns of Bilingual Readers." *NABE Journal* 3:3 (Spring 1979), 15-25.

Goodman, K. S. "Analysis of Oral Reading Miscues: Applied Psycholinguistics." In F. Smith, ed., *Psycholinguistics and Reading*. New York: Holt, 1973.

Goodman, Y., and Burke, C. *Reading Miscue Inventory: A Procedure for Diagnosis and Evaluation*. New York: Macmillan Co., 1972.

Gregg, L. W. and Steinberg, E. R. *Cognitive Processes in Writing*. Hillsdale, New Jersey: Lawrence Erlbaum Associates, 1980.

Greenfield, L. and Fishman, J.A. "Situational Measures of Normative Language Views of Person, Place and Topic Among Puerto Rican Bilinguals". In J.A. Fishman, R.L. Cooper, R. Ma, *et. al. Bilingualism in the Barrio*. Indiana U. Publications, Language Science Monograph #7. The Hague, Netherlands: Mouton and Co., 1971, 233-251.

Gunther, V. A. *Comparison of Bilingual Oral Language Reading Skills Among Limited English Speaking Children from Spanish Speaking Backgrounds*. Doctoral Dissertation, Northwestern University, Evanston, Illinois, 1981.

Hakuta, K. "Prefabricated Patterns and the Emergency of Structure in Second Language Acquisition," *Language Learning*, 24: (1974), 287-297.

– – – and Cancino, H. "Trends in Second Language Acquisition Research." *Harvard Educational Review*. 47 (1977), 294-316.

Halliday, M. A. K. *Exploration in the Function of Language.* New York: Elsevier North Holland, Inc., 1973.

Hatch, E. M. "Discourse Analysis and Second Language Acquisition." In. E. M. Hatch, ed. *Second Language Acquisition.* Rowley, Mass.: Newbury House Publishers, Inc., 1978, 401–435.

― ― ―. *Psycholinguistics: A Second Language Perspective.* Rowley, Mass.: Newbury House Publishers, Inc., 1983.

Haugen, E. I. *Bilingualism in the Americas: A Bibliography and Research Guide.* American Dialect Society, 26, (1956) 159.

Hernández-Chvez, E., Burt, M. K. and Dulay, H. C. "Language Dominance and Proficiency Testing: Some General Considerations. *NABE Journal,* 3:1 (Fall, 1978), 41–54.

Hernández, H. "Language Use Patterns in ESL and SSL Lessons." Unpublished paper, Stanford University, 1979.

― ― ―. *English as a Second Language Lessons in Bilingual Classrooms: A Discourse Analysis.* Doctoral Dissertation, Stanford University, 1981.

Hinofotis, F.B. "Lexical Dominance: A Case Study of English and Greek." *In Occasional Papers on Linguistics,* no. 1. Carbondale, Illinois: Southern University, Department of Linguistics, 1977, 241–245.

Holmes, J. "Sociolinguistic Competence in the Classroom." In Richard, J. C., ed. *Understanding Second and Foreign Language Learning.* Rowley, Mass. Newbury House Publishers, 1978, 134–162.

Hornby, P.A. "Achieving Second Language Fluency Through Immersion Education." *Foreign Language Annals,* 13 (April 1980), 107–113.

Howder, M. L. "Language-Related Issues Gain Momentum." *NCBE Forum,* 3:6 (July/August 1980), pp. 2, 4.

Huang, J. and Hatch, E. "A Chinese Child's Acquisition of English." In E. M. Hatch, ed. *Second Language Acquisition.* Rowley, Mass.: Newbury House, 1978, 118–131.

Hudson, R.A. *Soicolinguistics.* New York: Cambridge University Press, 1980.

Huerta, A.G. *Code Switching Among Spanish-English Bilinguals: A Sociolinguistic Perspective.* Doctoral Dissertation, University of Texas at Austin, 1978.

Hunt, K.W. *Grammatical Structures Written at Three Grade Levels.* (NCTE Research Report No. 3), Urbana, Illinois: National Council of Teachers of English, 1965.

Hymes, D. "Competence and Performance in Linguistic Theory" In B. Huxley and E. Ingram, eds. *Language Acquisition: Models and Methods.* New York: Academic Press, 1971.

Ianco-Worrall, A.D. "Bilingualism and Cognitive Development." *Child Development,* 43 (1972), 1390–1400.

Illyin Oral Interview. Rowley, Mass. Newbury House Publishers, Inc., 1976.

Imedadze, N. V. "On the Psychological Nature of Child Speech Formation Under Condition of Exposure of Two Languages." In E. M. Hatch, ed. *Second Language Acquisition.* Rowley, Mass.: Newbury House, 1978, 33–36.

Izzo, S. *Second Language Learning: A Review of Related Studies.* Rosslyn, Virginia: National Clearninghouse for Bilingual Education, 1981.
Jacobs, G.H. "An American Foreign Language Immersion Program: How To." *Foreign Language Annals,* 11:4 (1978), 4.
Jacobson, R. "Can Bilingual Teaching Techniques Reflect Bilingual Community Behaviors? - A Study in Ethnoculture and Its Reationship to Some Amendments Contained in the New Bilingual Education Act." In Padilla, R.V., ed. *Ethnoperspectives in Bilingual Education Research,* Vol. 1 Ypsilanti, Michigan: Eastern Michigan University, 1979, 483-497.
John, V. P. and Horner, V. M. *Early Childhood Bilingual Education,* New York: Modern Language Association, 1971.
Johnson, D.M. *Peer tutoring, Social Interaction and the Acquisition of English as a Second Language by Spanish-Speaking Elementary School Children.* Stanford University, Unpublished doctoral dissertation, 1980.
Johnson, M.C. *An Investigation of the Extent of Standard English and Black English Used by Children from Schools of Varying Racial Composition.* College Park, MD: University of Maryland, 1971.
Johnson, P. "Effect on Reading Comprehension of Building Background Knowledge." *TESOL Quarterly,* 16:4 (December 1982), 503-516.
Jones, R.L. and Spolsky, B., eds. *Testing Language Proficiency.* Washington, D.C. Center for Applied Linguistics, 1975.
Jones, W.R. "A Initial Study of Bilingualism and Non-verbal Intelligence." *British Journal Educational Psychology.* 30 (1960), 71-76.
– – –. *Bilingualism in Welsh Education.* Cardiff: University of Wales Press, 1966.
Keller, G.D. "The Ultimate Goal of Bilingual Education with Respect to Language Skills." In J.A. Fishman and G.D. Keller, eds. *Bilingual Education for Hispanic Students in the United States.* New York: Teachers College, Columbia University, 1982, 71-90.
Kenefick, B. *Language Functions of First-Grade Children With and Without Teacher Presence: An Empirical and Phenomological Study.* Unpublished. Ph.D. Dissertation, Columbia University, 1977.
Kessler, C. and Quinn, M.E. "Positive Effects of Bilingualism on Science Problem Solving Abilities." In Alatis, J.E., ed. *Current Issues in Bilingual Education.* Washington, D.C. Georgetown University Press, 1980, 295-308.
– – – and Quinn, M.E. "Bilingualism and Science Problem-Solving Ability." In Fisher, J.C., Clark, M.A., and Schachter, J. eds. *On TESOL '80. Building Bridges: Research and Practice in Teaching English as a Second Language.* Washington, D.C.: TESOL, 1981.
Kloss, H. "Notes Concerning a Language - Nation Typology." In Fishman, J.A. *et. al.* eds. *Language Problems of Developing Nations,* 1968, 69-86.
Krashen, S.D. "Bilingual Education and Second Language Acquisition Theory." In *Schooling and Language Minority Students: A Theoretical Framework.* Los Angeles: Evaluation, Dissemination, and Assessment Center, 1981, 51-79.

Kuhlman, N.A. "State Competency Writing Tests: What Do We Learn?" Paper presented at TESOL Annual Conference, Honolulu, 1982.

Kwok, I.S. *The Relationship of Langugae Orientation and Racial/Ethnic Attitude Among Chinese American Primary Grade Children.* Doctoral Dissertation, University of the Pacific, 1979.

Lalas, J. W. "The Influence of Prior Experience in ESL Reading." *Bilingual Journal*, 6:1 (Fall 1982), 10–12.

Lambert, W.E. "Culture and Language as Factors in Learning and Education." In A. Wolfgang, ed. *Education of Immigrant Students.* Toronto: Ontario Institute for Studies in Education, 1975.

– – –. "Culture and Language as Factors in Learning and Education." In Eckman, F., ed. *Current Themes in Linguistics: Bilingualism, Experimental Linguistics and Language Typologies. Washington, D.C. Hemisphere Publishing, 1977.*

– – –. "The Effects of Bilingualism on the Individual: Cognitive and Siciocultural Consequences." In Hornby, *P.A., ed. Bilingualism—Psychological, Social and Educational Implications.* New York, N.Y.: Academic Press, Inc. 1977, 15–28.

– – –. "The Two Faces of Bilingual Education." *NCBE Forum*, 3 August, 1980.

– – –, *et. al.,* "Evaluative Reactions to to Spoken Languages." *Journal of Abnormal and Social Psychology*, 60 (1960), 44–51.

– – –. Frankel, W. and Tucker, G.R. "Judging Personality Through Speech: A French-Canadian Example." *Journal of Communication*, 16 (December 1966), 305–321.

– – – and Tucker, G.R. *Bilingual Education of Children: The St. Lambert Experiment.* Rowley, Mass.: Newbury, 1972.

Laosa, L. M. "Bilingualism in Three United States Hispanic Groups: Contextual Use of Language by Children and Adults in Their Families." *Journal of Educational Psychology*, 67:5 (1975), 617–627.

Laswell, B.S. *The Functions of Language in Discussions: A Structuralist Approach.* Stanford University, Unpublished Doctoral Dissertation, 1979.

Leback, S.M. *Report on the Culver City Immersion Program.* Unpublished M.A. Thesis, UCLA, 1974.

Legarreta, D. "Language Choice in Bilingual Classrooms." *TESOL Quarterly*, 11:1 (March 1977), 9–16.

– – –. "The Effects of Program Models on Language Acquisition by Spanish-Speaking Children." *TESOL Quarterly*, 13:4 (December 1979), 521–534.

Legarreta-Marcaida, D. "Effective Use of the Primary Language in the Classroom" In *Schooling and Language Minority Students: A Theoretical Framework.* Los Angeles: Evaluation, Dissemination and Assessment Center, California State University, Los Angeles, 1981, 83–116.

Leopold, W.F. *Speech Development of Bilingual Child*, 4 vols. Evanston, Illinois. Northwestern University Press, 1939–1949.

– – –. "A Child's Learning of Two Languages" In Hatch, E.M., ed. *Second Language Acquisition*. Rowley, Massachusetts: Newbury House Publishers, 1978, 23–32.

Leslie, D. *Bilingual Education and Native Americans*. University of Alberta Research Report, 1977.

Levy, R.S. *An Analysis of the Effects of Language Acquisition Context Upon the Dual Language Development of Non-English Dominant Students*. New York: Arno Press, 1978.

Lewis, D.G. "Differences in Attainment Between Primary Schools in Mixed Language Areas: Their Dependence on Intelligence and Linguistic Background." *British Journal of Education Psychology*, 30 (1960), 63–70.

Lewis, E.G. "Bilingualism and Bilingual Education - The Ancient World to the Renaissance." In B. Spolsky and R. Cooper, eds. *Frontiers of Bilingual Education*. Rowley, Mass.: Newbury House Publishers, Inc. 1978, 22–93.

Lombardo, M. "Research Studies on the Approaches to Beginning Reading for Bilingual Students." *NABE News*, 3:4 (March 1980), 3–4, 18.

Ma, R. and Herasimchuk, E. "Linguistic Dimensions of a Biingual Neighborborhood" In J.A. Fishman, *et. al.,* eds. *Bilingualism in the Barrio* (Final Report). Washington, D.C.: U.S. Office of Education, 1968.

Mackey, W.F. *Bilingualism as a World Phenomenon*. Montreal: Harvest House, 1967.

– – –. "A Typology of Bilingual Education." In T. Anderson and M. Boyer, *Bilingual Schooling in the United States*, 2 vols., Washington, D.C. Government Printing Office, vol. 2, 1971, 63–82.

– – – and Ornstein-Galicia, J. *The Bilingual Education Movement: Essays on Progress*. El Paso: Texas Western Press, University of Texas, 1977.

Macnamara, J. *Bilingualism in Primary Education*. Edinburg: Edinburg University Press, 1966.

– – –. The Bilingual's Linguistic Performance: A Psychological Overview. *Journal of Social Issues*, 23 (1967), 58–77.

Malherbe, E.G. *The Bilingual School: A Study of Bilingualism in South Africa*. London: Green, 1946.

Marrow, K. *Techniques of Evaluation for a Notional Syllabus*. London: Royal Society of Arts, 1977.

McClure, E. "Aspects of Code Switching in the Discourse of Bilingual Mexican American Children." In Saville-Troike, M., ed. *Linguistics and Anthropology*. Washington, D.C.: Georgetown University Press, 1977.

– – – and Wentz, J. "Chicano Children's Code-Switching: An Overview." In Lafontaine, H., Persky, B. and Golubihick, L.H., eds. *Bilingual Education*. Wayne, New Jersey: Avery Publishing Group Inc., 1978, 180–184.

McLaughlin, B. "Differences and Similarities between First and Second Language Learning." In Winitz, H. ed. *Native Language and Foreign Language Acquisition*. New York: New York Academy of Sciences. 1981, 23–32.

McLennan, R. L. *Student/Teacher Interaction as a Function of Language Choice: An Observational Study*. Doctoral dissertation, Stanford University, 1978.

Mehan, H. "Ethnography." In *Bilingual Education Current Perspectives,* vol. 1, Arlington, Virginia. Center for Applied Linguistics, 1977.

— — —. *Learning Lessons.* Cambridge, Mass.: Harvard Press, 1979.

Meléndez, W. *The Effect of the Language of Instruction on the Reading Achievement of Limited English Speakers in Secondary Schools.* Doctoral dissertation. University of the University of the Pacific at Stockton, 1980.

Merino, B.J. "Order and Pace in the Syntactic Development of Bilingual Children." In Fishman, J.A. and Keller, G.D. *Bilingual Education for Hispanic Students in the United States.* New York: Teachers College, Columbia University, 1982, 446–464.

— — —. Politzer, R. L. and Ramírez, A. G. "The Relationship of Teachers Spanish Proficiency to Pupils' Achievement." *NABE Journal* 3:2 (Winter 1979), 21–38.

Milk, R. D. *"An Analysis of the Functional Allocation of Spanish and English in a Bilingual Classroom."* Unpublished manuscript, Stanford University, 1978.

— — —. *Variation in Language Use Patterns Across Different Group Settings in Two Bilingual Second Grade Classrooms.* Doctoral dissertation, Stanford University, 1980.

Mosely, F.J. *Bilingual-Multicultural Education: A Comparative Study of the Academic Growth of Bilingual Instructed Fourth and Sixth Grade Pupils to That of Monolingually Instructed Fourth and Sixth Grade Pupils.* Doctoral dissertation. The University of Akron, Ohio, 1983.

Modiano, N. "Bilingual Education for Children of Linguistic Minorities." *America Indigena,* 28 (1968), 405–414.

— — —. *Indian Education in the Chiapas Highlands.* New York: Holt Rhinehart, 1973.

Mulford, R. and Hecht, B. "Learning to Speak Without an Accent: Acquisition of a Second Language Phonology." Paper presented to the Fourth Annual Conference on Language Development. Boston University 1979.

Muñoz-Hernández, S. *A Description of Verbal Behaviors of Hispanic Teachers and Students in Fifth Grade Social Studies Classrooms.* Unpublished doctoral dissertation, Columbia University 1980.

Ney, J. W. "Miscue Analysis: The Writing of Three Hispanic-American Students in a Class of Twenty Fourth Graders." Tempe, Arizona, 1977 (ERIC-ED 161077).

Ng, B. *An Analysis of the Compositions of Bilingual Children in the Fifth Grade.* Doctoral dissertation, University of California, 1966.

Nygren-Junkin, L. *The Interaction Between French and English in the Speech of our Bilingual Children.* Unpublished Masters Thesis: Ontario Institute for Studies in Education, Toronto, Ontario, 1977.

O'Donnell, R.C., Griffin, W.J. and Norris, R.F. *Syntax of Kindergarten and Elementary School Children: A Transformational Analysis.* (NCTE Research Report No. 8), Urbana, Illinois: National Council of Teachers of English, 1967.

Office of Bilingual Bicultrual Education, *Basic Principles for the Education of Language Minority Students: An Overview.* Sacramento: State Department of Education, 1982.

Oller, J. W. *Language Tests at School.* London: Longman Group Ltd., 1979.

– – – and Perkins, K. *Language in Education: Testing the Tests.* Rowley, Mass.: Newbury House Publishers, Inc., 1978.

Olmedo-Williams, I. "Functions of Code-Switching in a Spanish-English Bilingual Classroom". Paper presented at the First Delaware Symposium on Language Studies, University of Delaware, Newark, 1979.

Olson, D. R. "From Utterance to Text: The Bias of Language in Speech and Writing." *Harvard Educational Review,* 47:3 (1977), 257–281.

Omark, D. R. "Pragmatics and Ethological Techniques for the Observational Assessment of Children's Communicative Abilities." In Erickson, J. G. and Omark, D. R., eds. *Communication Assessment of the Bilingual-Bicultural Child.* Baltimore, MD.: University Park Press, 1981, 249–284.

O'Neill, G.J. *Negro Nonstandard Grammatical Items in the Speech of Negro Elementary School Children as Correlates of Age, Grade and Social Status.* Los Angeles: University of Southern California, 1972.

Overall, P.M. *An Assessment of the Communicative Competence in English of Spanish-Speaking Children in the Fourth and Sixth Grades.* Stanford University, Unpublished doctoral Dissertation, 1978.

Oxford, R. *et. al.* "Projections of Non-English Language Background and Limited English Proficient Persons in the United States to the year 2000: Education Planning in the Demographic Context." *NABE Journal,* 5:3 (Spring 1981), 1–30.

Padilla, A.M. and Liebman, E. "Language Acquisition in the Bilingual Child." *Bilingual Review,* 2:1–2 (1975), 34–55.

Palmer, A. "Compartmentalized and Integrated Control: An Assessment of Some Evidence for Two Kinds of Competence and Implications for the Classroom." *Language Learning,* 29:1 (1979), 169–180.

Paulston, C.B. *Implications of Language Learning Theory for Language Planning: Concerns in Bilingual Education.* Arlington, Virginia: Center for Applied Linguistics, 1975.

– – –. *Bilingual Education. Theories and Issues.* Rowley, Massachusetts: Newbury House Publishers, Inc., 1980.

Peal, E. and Lambert, W.E. "The Relation of Bilingualism to Intelligence." *Psychological Monographs,* 76 (1962), 1–23.

Peña, A.A. *A Comparative Study of Selected Syntactical Structures of the Oral Language Status in Spanish and English of Disadvantaged First-Grade Spanish Speaking Children.* Doctoral dissertation, University of Texas at Austin, 1967.

Peñalosa, F. *Chicano Sociolinguistics.* Rowley, Mass.: Newbury House, 1980.

Perkins, J.A. *et. al. Strength Through Wisdom: A Critique of U.S. Capability.* Washington, D.C.: U.S. Government Printing Office, 1979.

Phillips, J. Mc. *Code-Switching in Bilingual Classrooms.* Masters Thesis, California State University, Northridge, 1975.

Plann, S. *The Spanish Immersion Program: Towards Native-like Proficiency or a Classroom Dialect.* Masters Thesis, UCLA, 1976.

— — —. "Morphological Problems in the Acquisition of Spanish in an Immersion Classroom." In R.W. Anderson ed., *The Acquisition and Use of Spanish and English as First and Second Languages.* Washington, D.C.: TESOL, 1979, 119–132.

Pletcher, B., et. al. *A Guide to Assessment Instruments for Limited English Speaking Students.* New York: Santillana Publishing Company, Inc., 1978.

Politzer, R. L. *Linguistic and Communicative Competence, Language Dominance, Selected Pupil Characteristics and Their Relation to Achievement of Bilingual Pupils,* Final Project Report NIE G-79-0130. Washington, D.C.: National Institute of Education, Department of Education, 1982.

— — — and Ramírez, A.G. "An Error Analysis of the Spoken English of Mexican-American Pupils in a Bilingual and Monolingual School Setting" *Language Learning,* 23:1 (June 1973), 39–62.

— — — and Ramírez, A.G. Judging Personality from Speech: A Pilot Study of the Effects of Bilingual Education on Attitudes Toward Ethnic Groups. Research and Development Memorandum No. 106. Stanford University Center for Educational Research, 1973 (ERIC ED 076278).

— — —. Shohamy, E. and McGroarty, M. "Validation of Linguistic and Communicative Oral Language Tests for Spanish-English Bilinguals." Paper presented at TESOL Annual Conference, Ann Arbor, Michigan, March, 1981.

Pozzi-Escot, I. "Report on the Research Carried Out by the Linguistics Development Plan of the National University of San Marcos." Paper presented at the Seminar on Bilingual Eduation, Lima, Peru, January, 1972.

Ramírez, A.G. *The Spoken English of Spanish-Speaking Pupils in a Bilingual and Monolingual School Setting: An Analysis of Syntactic Development,* (Technical Report No. 40). Stanford University Center for Educational Research, 1974.

— — —. "Language Dominance and Pedagogical Considerations." In E. J. Briere, ed. *Language Development in a Bilingual Setting.* Los Angeles: National Dissemination and Assessment Center, 1979a, 156–167.

— — —. "Attitudes Toward Speech Variation Among Spanish/English Bilingual Pupils: Some Implications for the Teacher and Learner," *Bilingual Education Paper Series,* 2:7 (1979b), Los Angeles: National Dissemination and Assessment Center, California State University.

— — —. "Teaching Reading in Spanish - A Study of Teacher Effectiveness." *Reading Improvement,* 16:4 (Winter 1979c), 304–313.

— — —. Acquisition of Spanish Grammar by Native-Speaking Pupils in a Spanish Immersion School Program, Grades K–4. Albany, N.Y. State University of New York, Teacher Education Department, 1980a, mimeo.

— — —. A Comparative Study of the Written English of English-Speaking Pupils in a Traditional Elementary School and a Spanish Immersion Program, Albany, New York: State University of New York, Teacher Education Department, 1980b, mimeo.

– – –. "Language in Bilingual Classrooms," *NABE Journal*. 4:3 (1980c), 61-79.

– – –. Language Attitudes and the Speech of Spanish-English Bilingual Pupils. In *Latino Language and Communicative Behavior*, R. P. Duran, ed. Norwood, New Jersey: Ablex, 1981, 217-235.

– – –. "Pupil Characteristics and Performance on Linguistic and Communicative Language Measures" In Rivera, C. *Models of Communicative Competence Measurement*. Clevedon, England: Multilingual Matters, Ltd., 1984, 82-105.

– – – and Politzer, R.L. "The Acquisition of English and the Maintenance of Spanish in a Bilingual Education Program," *TESOL Quarterly*, 9:2 (June 1975a), 113-124.

– – – and Politzer, R.L. "The Development of Spanish) English Bilingualism in a Dominant Spanish-Speaking Environment," *ATIBOS: Journal of Chicano Research*. (Summer 1975b), 31-51.

– – – and Politzer, R.L. "Comprehension and Production in ESL by Elementary School and Adolescents." In Hatch E.M., ed. *Second Language Acquisition*. Rowley, Mass.: Newbury House Publishers, 1978, 313-332.

– – –. Arce-Torres, E. and Politzer, R.L. "Language Attitudes and the Achievement of Bilingual Pupils in English Language Arts" *The Bilingual Review/La revista bilingüe*, 5:3 (September-December 1978), 190-206.

– – – and Stromquist, N.P. "ESL Methodology and Student Language Learning in Bilingual Elementary Schools." *TESOL Quarterly*, 13:2 (June 1979), 145-158.

– – – and Kim, B.W. "The Development of Conversational Abilities in ESL among Korean Children." Albany,: State University of New York, School of Education, 1982, Mimeo.

– – – and Milk, R.D. "Bilingual Elementary Teachers' Attitudes Toward Varieties of Spanish." Paper presented at the Conference on Dimensions of Bicultural Experience, State University of New York at Albany, April 1982.

– – –. Milk, R.D. and Sapiens, A. "Intergroup Differences and Attitudes Toward Varieties of Spanish Among High School Bilingual Pupils from California and Texas." *Hispanic Journal of Behavioral Sciences*, 5:4 (December 1983), 417-429.

Ramírez, M. "How Bilingual Multicultural Education Can Save the World." *Proceedings of the Eighth Annual International Bilingual Bicultural Education Conference*. Rosslyn, Virginia: National Clearninghouse for Bilingual Education, 1981, 15-20.

Ramos, M. *et al., The Determination and Implementation of Language Policy*. (Philippines Center for Language Study, Monograph Series no. 2). Quezon City, Philippines: Aleman Phoenix, 1967.

Rand, E. "Bilingual Education: Contributing to Second Language Programs in the Elementary Schools." *NCBE Forum*, 4:9 (November-December 1981), 3, 6.

Randeria, K.E. and Hornby, P.A. Plattsburgh/Quebec FLIP Exchange Program: An Evaluation. Plattsburgh, New York: State University College, Educational Research and Demonstration Center, 1982.

Report of the Minnesota State Board of Education's Curriculum Development Task Force on Contemporary World Studies. St. Paul: Minnesota State Board of Education, 1981.

Report to Parents of FLIP Students. Plattsburgh, N.Y.: State University College, Educational Research and Demonstration Center, 1981.

Rhodes, N.C. "Foreign Languages in the Elementary School: A Status Report." *ERIC Clearinghouse on Languages and Linguistics*, 5:1 (September 1981), 1,6.

Richards, J.C. "Social Aspects of Language Learning." Paper presented at the TESOl Convention, Washington, D.C., March 1972.

— — —, ed. *Understanding Second and Foreign Language Learning.* Rowley: Newbury House Publishers, Inc., 1978.

— — — and Rodgers, T. "Method: Approach, Design and Procedure." *TESOL Quarterly*, 16:2 (June 1982), 153–168.

Rodríguez - Brown, F.V. *The Effect of Language Used for Early Reading. Instruction: A Bilingual Perspective* (Final Project Report NIE-G-78-0134). University of Illinois-Chicago Circle and Bilingual Education Service Center, September 1979.

— — — and Elías-Olivares, L. "A Search for Congruence in Language Proficiency Testing: What the Tests Measure — What the Child Does." Paper presented at AERA Annual Meeting, Los Angeles, April, 1981.

Rodríguez, R.J. *A Comparison of the Written and Oral English Syntax of Mexican American Bilingual and Anglo American Monolingual Fourth and Ninth Grade Students.* Unpublished doctoral dissertation, University of New Mexico, 1974.

Rosier, P. *A Comparative Study of Two Approaches of Introducing Initial Reading to Navajo Children: The Direct Method and the Native-Language Method.* Doctoral dissertation. Northern Arizona University, Flagstaff, Arizona, 1977.

Rustow, D. "Language, Modernization, and Nationhood - An Attempt at Typology." In Fishman, J.A. et. al., eds. *Language Problems of Developing Nations,* 1968.

Ryan, E.B. and Carranza, M.A. Ingroup and Outgroup Reactions to Mexican American Language Varieties. In Giles, H., ed. *Language Ethnicity and Intergroup Relations.* New York: Academic Press, 1977.

Samuels, D.D. and Griffore, R.J. "The Plattsburgh French Language Immersion Program: Its Influence on Intelligence and Self-Esteem." *Language Learning*, 29:1 (June 1979), 45–52.

Sancho, A.R., *Bilingual Education: A Three Year Investigation Comparing the Effects on Maintenance and Transitional Approaches on English Language Acquisition and Academic Achievement of Young Bilingual Children.* Doctoral dissertation Claremont Graduate School, 1980.

Sapeins, A. "Discourse Analysis of a Bilingual Secondary Social Studies Classroom." Unpublished Manuscript, Stanford University, School of Education, 1978.

– – –. *Instructional Language Strategies in Bilingual Chicano Peer Tutoring and Their Effect on Cognitive and Effective Learning Outcomes.* Stanford University, Unpublished doctoral dissertation, 1982.

Saravia-Shore, M. "An Ethnographic Evaluation/Research Model for Bilingual Programs." In Padilla, R.V., ed. *Bilingual Education and Public Policy in the United States.* Ypsilanti, Michigan,: Eastern Michigan University, Department of Foreign Languages and Bilingual Studies, 1979, 328-348.

Savignon, S.J., *Communicative Competence: An Experiment in Foreign Language Teaching.* Philadelphia, PA.: Center for Curriculum Development, 1972.

Saville-Troike, M. "The Development of Bilingual and Bicultural Competence in Young Children." ERIC Clearninghouse on Elementary and Early Childhood Education, 1982 (ERIC ED 206 376).

Schon, I., Hopkins, K.D. and Davis, A.W. "The Effects of Books in Spanish and Free Reading time on Hispanic Students' Reading Abilities and Attitudes." *NABE Journal,* 7:1, (Fall 1982), 13-20.

Schooling and Language Minority Students: A Theoretical Framework. Los Angeles: Evaluation, Dissemination and Assessment Center, California State University, Los Angeles, 1981.

Schumann, J.H. "Second Language Acquisition Research: Getting a More Global Look at the Learner." *Language Learning,* Special Issue No. 4 (1976), 16-28.

– – –. "The Acculturation Model of Second Language Acquisition." In Gingras, R.D., ed. *Second Language Acquisition and Foreign Language* Teaching. Arlington, VA.: Center for Applied Linguistics. 1978, 27-50.

Scott, S. *The Relation of Divergent Thinking to Bilingualism: Cause or Effect.* Unpublished research report, McGill University, 1973.

Searle, J. *Speech Acts.* London: Cambridge University Press, 1969.

Segligman, C.R., Tucker, G.R., and Lambert, W.E. "The Effects of Speech Style and Other Attributes on Teachers' Attitudes Toward Pupils." *Language in Society,* 1 (1972), 131-142.

Shultz, J. "Language Use in Bilingual Classrooms." Presentation at TESOL Conference, Los Angeles, California, 1975.

Shuy, R.W. "On the Relevance of Recent Development in Sociolingustics: The Study of Language Learning and Early Education." *NABE Journal,* 4 (1979), 51-72.

Silverman, R.J., *et. al. Oral Language Tests for Bilingual Students.* Portland: North West Regional Laboratory, 1976.

Sinclair, J. and Coulthard, M. *Towards an Analysis of Discourse: The English Used by Teachers and Pupils.* London: Oxford University Press, 1975.

Stafford, K.R. Problem-Solving as a Function of Language. *Language & Speech,* 11 (1968), 104-122.

Stahl, A. "The Structure of Children's Composition: Developmental and Ethnic Differences." *Research in the Teaching of English*, 11:2 (Fall 1977), 156–163.

Stallings, J. and Kaskowitz, D. *Follow-Through Classroom Observation Evaluation 1972–1973*. Menlo Park, CA.: Stanford Research Institute, 1974.

Steffensen, M.S., Joag-Dev., C. and Anderson, R.D. "A Cross-Cultural Perspective on Reading Comprehension." *Reading Research Quarterly*, 15 (1979), 10–29.

Stern, H.H. "Bilingual Schooling and Foreign Language Education: Some Implications of Canadian Experiments in French Immersion." In J.E. Alatis, ed. *International Dimensions of Bilingual Education*. Washington, D.C. Georgetown University Press, 1978, 165–188.

Stevenson, D.K. "Beyond Faith and Face Validity: The Multitrait-Multimethod Matrix and the Convergent and Discriminant Validity of Oral Proficiency Tests." Paper presented at the TESOL convention, Boston, Mass., 1979.

Stockwell, R.P., Bowen, J.D. and Martin, J.W. *The Grammatical Structures of English and Spanish*. Chicago: University of Chicago Press, 1965.

Stubbs, Michael, *Language, Schools and Classrooms*. Longon: Methuen and Co. Ltd., 1976.

Swain, M.K. *Bilingualism as a First Language*. Unpublished doctoral dissertation. University of California at Irvine, 1972.

– – –. "Bilingualism, Monolingualism and Code Acquisition". In W.F. Mackey and T. Anderson, eds. *Bilingualism in Early Childhood*. Rowley, Mass.: Newbury House, 1977, 28–35.

– – –. "Future Directions in Second Language Research." In C.A. Henning, ed. *Proceedings of the Los Angeles Second Language Research Forum*. Los Angeles: University of California at Los Angeles, 1977.

– – –. "Bilingual Education for the English-Speaking Canadians." In J.E. Alatis, ed. *International Dimensions of Bilingual Education*. Washington, D.C.: Georgetown University Press, 1978, 141–154.

– – –. "French Immersion: Early, Late or Partial?" *The Canadian Modern Language Review*, 34:3 (February 1978), 577–585.

– – –. "Time and Timing in Bilingual Education." *Language Learning*, 31:1 (June 1981), 1–15.

– – – and Lapkin, S. *Evaluating Bilingual Education: A Canadian Case Study*. Clevedon England: Multilingual Matters, Ltd., 1982.

Tannen, D. "What's in a Frame? Surface Evidence for Underlying Expectations." In R.O. Freddle, ed. *New Directions in Discourse Processing*. Norwood: Ablex, 1979.

Thonis, E.W. "Reading Instruction for Language Minority Students." In *Schooling and Language Minority Students: A Theoretical Framework*. Los Angeles: Evaluation, Dissemination and Assessment Center, California State University, Los Angeles, 1981, 147–181.

Tinkunoff, W. J. *Descriptive Study of Significant Bilingual Instructional Features*. San Francisco: Far West Laboratory for Educational Research and Development, 1982.

Torrance, E.P. "Creative Functioning of Monolingual and Bilingual Children in Singapore." *Journal of Educational Psychology*, 61 (1970), 72–75.

Townsend, D. R. *A Comparison of the Classroom Interactional Patterns of Bilingual Early Classroom Teachers*. Doctoral dissertation, University of Texas at Austin, 1974.

— — — and G. Zamora, "Differing Interaction Patterns in Bilingual Classrooms." *Contemporary Education*, 46:3 (Spring 1975), 196–202.

Troike, R.C. "Research Evidence for the Effectiveness of Bilingual Education." *NABE Journal*, 3:1 (Fall 1978), 13–24.

Trueba, H.T. "The Meaning and Use of Context in Ethnographic Research: Implication for Validity." *NABE Journal*, 6:2–3 (Winter/Spring 1981–82), 21–34.

— — — and Wright, P.G. "A Challenge for Ethnographic Researchers in Bilingual Settings: Analyzing Spanish/English Classroom Interaction." *Journal of Multilingual and Multicultural Development*, 2:4 (1981), 243–257.

— — —, *et. al.* "The Acquisition of English for Bilingual Students: Some Thoughts on the Nature, Process and Outcomes of Literacy". San Diego State University, Center for Ethnographic Research, 1982.

Tucker, G.R. "Methods of Second Language Teaching." *Modern Language Journal,* 31:2 (November 1974), 102–107.

— — —. Otanes, F.T. and B.P. Sibayan. "An Alternate Approach to Bilingual Education." In Alatis, J.E., ed. *Report of the 21st Annual Round Table Meeting on Linguistics and Language Studies*, Georgetown University Press, Washington, D.C. 1970, 281–299.

Ulibarri, D.M., Spencer, M.L. and Rivas, G.A. "Language Proficiency and Academic Achievement: A Study of Language Proficiency Tests and Their Relationship to School Ratings as Predictors Academic Achievement." *NABE Journal*, 5:3 (Spring 1981), 47–60.

Urzua, C. "An Interaction Model of Curriculum Design for Young Second Language Learners." Paper presented at the Summer TESOL Meeting in Albuquerque, 1980.

Valdés-Fallis, G. *Code-Switching and the Classroom Teacher*. (Language in Education: Theory and Practice Series, No. 4). Arlington, VA.: Center for Applied Linguistics, 1978.

— — — Lozano, A.G., and Garcia-Moya, R., eds. *Teaching Spanish to the Hispanic Bilingual: Issues Aims, and Methods*. New York: Teachers College, Columbia University, 1981.

Valencia, A. "Bilingual/Bicultural Education: A Prospective Model in Multicultural America." In Alatis, J. and Twaddel, K., eds. *English as a Second Language in Bilingual Education*. Washington, D.C.: TESOL, 1976, 301–312.

Valette, R.M. *Modern Language Testing,* 2nd ed. New York: Harcourt Brace and World, 1977.

Veltman, C.J. *The Retention of Minority Language in the United States.* Washington, D.C.: National Center for Educational Statistics, 1980.

Volterra, V. and Taeschner, T. "The Acquisition and Development of Language by Bilingual Children." *Journal of Child Language,* 5 (1978), 311–326.

Vorih, L. and Rosier, P. "Rock Point Community School: An Example of a Navajo-English Bilingual Elementary School Program." *TESOL Quarterly,* 12:3 (September 1978), 263–271.

Waldman, E. *Cross-Ethnic Attitudes of Anglo Students in Spanish Immersion, Bilingual, and English Schooling.* Unpublished M.A. Thesis, UCLA, 1975.

Walters, J. "Language Variation in the Assessment of Communicative Competence." *Occasional Papers on Linguistics.* No. 6. Carbondale, Illinois: Southern Illinois University, Department of Linguistics, 1979, 293–305.

Wang, M., Rose, S. and Marwell, J. *The Development of the Language Communication Skill Tasks.* Pittsburgh: Learning and Research and Development Center, 1973.

Wiedemann, L. *Portugal vs United States Experience in the Elementary School as a Factor in School Performance of Portuguese-Americans.* Doctoral dissertation, Stanford University, 1982.

Wiemann, J.W. and Backlaud, P. "Current Theory and Research in Communicative Competence." *Review of Educational Research,* 50:1 (1980), 185–200.

Williams, F. *et. al. Explorations of the Linguistic Attitudes of Teachers.* Rowley: Newbury House Publishers, Inc., 1976.

Wise, M.R. "Utilizing Languages of Minority Groups in a Bilingual Experiment in the Amazonian Jungle of Peru." *Community Development Journal,* 4 (1969), 117–122.

Wode, H. "Developmental Sequences in Naturalistic L_2 Acquisition." In E.M. Hatch, ed. *Second Language Acquisition.* Rowley, Mass.: Newbury House Publishers, 1978, 101–107.

Yoshida, M. "The Acquisition of English Vocabulary by a Japanese Speaking Child." In E.M. Hatch, ed. *Second Language Acquisition.* Rowley, Mass.: Newbury House, 1978, 91–100.

Zappert, L.T. and Cruz, B.R. *Bilingual Education: An Appraisal of Empirical Research,* Berkeley: Bahia, Inc., 1977.

Zentella, A. C. "Ta Bien, You could answer me in cualquier idioma: Puerto Rican Code-switching in Bilingual Classrooms." Presentation at ETS Conference on Chicano and Latino Discourse Behavior, Princeton, New Jersey, 1978.

Zirkel, P. A. "A Method for Determining and Depicting Language Dominance." *TESOL Quarterly,* 8:1 (March 1974), 7–16.

SUBJECT INDEX

AUTHOR INDEX